Information on Music: A Handbook of Reference Sources in
European Languages, Volume II

INFORMATION ON MUSIC:
A HANDBOOK OF REFERENCE SOURCES IN EUROPEAN LANGUAGES

Information on Music:

A Handbook of

Reference Sources

in European Languages

Volume II, The Americas

Guy A. Marco
Chief, General Reference and Bibliography Division
Library of Congress

Ann M. Garfield

Sharon Paugh Ferris

1977

LIBRARIES UNLIMITED, INC., Littleton, Colo.

LIBRARIES UNLIMITED, INC.
P.O. Box 263
Littleton, Colorado 80160

Library of Congress Cataloging in Publication Data   (Revised)

Marco, Guy A
    Information on music.

    Vols, 2-   by G. A. Marco, A. M. Garfield, and S. P.
Ferris.
    Includes indexes.
    CONTENTS: v. 1. Basic and universal sources.--v. 2.
The Americas.
    1. Music--Bibliography. 2. Music--Discography--
Bibliography. 3. Bibliography--Bibliography--Music.
I. Ferris, Sharon Paugh. II. Garfield, Ann M.
III. Title.
ML113.M33   016.78   74-32132
ISBN 0-87287-141-X

TABLE OF CONTENTS

ACKNOWLEDGMENTS

Many libraries provided the resources needed to compile this volume, and many librarians the indispensable personal assistance: Library of Congress, Music Division (Don Leavitt, Betty Aumann, Barbara Henry, Joe Hickerson, Wayne Shirley); Ohio State University, School of Music Library (Olga Buth); Northwestern University, School of Music Library (Don Roberts, Connie Nisbet, Stephen Fry—now at UCLA); Eastman School of Music (Charles Lindahl); Kent State University (Jane Benson, Virginia Crowl, Sue Rosenberger, Hazel Young); Cleveland Public Library (Rosemary McAttee). Robert Murrell Stevenson, University of California at Los Angeles, read the sections on Latin American countries and offered valuable advice. Maria Calderisi, National Library of Canada, read the Canadian chapter and improved it greatly with her suggestions. Eugene Sheehy, Columbia University Libraries, kindly let us see the proofs to certain chapters of the forthcoming edition of *Guide to Reference Books* (Winchell). Carole Franklin (Pennsylvania State University) assisted with the U.S. folk music and popular music sections; Dominique-René de Lerma (Morgan State University) read and ameliorated the unit on black music in the United States. Other information was provided by Nancy Kent (Harvard), Eldo Neufeld (University of British Columbia) and Jack Ralston (University of Missouri at Kansas City). Ulo Valdma, graduate assistant, Kent State University, did a great deal of important verifying and searching for elusive data. Other help was given by graduate assistants Althea Aschmann and Gonzalo López. Liz Sheaffer and Rosemary Fithian did a good share of the typing. Thanks are also due to Barbara Sexton, Joan Garfield, David Olszewski and Olga Wynnytsky.

INTRODUCTION

Although we had intended for the second volume in this series to encompass information sources for individual countries and regions throughout the world, it soon became apparent that the resulting tome would be too massive for convenient use. We have accordingly limited ourselves, in the present compilation, to materials concerning the Western hemisphere. It appears that Europe will fit neatly into a book of its own, which will be Volume III, and the rest of the world will occupy Volume IV.

The works cited were drawn from a sizeable universe. As a beginning, the *Library of Congress Catalog–Books: Subjects* was searched, 1950-1975, and all entries under appropriate headings were noted. Bibliographies in the *Harvard Dictionary of Music*, and in *Musik in Geschichte und Gegenwart* were also checked. All titles of potential significance were examined by one or more of the three authors. Catalogs and shelves in major libraries were also scrutinized, and various experts were consulted. Advertisements and publisher announcements were taken into account. Perhaps a tenth of the material considered for inclusion finally found its way into these pages.

Conceptually, we have maintained the philosophy of the first volume. "Excellence, convenience, and uniqueness" remain the criteria for inclusion. All written formats have been considered eligible for listing: books on musical topics, books of a general nature with some musical information in them, journals, and articles in journals, dissertations and other graduate-level student works, and even unpublished card files.

The kind of information we have tried to illuminate is the body of basic facts regarding the musical realm; we have not explored the arcane range of musicological investigation, and we have included only those specimens of learned research which also provided useful information at a relatively unspecialized level. But bibliographies are identified that can form the entrance points into research areas of any desired complexity or minuteness. That particular framework was continually tested as we brought together materials on individual countries, and in certain cases the frame had to be twisted: we did not always find a unified literature that could be rationally categorized. Sometimes we have had to include works dealing with very technical problems, simply because nothing else was available in the national/topical combination under consideration. Always we have tried to relate our choices to the requirements and convenience of the fact-searcher—and consequently we have given preference to writings with good reference features (such as indexes and bibliographies) and writings that are descriptive of the most recent situations. The annotations are intended to identify these elements and to be as specific as possible about the character and quantity of factual content.

Form of presentation, as in Volume I, generally follows that of the Library of Congress; most entries for monographs are taken nearly verbatim from LC cards. For journal articles, the LC style as given in the *Handbook of Latin American Studies* was the guide. Some modification of LC style will be found (e.g., in capitalization practice for English titles, in the manner of handling reprint editions, in the treatment of joint authors).

One feature not present in the first volume will be worth a comment. Each entry number carries, on the line beneath, a code for the language(s) of the work—this useful idea was borrowed from *RILM Abstracts*. While the language of a work is often obvious, to most readers, from the title itself, it is not always apparent from the title that summaries and other text may be found in a different language; and it will also be noticeable in Volume III, Europe, that many readers may need this assistance even to recognize the title language. Language codes used in this volume are: Du (Dutch), En (English), Fr (French), Ge (German), It (Italian), Pr (Portuguese), Ru (Russian) and Sp (Spanish).

The typical entry gives this information: author, title, edition statement, place of publication, publisher, date, pagination, Library of Congress printed card number, International Standard Book Number, and Library of Congress classification number.

Despite an attempt to represent various languages, for the added convenience of readers in diverse countries, we have not found many useful books about the United States in languages other than English. The writings about Canada are nearly all in English and/or French; and the literature on Latin America is almost entirely Spanish, English, or Portuguese.

Under each regional or national heading, the materials are presented in a standard sequence. Although not all subdivisions are used under each heading, the outline below shows the order of the subdivisions:

The Language of Music (dictionaries of terms)

Direct Information Sources (writings about music)

> Introductions and General Surveys (may include dictionaries of topics, and encyclopedias; and in certain countries may include certain historical studies which are useful for a panoramic view of the national music experience)
> Collections of Essays, Articles, etc.
> Folk Music and Folksong
> Popular Music
> Instrumental Music (may be further subdivided by instrument or combination; includes orchestral music)
> Opera and Vocal Music
> Church and Religious Music
> Music Theory and Musicology
> Historical Studies, Chronologies, Contemporary Narratives
> Regional and Local Histories
> Music Printing and Publishing
> Directories
> Periodicals and Yearbooks
> Instruments
> Performing Groups
> Iconographies
> Miscellaneous

Biographical Sources

Guides to Other Sources (bibliographies, indexes)

> Bibliographies of Bibliographies
> Selective and Critical Guides
>> General
>> Folk Music and Folksong

> Popular Music
> Instrumental Music
> Opera and Vocal Music
> Church and Religious Music
> Other Topics
>
> General Lists and Library Catalogs
> Annual and Periodic Lists
> Periodical Indexes
> Dissertations and Theses
> Reviews of Books
> Other Indexes

Lists of Music

> Bibliographies of Lists of Music
> Selective and Critical Lists
> > General
> > Folk Music and Folksong
> > Popular Music
> > Instrumental Music
> > Opera and Vocal Music
> > Church and Religious Music
> > Other Topics
>
> General Lists and Library Catalogs
> Lists of Manuscript Music
> Lists of Early Music (to 1800)
> Lists of 19th and 20th Century Music
> Thematic Indexes
> Annual and Periodic Lists
> Other Lists

Discographies

Within each division and subdivision, the entries are usually arranged so that more general titles appear first, and more specific titles later; or with the most useful materials first; or in other affinity groupings as suggested by the subject at hand. In a few cases the works are simply given in alphabetical order by author.

It was clear to us, and to several reviewers, that the subject indexing of Volume I was unsatisfactory. Ergo, we have constructed for the present volume a detailed subject index, utilizing the subject-heading structure of the Library of Congress, and have incorporated into it all the works of Volume I. The author-title index is also cumulative, covering both volumes.

Several bibliographic source-works are cited regularly in shortened style:

ARBA   *American Reference Books Annual* (1970, 1971, 1972, 1973, 1974, 1975, 1976). Edited by Bohdan S. Wynar. Littleton, Colo.: Libraries Unlimited, 1970– .

Chase   Gilbert Chase, *A Guide to the Music of Latin America.* 2d ed. Washington: Pan American Union and Library of Congress, 1962. (Reprint–New York: AMS Press, 1972). See entry *0891.*

Duckles 74 Vincent Duckles, *Music Reference and Research Materials.* 3d ed. New York: Free Press, 1974. See entry *0216*, Volume I.

Jackson Richard Jackson, *United States Music: Sources of Bibliography and Collective Biography.* New York: Institute for Studies in American Music, Department of Music, Brooklyn College of the City University of New York, 1973. See entry *0786c.*

Winchell 67 Constance Winchell, *Guide to Reference Books.* 8th ed. Chicago: American Library Association, 1967. Supplements covering 1965/66, 1967/68, 1969/70.

Sheehy 76 Eugene P. Sheehy, *Guide to Reference Books.* 9th ed. Chicago, American Library Association, 1976. Mr. Sheehy kindly provided some proof pages for our use before the ninth edition was published; certain "76" numbers have been drawn from those proof pages.

These source-works have numbered items; the appropriate number after the source title is usually self-explanatory—but notice that Winchell's supplement numbers begin with the number of the supplement (Winchell 67-2BH100—item BH100 in the second supplement, 1967/68). ARBA 1970 did not have item numbers, so citations thereto are given only by volume and page.

To close this introduction, I wish to introduce two co-authors for the present volume: Ann Garfield (Cleveland Public Library) and Sharon Paugh Ferris—my assistant in Volume I—(Massillon, Ohio, Public Library). Ann worked mostly on Latin American materials, Sharon on North American. They deserve the major share of credit for whatever utility our work may have, but I retain for myself the responsibility for any errors and omissions which may be encountered. Readers who notice such flaws are requested to communicate with me, so that corrections can be inscribed in the "update" section of the next volume.

Guy A. Marco
Chief, General Reference and Bibliography Division
Library of Congress

O amazement of things! even the least particle!
O spirituality of things!
O strain musical, flowing through ages and continents—
    now reaching me and America!
I take your strong chords—I intersperse them, and cheerfully
    pass them forward.

                                        Whitman

CHAPTER 1

UPDATE OF VOLUME I

This chapter is a supplement to Volume I, listing new titles for that volume. The appendix to Volume II (page 211) lists revisions for Volume I, correcting and amplifying entries from 0001 through 0503.

THE LANGUAGE OF MUSIC

0504 Risatti, Howard. **New Music Vocabulary: A Guide to Notational Signs for**
En **Contemporary Music.** Urbana: University of Illinois Press, 1975. 219p.
LC 73-81565. ISBN 0-252-00406-X. ML 431 R6
ARBA 76–1001
A dictionary of symbols found in some 600 scores. Alternative notations for the same passage shown; index by instrument and technical device. While the signs given are not to be found in standard music dictionaries, the effects they represent can, in many cases, be just as well written in conventional notation.

0505 Fink, Robert; Ricci, Robert. **The Language of Twentieth-century Music;**
En **a Dictionary of Terms.** New York: Schirmer Books; London: Collier
Macmillan Publishers, 1975. vii, 125p. LC 74-13308. ISBN 0-02-870600-5.
ML 100 F55
This work contrasts with the preceding (*0504*) in presenting the critical vocabulary *about* modern music, rather than the composers' vocabulary as found in the actual scores. It gives the basic terms of chance music, computer music, electronic music, rock, serial music, film music and jazz; about 1,000 terms in all. An interesting appendix groups the terms topically.

0506 Gold, Robert S. **Jazz Talk; a Dictionary of Colorful Language That Has**
En **Emerged from America's Own Music.** Indianapolis, New York: Bobbs-
Merrill Co., 1975. xii, 322p. LC 74-17642. ISBN 0-672-52093-1.
An excellent dictionary of about 1,000 terms, based on the author's *Jazz Lexicon* (Knopf, 1964; Duckles 74-287). Words are carefully defined and discussed, then put into chronological context with a series of dated quotations. Quotation sources include newspapers, popular magazines, novels, biographies and works on jazz. The sources are gathered into a nine-page bibliography.

DIRECT INFORMATION SOURCES

0507 Vinton, John. **Dictionary of Contemporary Music.** New York: E. P. Dutton,
En 1974. xiv, 834p. ISBN 0-525-09125-4. LC 73-78096.
ARBA 75–1143 ML 100 V55
An important handbook of about 1,000 articles on topics, countries, terms and persons, all in the general framework of 20th-century serious music of the West.

Entries are signed, by various expert authors, and include bibliographies. Principal works are listed for composers. A six-page list of publishers is a useful bonus. No photos, no musical examples, and no index. Many national and topical articles are cited elsewhere in this and subsequent volumes.

0508 Hague. Gemeentemuseum. **European Musical Instruments in Prints and**
En **Drawings.** Zug, Switzerland: Inter Documentation Company AG, 1972.
Microfiche. (Répertoire international d'iconographie musicale—RidiM,
Musicology SA 1)
See entry *0114.* See p. 32 of Volume I for some facts on RidiM. The
present work offers 600 prints and drawings dating from the sixteenth through
the nineteenth century. Indexed by artist and by instrument. See also *0509.*

0509 Hague. Gemeentemuseum. **Portraits of Composers and Musicians.** Zug,
En Switzerland: Inter Documentation Company AG, 1974. Microfiche.
(Répertoire international d'iconographie musicale—RidiM, Musicology
SA 2)
See p. 32 of Volume I for some facts on RidiM. This work consists of 830
prints, drawings, and paintings of composers and musicians from Germany,
Netherlands, France, Italy, England, and Eastern Europe.

0510 **Encyclopédie des musiques sacrées**, publiée sous la direction de Jacques
Fr Porte. Paris: Éditions Labergerie, 1968-70. 4v. LC 70-211374.
Duckles 74—315 ML 102 E53
A major work of multiple authorship. Covers, in addition to numerous
aspects of Western and Oriental religious music, various folkloric considerations.
Historical articles, and excellent articles on individual countries. Some articles will
be cited later in this and later volumes. Bibliographies; no general index.

0510a **Ethnomusicology.** v.1— . 1953— . Ann Arbor, Mich.: Society for Ethno-
En musicology. (3 per year) LC 56-12963. ML 1 E77
In addition to scholarly articles on folk music of the world, each issue
features a valuable bibliography-discography section (classified, in all languages
with transliterations to Roman alphabet, with full imprint data and occasional
explanatory comments). This listing occupies 35 pages of the May 1976 issue.
There are also long, reliable reviews of books and recordings.

0511 **Praeger History of Western Music.** Ed. Frederic W. Sternfeld. New York:
En Praeger, 1973. 2v.
ARBA 75—1151
Intended to include five volumes, but appears to have ceased. The following
have appeared: *Music from the Middle Ages to the Renaissance* (524p.; LC 73-180323;
ML 172 S85), Vol. 1; and *Music in the Modern Age* (515p.; LC 78-190596; ML 197
S7655 M9), Vol. 5. Both volumes are made up of contributions by various authors,
many of them leading authorities. Particular treatment of individual countries.
Strong bibliographies and discographies. Volumes and sections will be cited later
under appropriate countries or topics.

The following are important guides to periodicals:

0512 **Union List of Serials in Libraries of the United States and Canada.** 3d ed.
En New York: H. W. Wilson, 1965. 5v. LC 65-10150. Z6945 U45
Sheehy 76—AE133
A list of more than 156,000 titles of periodicals and continuations, located in 956 libraries. Bibliographic data, and indication of holdings in particular libraries. Covers titles issued up to December 1949. See following item.

0513 **New Serial Titles: a Union List of Serials Commencing Publication after**
En **December 31, 1949; 1950-1970 Cumulative.** Washington: Library of Congress; New York: R. R. Bowker, 1973. 4v. LC 53-60021. ISBN 0-8352-0556-8; ISSN 0028-6680. Z6945 N44
Sheehy 76—AE134; ARBA 75—41
Periodical holdings of more than 800 U.S. and Canadian libraries, arranged by title. The basic publication is issued monthly, with quarterly and annual cumulations; the work cited here is the principal cumulation—which supersedes all earlier issues through 1970. Data given will vary according to availability of information; the ideal entry gives publisher and place, beginning (and ending) dates, Dewey classification number, library locations and holdings, ISSN (International Standard Serial Number), and code for country; for titles issued monthly or quarterly, the frequency of publication is provided.

0514 **New Serial Titles 1950-1970 Subject Guide.** New York: R. R. Bowker,
En 1975. 2v. LC 75-15145. ISBN 0-8352-0820-6.
ARBA 76—26
A Dewey-classified arrangement of the titles in the preceding work (*0513*). Under each class number, entries appear in order by country, then by title. There are about 2,250 items in the music class, grouped by countries.

0515 **Ulrich's International Periodicals Directory: a Classified Guide to Current**
En **Periodicals, Foreign and Domestic.** 16th ed. New York: R. R. Bowker, 1975. 2,289p. (A Bowker Serials Bibliography) LC 32-16320. ISBN 0-8352-0824-9. Z 6941 U5
Sheehy 76—AE10; ARBA 76—27
About 57,000 titles, in subject groupings. Gives publishing information and (with variable dependability) identifies indexes that include each periodical. About 400 entries in music area. Journals that have ceased publication are listed in a separate section.

The following periodical is international in scope:

0515a **Cash Box; International Music Record Weekly.** v.1— . 1942— . New York:
En Cash Box Publishing Co. (weekly) ISSN 0008-7289. ML 13 C3
Record industry news, advertisements; poll winners; golden record albums; million sellers; publishers hitting "top 100"; directories of record manufacturers, importers, studios, pressers, etc. Most coverage for United States, but also considerable information on United Kingdom, Japan, Argentina; some notices for other countries.

BIOGRAPHICAL SOURCES

0516   **Biographical Dictionaries Master Index–1975-1976.** Ed. Dennis LaBeau
En   and Gary C. Tarbert. Detroit: Gale Research Co., 1976. 3v. LC 75-19059.
        ISBN 0-8103-1077-5.   Z5305 U5 B56
        An index to some 800,000 names of persons for whom biographical
information appears in about fifty sources. Reference sources covered include
the Marquis series (*Who's Who in America,* etc.) and specialized works in subject
fields. Music titles include the *Encyclopedia of Folk, Country and Western Music*
(*0613*), *Who's Who of Jazz* (*0672*), and *Who's Who in Music and Musicians'
International Directory* (*0149*).

0517   Douglas, John R. "Publications Devoted to Individual Musicians: a
En   Checklist." **Bulletin of Bibliography & Magazine Notes,** 33-3 (April-June
        1976), 135-39.
        Lists of journals, newsletters, and other publications issued by organiza-
tions centered on certain composers or other musicians. There are 52 musicians
thus honored, from J. S. Bach to Eugene Ysaÿe.

0518   Hixon, Donald L.; Hennessee, Don. **Women in Music: a Biobibliography.**
En   Metuchen, N.J.: Scarecrow Press, 1975. xiii, 347p. LC 75-23075. ISBN
        0-8108-0869-2.   ML 105 H6
        ARBA 76–1002
        An index to locations of biographical data, covering Grove's *Dictionary*
(*0059*), Thompson's *International Cyclopedia* (*0065*), Baker's *Biographical
Dictionary* (*0175*) and 45 other standard sources. More than 5,000 names; brief
entries for each, giving birth/death dates, musical occupation, and citations to
sources. Useful classified list; accompanists, composers, contraltos, critics, editors,
glass harmonica players, and even librarians. "No effort has been made to reconcile
the different transliteration systems among the sources treating Slavic names."

GUIDES TO OTHER SOURCES

0519   Hughes, Andrew. **Medieval Music: the Sixth Liberal Art.** Toronto; Buffalo:
En   University of Toronto Press, 1974. xii, 326p. (Toronto Medieval Bibliog-
        raphies, 4) LC 73-85087. ISBN 0-8020-2094-1.   ML 114 H8
        ARBA 76–988
        A selective, annotated bibliography of 2,003 numbered items, grouped
under such topics as notation, rhythm, iconography, treatises, and individual
composers or regions. Author and subject-title indexes. This is the most valuable
guide to the writings on medieval music: easy to use, authoritative, and illuminating.

0520   Garfield, Ann. **A Subject Index of Six British Music Periodicals, 1927-37.**
En   Unpublished paper, Kent State University, School of Library Science, 1975.
        viii, 189p.
        A very detailed index, using Library of Congress subject headings, of
British Musician, Chesterian, Music and Letters, Musical Times, Proceedings of the

Royal Musical Association and *Sackbut*. Connects the indexes of Blom (*0306*) and Daugherty (*0307*).

0521   Gillis, Frank; Merriam, Alan P. **Ethnomusicology and Folk Music; an**
En   **International Bibliography of Dissertations and Theses.** Middletown, Conn.:
        Wesleyan University Press, 1966. 148p. LC 66-23459/MN.

        Duckles 74—654   ML 128 E8 G5

        Developed from lists which had appeared in *Ethnomusicology*. Supplements published in later issues of that journal. Includes 873 entries, with subject, author, and institution index.

0521a   Sandberg, Larry; Weissman, Dick. **The Folk Music Sourcebook.** New York:
En   Alfred A. Knopf, 1976. x, 260, xv p. LC 75-34472. ISBN 0-394-49684-1.

                                                               ML 19 S26

        A very useful guide to the literature and discography of North American folk music, with directory information on organizations, festivals, folk music centers, periodicals, archives, etc. The scope of "folk music" is here inclusive of blues and ragtime, and other black-American genres; North American Indian music. The first part of the book presents concise background information on each of the styles (country blues, Chicago blues, piano blues, gospel music, Canadian folk music, fiddle music, etc.) and then offers a selective, annotated discography. The second part gives some biographical sketches, an annotated list of song books, a list of reference books (not reliable), and some articles on instruments and how to play them. The descriptive list of periodicals (more than 100) is available. Index of names and topics.

LISTS OF MUSIC

0522   Olmsted, Elizabeth, ed. **Music Library Association Catalog of Cards for**
En   **Printed Music, 1953-1972: a Supplement to the Library of Congress**
        Catalogs. Totowa, N.J.: Rowman & Littlefield, 1974. 2v. LC 73-17184.
        ISBN 0-87471-474-5.   ML 113 042
        ARBA 75—1138

        A composer list of 30,000 entries which were submitted to the National Union Catalog but which had not appeared in *Music, Books on Music, and Sound Recordings*, formerly *Music and Phonorecords* (*0387*). This is a rather informal catalog, with entries accepted as received from contributing libraries; cross references and tracings are lacking, and so is subject indexing. Nevertheless valuable for data on works and editions otherwise destined to blush unseen.

0523   Parsons, Denys. **The Directory of Tunes and Musical Themes.** Cambridge,
En   Eng.: S. Brown, 1975. 288p. LC 75-31448. ISBN 0-904747-00-X.

                                                               ML 128 I65 P33

        About 15,000 themes, vocal and instrumental, from serious and popular music. A very useful companion for the old indexes of Barlow and Morgenstern (*0444, 0445*) and Burrows and Redmond (*0446, 0447*). A novel method of indicating the contour of a melody without musical notation makes it possible to identify tunes.

DISCOGRAPHIES

0524 Gray, Michael; Gibson, Gerald. "Bibliography of Discographies Annual
En Cumulation." **ARSC Journal.**
This is a yearly feature in the official journal of the Association for
Recorded Sound Collections. It forms a useful supplement to Cooper (*0458*).

0525 Decca Record Co., Ltd. **Main Catalogue (Alphabetical and Numerical)**
En **up to and including September 1971.** London: Decca Record Co., Ltd.,
1972. Supplement, Oct. 72-Sept. 73 [1974?]
A very thorough inventory of Decca records in print. Serious music and
popular music; artist and title indexes, and numerical (chronological) lists. More
than 30,000 items included. Contents of albums given. Classified grouping of artists
(e.g., about 300 rock groups). Earliest serious music disc dates from 1958. Appendix
of about 60 popular albums from West Africa. Labels include Brunswick, Qualiton,
Telefunken, and Turnabout.

0526 Jepsen, Jorgen Grunnet. **Jazz Records 1942-1962: A Discography.** Holte,
En Denmark: Karl Emil Knudsen, 1963-71. 8v.   ML 156.4 J3J4

Duckles 74—1773
Publisher varies. The most extensive inventory. Arrangement by artist,
with information on recording dates and places, performers, matrix and release
numbers. Covers American and European labels. Supplements planned.

0527 New York Library Association. Children's and Young Adult Services
En Section. **Recordings and Cassettes for Young Adults.** New York: New
York Library Association, 1972. 52p.   ML 156.2 N38
Recommends 461 titles for a basic collection; covers rock, country, western,
jazz, and soul. Note companion publication for children, *0502*.

0528 **Media Review Digest.** 1973/74— . Ann Arbor, Mich.: Pierian Press, 1975— .
En (annual) ISBN 0-87650-053-X. LC 73-172772.   Z 5784 M9 M849
Supersedes *Multi Media Reviews Index*, same publisher. Issued in two
parts: 1) Films and filmstrips, and miscellaneous media; 2) Records and tapes.
Subject indexes and supplements for each part. Reviews in about 70 sources are
cited, with + and - signs to indicate reviewer opinions. (Names of reviewers given).
Popular and serious music covered.

0529 Halsey, Richard Sweeney. **Classical Music Recordings for Home and
Library.** Chicago: American Library Association, 1976. 340p. LC 75-
40205. ISBN 0-8389-0188-3.
ARBA 77   ML 111.5 H34
A 4,101 item discography, intended to identify the basic stock for a serious
music collection. The list is arranged by genre, then by composer; there is a title
index, and an index by manufacturer number. Timing is given for each piece. Some
information on recording cataloging and classification, and ordering, is provided.

The work is marred by the unfortunate inclusion of the author's qualitative ratings of all selections; these indicators of his personal taste are mostly foolish, and potentially misleading to the non-musical reader.

Two other discographical works have been announced:

0530　Eastman School of Music, Rochester, New York. **Sibley Music Library**
En　　**Catalog of Sound Recordings.** Boston: G. K. Hall. ISBN 0-8161-0063-2.
　　　To be available in 1977. Entries for 25,000 recordings, primarily Western classical music. Individual compositions in composite releases are identified through analytic entries. (Information from publisher's announcement.)

0531　Indiana University. Archives of Traditional Music. **Catalog of Phonorecord-**
En　　**ings of Music and Oral Data.** Boston: G. K. Hall. ISBN 0-8161-1120-0.
　　　Data on a collection of 6,000 cylinders, 25,000 discs and 18,000 tapes, presented in the usual G. K. Hall format: photoduplication of actual catalog cards.

CHAPTER 2

NORTH AMERICA

GENERAL

A few titles of wide geographic scope are presented here, all of them pertaining to aspects of folk music. Works primarily about Canada, with some attention to the United States, are entered under Canada; and works primarily about the United States, with some attention to Canada, are entered under United States.

0532   Nettl, Bruno. **Folk and Traditional Music of the Western Continents.** (*0103*).
En   LC 72-10010. ISBN 0-13-322941-6.   ML 3549 N5
        Includes excellent survey chapters on "Folk Music in Modern North
America," "The American Indians," and "Afro-American Folk Music in North and
Latin America." Styles, instruments, role of music in the various cultures. Drawings,
musical examples, selective bibliographies and discographies for each chapter.
Indexed.

0533   Collaer, Paul. **Music of the Americans; an Illustrated Music Ethnology of**
En   **the Eskimo and American Indian Peoples.** New York: Praeger, 1973.
        207p. LC 70-112028.   ML 3547 C64
        A translation of Collaer's *Amerika: Eskimo und indianische Bevölkerung*,
        1966 (*0119*). Excellent collection of illustrations—instruments, dances,
ceremonies—with scholarly commentaries. Prefatory discussion of anthropology
and culture in the pre-European settlements, with maps. Bibliography of 901
entries; index.

0534   Nettl, Bruno. **North American Indian Musical Styles.** Philadelphia:
En   American Folklore Society, 1954 [i.e., 1955]. ix, 51p. (Memoirs of the
        American Folklore Society, v.45) LC 55-14188.   GR 1 A5 vol.45
        A study of 80 tribes in the regions north of Mexico. Historical and technical
aspects are covered. See also next entry, *0535*.

0535   Nettl, Bruno. "Musical Areas Reconsidered." In: **Essays in Musicology, in**
En   **Honor of Dragan Plamenac on His 70th Birthday.** Ed. Gustave Reese and
        Robert J. Snow. Pittsburgh: University of Pittsburgh Press, 1969. pp. 181-89.
        LC 68-12731. ISBN 8-229-1068-5.   ML 3797.1 R44
        "Reference is made to the author's earlier publication . . . (*0534*). The
article provides a critique, some new material, and suggests a revision of the conclu-
sions." (Author abstract in *RILM Abstracts*).

0536   Haywood, Charles. **A Bibliography of North American Folklore and Folksong.**
En   2d rev. ed. New York: Dover Publications, 1961. 2v. (xxx, 1,301p.)
        LC 62-3483.   Z 5984 US H32
        Duckles 74—678

(1st ed. 1951) Based on 1951 Ph.D. dissertation, Columbia University. Vol. 1: non-Indian peoples north of Mexico; Vol. 2: Indians north of Mexico. An exhaustive, if not comprehensive, listing of published writings in classified arrangement, with folklore separated from folk music entries. Discographies, mostly of 78 rpm's. Note that second edition was principally a corrected reprint, and that no literature subsequent to 1951 is presented in it. Index of persons, places, and topics.

0537   Hickerson, Joseph Charles. "Annotated Bibliography of North American
En   Indian Music North of Mexico." Unpublished Master's Paper, Indiana
       University, 1961. xi, 464 leaves.   ML 128 F75 H45
       An exhaustive list of writings which describe and/or discuss the music of individual tribes or of larger areas. Reviews of books and recordings are included. Published collections of Indian melodies have been listed. Categories omitted are unpublished theses and dissertations, and commercial recordings. An historical survey of research in North American Indian music precedes the bibliography. There is an index by tribe or area.

0538   Cavanagh, Beverly. "Annotated Bibliography: Eskimo Music." **Ethno-**
En   **musicology**, 16 (Sept. 1972), 479-87.
       About 100 items. Covers Greenland, the Arctic, and Alaska.

0539   New York (City). Public Library. Reference Department. **Dictionary**
. En   **Catalog of the History of the Americas.** Boston: G. K. Hall, 1961. 28v.
       ISBN 0-8161-0540-5. Supplement, 1974. 9v. ISBN 0-8161-0771-8.
                                                    Z 1201 N48
       An author-title-subject catalog of a major collection. Includes nine entries for Eskimo music; 215 entries for North American Indian music; 33 for Indian musical instruments; plus many other entries under related headings. Journal articles are included.

0540   Society for Ethnomusicology. **Directory of Ethnomusicological Sound**
En   **Recording Collections in the U.S. and Canada.** Ed. Ann Briegleb. Ann
       Arbor, Mich.: Society for Ethnomusicology, 1971. 49p. (Special Series,
       no. 2) LC 72-179153.   ML 19 S64
           Duckles 74—1790
       An inventory of 124 collections, arranged by state.

0541   **Archives of Recorded Music. Archives de la musique enregistrée.** Paris:
En/Fr UNESCO, 1952– .
           Duckles 74—1785/89
       Issued in series; Series A—Occidental music; Series B—Oriental music; Series C—Ethnographical and Folk music. Individual volumes will be cited as appropriate, later in the present work.

CANADA

THE LANGUAGE OF MUSIC

There is no specifically Canadian term dictionary. The English and French vocabularies are covered by the standard dictionaries (*0001-0010*).

DIRECT INFORMATION SOURCES

Introductions and General Surveys

0542   Kallmann, Helmut. "Kanada." **MGG** (*0058*), VII, cols. 499-507.
En   A good general study, emphasizing historical development. Art music only; nothing on folk song. Bibliography of 13 items.

0543   Beckwith, John. "Canada." **Dictionary of Contemporary Music** (*0507*),
En   119-124.
A review of the current scene and of recent developments; principal composers and major works cited.

0543a   MacMillan, Keith. "Canadian Music." **The International Cyclopedia of**
En   **Music and Musicians**, 10th ed. (*0065*), 345-353.
A good general overview, touching on all aspects of music in Canada.

Collections of Essays, Articles, etc.

0544   MacMillan, Ernest. **Music in Canada**. Toronto: University of Toronto Press,
En   1955. 232p. LC 55-4629.   ML 205 M3
Various topics and authors. Folk music, composition, orchestras, choral music, opera, ballet, radio music, music education, recordings, film music, church music, festivals. Indexed.

0545   Walter, Arnold. **Aspects of Music in Canada**. Toronto: University of Toronto
En/Fr   Press, 1969. 336p. LC 74-418249. ISBN 8020-1536-0.
ML 205 A86
A companion volume to the preceding title, with similar format and coverage. Particularly useful essays on folk music, important orchestras and opera companies, leading soloists, music education, musical organizations. Indexed. The French version: *Aspects de la musique au Canada* (Montréal: Centre de Psychologie et de Pédagogie, 1970). Only the French edition has a bibliography (about 100 items).

Folk Music and Folksong

0546   **Ethnomusicology**, 16-3 (Sept. 1972).   ML 1 E77
En   Issue devoted to Canada. Topics and reports cover field research projects, Anglo-Canadian folk music, and French-Canadian folk music. Bibliography; discography. Certain articles will be cited individually later.

0547   Barbeau, Marius. "Folk Music: Canadian." **Grove's** (*0059*), III, 211-214.
En   Survey of Canadian Indian music, French-Canadian music, and Anglo-Canadian music. Brief bibliographies.

0548   Brassard, François. "French-Canadian Folk Music Studies: A Survey."
En   *0546*, pp. 351-359.
       A chronological view of major studies and principal publications of folk song collections.

0549   Creighton, Helen. "Canada's Maritime Provinces—an Ethnomusicological
En   Survey." *0546*, pp. 404-14.
       Considers folk music of British, Acadian-French, Gaelic, Indian and Negro ethnic groups in the Maritime Provinces. Brief bibliographies and discographies.

0550   Fowke, Edith. "Anglo-Canadian Folksong: a Survey." *0546*, pp. 335-50.
En   History of folk song collecting, with titles of major collections and some discussion of the songs. More than 100 items, spanning the period 1918-1971. Discography of 15 entries.

0551   Peacock, Kenneth. "Establishing Perimeters for Ethnomusicological
En   Research in Canada: On Going Projects and Future Possibilities at the Canadian Centre for Folk Culture Studies." *0546*, pp. 329-334.
       A review of research up to this time, with comments on current and planned studies. Useful chart presents the cultures of Canada related to holdings of instruments, songs and other music at the Centre.

Historical Studies, Chronologies, Contemporary Narratives

0552   Kallmann, Helmut. **A History of Music in Canada 1534-1914.** 2d ed.
En   Toronto: University of Toronto Press, 1969. xiv, 311p. ISBN 8020-5089-1.   ML 205 K34
       A scholarly narrative of folk, church, and art music. Westward expansion of culture; early 20th-century performances and artists. Appendix of books with music published in Canada before 1850. Bibliography of 14 pages, but not annotated. Facsimiles, music examples, indexed.

0553   Lasalle-Leduc, Annette. **La vie musicale au Canada français.** Québec:
Fr   Ministère des Affaires Culturelles, 1964.   ML 205.5 L33
       Currents and influences in French-Canadian musical life. Biographical information and portraits. Bibliography of French and English sources. Name index.

0554   Moogk, Edward B. **Roll Back the Years; History of Canadian Recorded**
En/Fr **Sound and Its Legacy: Genesis to 1930.** Ottawa: National Library of Canada, 1975. 443p. LC 75-514538.   ML 1055 M661
       Although this is a specialized study, it offers much information on Canadian artists and musical activity for the period covered. Numerous documents and portraits

of musicians. A very useful discography of Canadian-born or resident performers; another for composers; and one of early recordings. A 7" disc accompanies the volume, offering excerpts from historic recordings. Includes about 7,700 entries for performers; plus citations of some 860 recordings of 224 Canadian compositions. Issued also in French version: *En remontant les années: l'histoire et l'héritage de l'enregistrement sonore au Canada, des débuts à 1930.*

0555   Amtmann, Willy. **Music in Canada 1600-1800.** Cambridge, Ontario: Habitex
En   Books, 1975. ISBN 0-88912-020-x.   ML 205 A4
        A study of primary sources (journals, annals, etc.) and a report of musical information found in them. A section on music in old Quebec: musicians, concerts, and opera. Bibliography of four pages. Indexed.

0556   Howell, Gordon Percy. "The Development of Music in Canada." Unpublished
En   doctoral dissertation, University of Rochester, 1959. 2v. (Micro-opaque of
        typescript—Rochester: University of Rochester Press, 1962; 7 cards)
                                                            Microcard M1 205
        A detailed and documented historical essay, with individual attention to the contributions of Healy Willan, Claude Champagne, John Weinzweig, Jean Papineau-Couture, and Barbara Pentland. Musical examples; bibliography (4 pages).

Music Printing and Publishing

0557   Canadian Music Publishers Association. **A Directory of the Members of**
En   **the Canadian Music Publishers Association and Their Exclusive Agencies.**
        5th ed. Toronto: Canadian Music Publishers Association, 1975. 14p.
        LC 79-434076.   ML 112 C25
        (1st ed. 1966) Lists the publishers and their agents; indicates which catalogs include educational material; cites the royalties and rentals involved.

0557a   Calderisi, Maria. **Music Publishing in Canada: 1800-1867.** Unpublished
En   Master's thesis, McGill University, 1976. 130p.
        Subdivided into three categories: book publishers, newspaper and periodical publishers. Includes a directory of sheet music publishers.

0557b   Kallmann, Helmut. "Canadian Music Publishing." **Papers of the Biblio-**
En   **graphical Society of Canada**, 13 (1974), 40-48.
        A useful and informative overview of the subject, from the beginning to the present.

Directories

0558   **Canadian Almanac & Directory.** Toronto: Copp Clark, 1976. LC 7-24314
En   ISBN 0-7730-40226.   AY 414 C2
        Sheehy 76—CG98
        Published since 1848. An annual directory with information on three music conservatories, one college, music publishers association and three and one-half

pages of listings of musical associations, orchestras, festivals. The entries give mailing addresses and executive directors.

0558a **Canadian Music Industry Directory.** v.1— . 1965— . Toronto: RPM Music
En   Publications. (annual; irregular)
    By the publishers of a trade weekly. Information on publishers, record companies, radio stations, agencies, awards, etc.

    Other directory information on Canada is available in several general sources: *Musical America: Directory Issue (0144)*, *Musical Courier Annual Directory of the Concert World (0145)* and *The Musician's Guide (0146)*.

Periodicals

0559   Kallmann, Helmut. "A Century of Musical Periodicals in Canada."
En   **Canadian Music Journal,** 1-1 (1956), 27-43; 1-2 (1957), 25-35.
      Duckles 74—624
    A historical survey, with a checklist of titles. About 70 periodicals listed, with library locations.

    The following journals and magazines are of value for information on the current scene, for popular and/or serious music events and personalities:

0560   **Beetle.** v.1— . 1970— .
En   Focus on Canadian pop/rock, with some attention to the United States and Britain. Record reviews included.

0561   **The Canada Music Book. Les cahiers canadiens de musique.** v.1— . 1970— .
En/Fr (semiannual)
    Indexed in *Music Index (0289)*. General articles, largely on Canadian topics, in French or English (untranslated).

0562   **The Canadian Composer. Le compositeur canadien.** v.1— . 1965— .
En/Fr Toronto: Composers, Authors and Publishers Association of Canada, Ltd. (monthly)
    Indexed in *Canadian Periodical Index (0593)*; *Music Index (0289)*. Articles on composers and artists, including popular and jazz performers as well as those in the classical field.

0563   **Canadian Music Journal.** v.1-6, 1956-62. Sackville, New Brunswick:
En   Canadian Music Council. (quarterly)   ML 5 C153
    Indexed in *Music Index (0289)*.

0564   **Coda: Canada's Jazz Magazine.** v.1— . 1958— . Toronto: Coda Publications.
En   (monthly)
    Indexed in *Music Index (0289)*. Coverage is international, with emphasis on Canadian topics and personalities.

0565   **Culture vivante.** v.1-8, 1966-73. Québec: Ministère des Affaires Culturelles.
Fr   (quarterly)
       Indexed in *Music Index (0289)*. Articles on the arts in Québec Province.

0566   **Canadian Folk Music Journal.** v.1– . 1973– . Toronto: Canadian Folk
En/Fr Music Society. (annual)
       Substantial articles on Canadian folk music in its broadest sense, in English
or in French (untranslated).

0567   **Music Scene. Scène musicale.** v.1– . 1967– . Don Mills, Ontario: BMI
En/Fr Canada Ltd. (bimonthly)
       Indexed in *Music Index (0289)*. Biographical articles, chronicles, brief
news items; amply illustrated. Emphasis on popular music. Important feature:
"New works accepted into the Library of the Canadian Music Centre," which
supplements the CMC printed catalogs (*0601-0605*).

0568   **Opera Canada.** v.1– . 1960– . Toronto: Canadian Opera Association.
En   (quarterly)   ML 5 058
       Indexed in *Music Index (0289)*.

0569   **Performing Arts in Canada.** v.1– . 1964– . Toronto: Performing Arts
En   in Canada. (quarterly)
       Indexed in *Music Index (0289)*; *Canadian Periodical Index (0593)*.

Instruments

0570   Kallmann, Helmut. **Canadian-built 19th-century Musical Instruments;**
En   **a Checklist.** 2d ed. Edmonton, Alberta: Edmonton Public Library, 1966.
       7 leaves. LC 68-105582/MN   ML 478 K34 1966
       An inventory of about 90 instruments located in private collections and
museums. Mainly keyboard instruments, especially reed organs. The only wind is
an alto horn; some strings. A few Eskimo and Indian examples.

BIOGRAPHICAL SOURCES

0571   Canadian Broadcasting Corporation. **Catalogue of Canadian Composers.**
En   Ed. Helmut Kallmann. 2d ed. Toronto: Canadian Broadcasting Corpora-
       tion, 1952. 254p. LC 54-24378. (Reprint–St. Clair Shores, Mich.:
       Scholarly Press, 1972) ISBN 0-403-01375-5.   ML 106 C3 C3
         Duckles 74–111; Sheehy 76–BH67
       (1st ed. 1947) Brief sketches on 356 persons, with lists of works; informa-
tion on the compositions includes dates, performing medium, duration, publisher.
Supplementary lists of United States composers born in Canada, composers who
resided in Canada, and Canadian composers of popular music; also publishers,
and composer organizations.

0572 Canadian Broadcasting Corporation. **Thirty-four Biographies of Canadian**
En/Fr **Composers. Trente-quatre biographies de compositeurs canadiens.** Montreal:
Canadian Broadcasting Corporation, 1964. Reprint—St. Clair Shores, Mich.:
Scholarly Press, 1972. 110p. LC 75-166224/MN ML 390 C26
Duckles 74—112; ARBA 74—1101
Long articles on 34 persons (all but five also covered by (*0571*). Photo-
graphs and classified lists of works.

0573 Canadian Music Library Association. **A Bio-bibliographical Finding List of**
En **Canadian Musicians and Those Who Have Contributed to Music in Canada.**
Ottawa: Canadian Library Association, 1961. 53p. LC 62-5031.
ML 106 C3 B5
An index to biographical data on some 2,000 individuals, found in about
100 books. Entries identify the person and give dates, professional activities, and
the citation.

0574 **Orchestral Music by Canadian Composers Available from BMI Canada Ltd.**
En Toronto: BMI Canada Ltd., [1960?] ML 128 O5 B2
Biographies of 20 composers, with lists of works.

0574a Macmillan, Keith; Beckwith, John. **Contemporary Canadian Composers.**
En Toronto: Oxford University Press, 1975. 248p. LC 76-351189. ISBN
0-19-540244-8. ML 106 C3 C66
Biographies of 144 serious-music composers active since 1920. Lists of
works are included, and bibliographies of writings by and about each individual.
For works cited, information given is date of composition and first performance,
timing, instrumentation, and publisher.

0575 Canadian Music Centre, Toronto. **Reference Sources for Information on**
En/Fr **Canadian Composers. Ouvrages de références sur les compositeurs canadiens.**
Toronto: Canadian Music Centre, 1970. 11 leaves. LC 71-571653/MN
ML 120 C2 C363
A guide to biographical material in books, encyclopedias, and periodicals.

0576 Soeurs de Sainte-Anne. **Dictionnaire biographique des musiciens canadiens.**
Fr 2d ed. Lachive: Soeurs de Sainte-Anne, 1935. LC 37-5374.
ML 106 C655
(1st ed. 1922) Popular-style biographical sketches, with portraits. No lists
of works, but some titles are cited. This was the earliest biographical dictionary of
Canadian music. It emphasizes persons from Quebec.

0577 Such, Peter. **Soundprints; Contemporary Composers.** Toronto: Clarke,
En Irwin, 1972. 171p. (Canadian Portraits [series]) LC 74-160082. ISBN
0-7720-0564-8. ML 390 S972 S7
Biographical essays on six composers: John Weinzweig, Harry Somers,
John Beckwith, Norma Beecroft, Walter Buczynski, and Murray Schafer. Portraits;
lists of works.

0578   **Creative Canada: A Biographical Dictionary of Twentieth-Century Creative**
En   **and Performing Artists.** Toronto: University of Toronto Press, 1971. 2v.
         LC 71-151387. ISBN 0-8020-3262-1.   NX 513 A1C7
         Persons entered have contributed to the cultural life of Canada. Musicians,
composers, and music historians are included. Each entry gives biographical background, education, home and business address, professional memberships, recordings,
compositions, writings. Volume 2 contains a cumulative index.

0579   Napier, Ronald. **A Guide to Canada's Composers.** Willowdale, Ontario:
En   Avondale Press, 1973. 50p. LC 73-80285. ISBN 0-9690452-1-2.
                                                           ML 21 N25
         Brief notices on 255 composers, with some emphasis on those living before
the contemporary period. Only facts given are dates, types of works composed (no
lists of actual titles), publishers, and performing rights holders.

         Two general biographical works are of considerable utility for locating
information on certain musicians.

0580   **Dictionary of Canadian Biography.** Toronto: University of Toronto Press,
En/Fr   1966– . (In progress)   F 1005 D49
         Sheehy 76–AJ101
         Also published in French: *Dictionnaire biographique du Canada* (Québec:
Les Presses de l'Université Laval). Three volumes published through 1974. A
scholarly work, comparable to the *Dictionary of American Biography (0778)*;
however, it is arranged by periods rather than alphabetically.

0581   **Canadian Who's Who.** Toronto: Trans-Canada Press, 1910– . (triennial)
En   Sheehy 76–AJ107   F 1033 C23
         Publisher varies. V. 13, 1973/1975. The most useful current guide, because
of its semiannual supplements and occupational indexes (which are issued in separate
booklets). A recent index listed 70 persons as musicians.

GUIDES TO OTHER SOURCES

Bibliographies of Bibliographies

0582   Lochhead, Douglas. **Bibliography of Canadian Bibliographies. Bibliographie**
En/Fr   **des bibliographies canadiens.** 2d ed. Toronto: University of Toronto Press,
         1972. xiv, 312p. LC 76-166933. ISBN 0-8020-1865-3.
         Sheehy 76–AA39   Z1365 AI 6
         (1st ed. 1960: Raymond Tanghe, *Bibliography of Canadian Bibliographies*).
This edition contains 2,325 entries, of which 21 are on music.

0583   Proctor, George A. **Sources in Canadian Music: a Bibliography of Bibliog-**
En/Fr   **raphies. Les sources de la musique canadienne: une bibliographie des**
         bibliographies. Sackville, New Brunswick: Ralph Pickard Bell Library,
         Mount Allison University, 1975. 38p.

A very useful survey of the major reference literature, in the form of a bibliographic essay; bibliography of 167 items. Valuable descriptive annotations and detailed publication data. Name and titles indexes.

0584 Bradley, Ian L. **A Selected Bibliography of Musical Canadiana.** Vancouver:
En Versatile Publishing, 1974. 106p.
An extensive classified bibliography of over 1,300 entries. A revised edition is in progress.

0585 "A Basic Bibliography of Musical Canadiana." Toronto, 1970. 38 leaves.
En ML 120 C3 B38
A checklist prepared for the 1970 conference of the American Musicological Society & College Music Society. It presents about 650 entries, in topical groups (bibliographies, theses, histories, biographies, ethnomusicology, etc.). (This paper is available from the Faculty of Music Library, University of Toronto.)

0586 Jarvi, Edith T.; Henderson, Diane. **Guide to Basic Reference Materials**
En **for Canadian Libraries.** 4th ed. Toronto: University of Toronto Press,
1974. 272p. LC 74-194685. ISBN 0-8020-3331-8. Z1035.1 J32
An annotated bibliography of 1,595 reference titles. Most titles are not Canadian publications. Fourteen entries, or approximately one-fourth of the entries for music in the humanities chapter, deal exclusively with Canadian music.

Folk Music and Folksong

0587 Guedon, Marie-Françoise. "Canadian Indian Ethnomusicology: Selected
En Bibliography and Discography." **Ethnomusicology**, 16-3 (Sept. 1972),
465-78.
Intended to be "an interim list." About 250 entries, in geographical groupings; occasional brief explanatory notes.

0588 Fowke, Edith. "A Reference List on Canadian Folk Music." **Canadian Folk**
En **Music Journal**, 1 (1973)
A selective list, revising an earlier compilation of 1966. Presents books, pamphlets, and journal articles. Also gives names of compositions based on folk songs. Discography.

0589 Estreicher, Zygmunt. "Eskimo-Musik." **MGG** (*0058*), III, cols. 1526-1533.
Ge A general survey and review of earlier research. One musical example, two photographs, one-half column bibliography.

0589a Mount Allison University. Library. **Catalogue of Canadian Folk Music in**
En **the Mary Mellish Archibald Library and Other Special Collections.**
Sackville, New Brunswick: Mount Allison University, 1974. 88p.
A classified bibliography of writings about Canadian folk music, with author, subject and title index (including material from periodicals), plus list of compositions, and discography.

See also Haywood, *0536*, especially vol. 1, pp. 422-28; and vol. 2, pp. 1078-1113, 1114-1129, 1130-1159. And Gillis (*0521*) cites 19 items under Canada.

Annual and Periodic Lists

Coverage of Canadian imprints for the last half century is provided in two works:

0590
En
Canadian Catalogue of Books Published in Canada, about Canada, as Well as Those Written by Canadians, with Imprint 1921-1949. Consolidated English language reprint edition, with cumulated author index. Toronto: Toronto Public Libraries, 1959. 2v.   Z1365 C222
  Sheehy 76—AA523
Continued by the following item.

0591
En
Canadiana. Ottawa: National Library of Canada, 1951— . (monthly; annual cumulations)   Z1365 C23
  Sheehy 76—AA532
Succeeds the preceding item. An excellent example of national bibliography. Lists, in classified arrangement, all material published in Canada: books, pamphlets, theses, new journals, microforms, films and filmstrips, government publications (national and provincial). Musical compositions included beginning 1953, sound recordings beginning 1970. Earlier coverage of music-score publication is found in *0599*.

The next title offers a convenient summary of currently available books:

0592
En
Canadian Books in Print. Subject Index. Toronto: University of Toronto Press, 1973— . ISBN 8020-4520-0.   Z 1365 C2197
A topical arrangement of the titles given in *Canadian Books in Print* (Winchell 76—AA531); includes material originally published in Canada or reissued by Canadian publishers. About 65 entries under music in 1975; some song-books listed, but no music scores. Earlier title: *Subject Guide to Canadian Books in Print*.

Periodical Indexes

0593
En/Fr
Canadian Periodical Index. Index de périodiques canadiens. 1928-32; 1938— . Ottawa: Canadian Library Association. (monthly, annual; cumulations for 1938-47 and 1948-59)   AI 3 C2422
  Sheehy 76—AE198, AE200
Publisher and title vary; see Winchell for the involved history. Currently listing articles, by author and subject, from some 88 journals. French see references to the English subject headings. Only two music journals covered: *Canadian Composer* (*0562*) and *Performing Arts in Canada* (*0569*), and both are also included in the *Music Index*. So the principal value of CPI is for location of articles on musical topics in general magazines and in journals of related disciplines.

The next two items are unpublished. They offer two approaches to the periodical literature which would not otherwise be available. The National Library does give postal reference service, and invites inquiries related to the two files.

0594   National Library of Canada. Music Division. "Index of Articles on
En   Canadian Musicians Found in Periodicals and Other Sources."
       Index card file, containing some 3,500 entries in 1976. Includes news
items and obituaries.

0595   National Library of Canada. Music Division. "Index of Pictures of
En   Canadian Musicians Found in Periodicals."
       Index card file, containing some 4,000 entries in 1976.

Dissertations

0596   Canadian Bibliographic Centre. **Canadian Graduate Theses in the**
En   **Humanities and Social Sciences, 1921-1946.** Ottawa: Printer to the King,
       1951. 194p. LC 53-18478.   Z5055 C2 088
       Sheehy 76–AH25
       A subject list, subdivided by institution, of 3,043 theses. Author index;
English and French subject indexes. Brief notes on content given. Only seven items
on music, of 3,043 total entries; useful for related-field materials.

0597   National Library of Canada. **Canadian Theses. Thèses canadiennes.**
En/Fr 1960/61– . Ottawa: Queen's Printer, 1962– . (annual)
       Sheehy 76–AH26   Z5055 C2 0885
       Arranged by Dewey classification, then by university. Author index. Total
of 78 musical works (48 master's and 30 doctoral) through 1969/70, which was
most recent issue seen.

LISTS OF MUSIC

Selective and Critical Lists

General

0598   BMI Canada, Ltd. **Yes, There Is Canadian Music.** 7th ed. Montreal,
En   Toronto: BMI Canada, Ltd., 1968. 103p. LC 72-491222.
                                                           ML 120 C2 B2
       (1st ed. 1952) Title varies. Lists of popular and serious music, with
discographies.

0599   Canadian Music Library Association. **Musical Canadiana; a Subject Index.**
En   Ottawa: Canadian Library Association, 1967. 62p. LC 68-114946.
                                                           ML 120 C2 C33

Music by Canadians, about Canada, or having some association with Canada; some 800 works given, all published prior to 1921. Includes a list of about 80 patriotic songs. There is no list of music published in Canada between 1921 and 1952. Beginning in 1953, *Canadiana* (*0591*) covers publication of music scores.

Instrumental Music

0600   Canadian League of Composers. **Catalogue of Orchestral Music, Including**
En   **Works for Small Orchestra and Band, Concertos, Vocal-Orchestral and**
        Choral-Orchestral Works. Toronto: Canadian League of Composers, 1957.
        58p. LC 61-20792.   ML 120 C2 C35
        Information given for each work: publisher, performing rights, instrumenta-
tion, descriptive notes. Arranged by composer, with index by format.

0601   Canadian Music Centre, Toronto. **Catalogue of Chamber Music Available**
En/Fr   **on Loan from the Library of the Canadian Music Centre.** Toronto:
        Canadian Music Centre, 1967. 288p. LC 68-141478/MN. Supplement,
        1973.   ML 120 C2 C357
        Works by 85 Canadian composers. Information given: instrumentation,
difficulty, duration, date of composition, performance history, recordings, publisher,
descriptive notes. Biographical sketches; discographies. See also *0567*.

0602   Canadian Music Centre, Toronto. **Catalogue of Orchestral Music at the**
En/Fr   **Canadian Music Centre, Including Orchestra, Band, Concertos, Operas**
        and Vocal-Orchestral. Catalogue des oeuvres disponibles au Centre
        Musical Canadien; orchestre, fanfare et harmonie, opéra, voix et orchestre.
        Toronto: Canadian Music Centre, 1963. Supplement, 1968. unpaged.
        LC 64-3280/MN   ML 120 C2 C36
        An updated version of *0600*. Same type of information, and same format.
See also *0567*.

0603   Canadian Music Centre, Toronto. **Catalogue of Canadian Keyboard Music**
En/Fr   **Available on Loan from the Library of the Canadian Music Centre. Catalogue**
        de musique canadienne à clavier disponible à titre de prêt à la bibliothèque
        du Centre Musical Canadien. Toronto: Canadian Music Centre, 1971. 91p.
        LC 74-130379.   ML 120 C2 C355
        Similar format to the preceding. Works for piano, organ, and harpsichord.
See also *0567*.

Opera and Vocal Music

0604   Canadian Music Centre, Toronto. **Canadian Vocal Music Available for**
En/Fr   **Perusal from the Library of the Canadian Music Centre. Musique vocale**
        canadienne. 2d ed. Toronto: Canadian Music Centre, 1971. 81p.
        LC 74-163963/MN   ML 128 V7 C24

(1st ed. 1967) Solo pieces, duets, trios, ensembles, and operas by Canadians. Information given for each work: publisher, form, accompaniment, and voice availability (high, medium, low). See also *0567*.

0605   Canadian Music Centre, Toronto. **Catalogue of Canadian Choral Music**
En   **Available for Perusal from the Library of the Canadian Music Centre.**
        2d ed. Toronto: Canadian Music Centre, 1970. 207p.

   Duckles 74–838   ML 128 V7 C25

   (1st ed. 1966) More than 700 Canadian works for adult choirs, in classified array. Information given: difficulty, accompaniment, duration, publisher. Composer index. See also *0567, 0600, 0602*.

Lists of Manuscript Music

0606   Canadian Music Centre, Toronto. **Catalogue of Microfilms of Unpublished**
En   **Canadian Music.** Toronto: Canadian Music Centre, 1970. 78 leaves.

                                                     ML 120 C3 C36

   About 1,200 works, in composer order and also by reel sequence. Works under composers are grouped by genre; information given includes date and instrumentation. About 90 composers, most of them contemporary.

DISCOGRAPHIES

   Many of the preceding items contain recording lists. See especially: *0549, 0550, 0554, 0578, 0588, 0591, 0598, 0601, 0602*.

UNITED STATES

   Note: there are many citations in this section to entries in Richard Jackson, *United States Music . . . (0786)*.

THE LANGUAGE OF MUSIC

   These items in Volume I display the basic American-English vocabulary: *0001-0006; 0011-0013; 0015-0017; 0025*. Useful works in the present volume are *0504, 0505, 0506*.

DIRECT INFORMATION SOURCES

Introductions and General Surveys

0607   "Vereinigte Staaten." **MGG** (*0058*), XI, columns 1467-1487.
Ge   Articles were written by American music authorities and translated for use in the *MGG*: 1) music before 1820, by Irving Lowens (one column bibliography);

2) 1820-1920, by H. Wiley Hitchcock (one-half column bibliography); 3) after
1920, by Nathan Broder (one-sixth column bibliography); 4) American radio and
television music, by Julius Mattfeld (no bibliography); 5) music education and
musicology, by Nathan Broder (no bibliography). Dependable surveys of main
figures, works, books, and trends. The article on the post-1920 era gives some
interesting 1963 statistics on numbers of musicians, music students, record sales,
etc. The study of radio and television is a strong presentation, with much detail
on persons and works. The final article mentions some important libraries, schools
of music, and a few musicological publications; it is not very substantial.

0608   Wörner, Karl H. "Amerika." **MGG** (*0058*), I, columns 418-427.
Ge   Survey of early compositions, books on music, and musical performances
in the United States. Comments on European (especially German) influences, both
musical taste and on composers. Names major festivals, organizations, awards,
journals. Nothing about America outside U.S.A. Bibliography: one-half column.

0609   Yellin, Victor. "United States." **Harvard Dictionary** (*0002*), pp. 882-889.
En   Compact survey of serious national music described in four time divisions:
1607-1790, 1790-1865, 1865-1929, 1930– . Folk music, black music, jazz, blues
mentioned. Bibliographies.

0610   **Grove's Dictionary of Music and Musicians. American Supplement.** Being
En   the sixth volume of the complete work. Waldo Selden Pratt, ed. Philadelphia:
        Theodore Presser Co., 1927. 412p.   ML 100 G884 1904 suppl.
        Grove's is described at *0059*. The idea of a specifically American supplement
seems quaint today, but it did represent a concession to the criticism that *Grove's*
was overwhelmingly Anglo-European. The *Supplement* still has considerable reference
value, primarily for material on individuals (700 biographical articles, with lists of
works; 1,700 persons briefly identified in a chronological register), and for information on performing organizations of the time. Canadians and some Latin Americans
included. Sixteen portraits, plus references to other portraits in the main set. One of
the longest articles, "Tune-Books," pp. 385-392, contains a useful selective list of
books with religious music, "largely condensed and rearranged from Metcalf,
American Psalmody . . . " (0792). No index.

Folk Music and Folksong

General

0611   Nettl, Bruno. **Folk Music in the United States; an Introduction.** 3d ed.
En   revised and expanded by Helen Myers. Detroit: Wayne State University
        Press, 1976. 189p. LC 76-84. ISBN 0-8143-1556-9.
                                                ML 3551 N47
        (1st ed. 1960) First two editions had title: *An Introduction to Folk Music
in the United States*. Considers the nature and styles of folk music in general, and
the specific American traditions (Indian, British, Afro-American, Hispanic-American,
and European). There is a useful bibliographic essay. Indexed.

0612   Lawless, Ray McKinley. **Folksingers and Folksongs in America; a Handbook**
En   **of Biography, Bibliography, and Discography.** Illustrated from paintings by
       Thomas Hart Benton and others, and from designs in Steuben glass. New
       rev. ed. with special suppl. New York: Duell, Sloan and Pearce, 1965.
       xviii, 750p. LC 65-21677/MN.   ML 3550 L4 1965
       Duckles 74–203; Jackson–34
       (1st ed. 1960) This is a reprint of the original edition, with a supplement
updating information on singers, books and magazines, and recordings; the supplement has its own index. The reprint section does include some corrections; and it
has its separate index. Includes biographical sketches of folksingers, facts about folk
instruments, list of folksong collections, list of song titles in collections.

0613   Stambler, Irwin; Landon, Grelun. **Encyclopedia of Folk, Country and**
En   **Western Music.** New York: St. Martin's Press, 1969. vii, 396p. Paperback
       reprint–1975. LC 67-10659.   ML 102 J3S78
       Duckles 74–209; Jackson–38
       About 500 topical and biographical articles, primarily in the country-
western field. Appendices of award winning songs and recordings.

       The next two items are major journals:

0614   **Journal of American Folklore.** v.1– . Apr/June 1888– . Richmond,
En   Virginia [etc.] : American Folklore Society. (quarterly) LC 17-28737.
                                                         GR 1 J8
       Place of publication varies. An important source of scholarly essays, some
of them on musical topics. An index to the first 70 years was issued in 1958 by the
Society.

0615   **Sing Out.** v.1– . May 1950– . New York: People's Artists, 1950– .
En   ML 1 S588
       Lawless (in *0612*) calls this the "oldest and . . . best of the 'little' magazines
in the field." Its major emphasis is American folk music; approach is popular rather
than academic.

       Other magazines with information on folk music are cited later: *0647-0652*.
And see also the annotated list of periodicals in Sandberg, *0521a*.

       Discographies in the general area of American folk music are found under
Discographies (see page 91).

Indian Music

0616   Densmore, Frances. **The American Indians and Their Music.** New York:
En   The Womans Press, 1926. 143p. LC 27-1524. Reprint–New York: Johnson
       Reprint Corp., 1970. (Series in American Studies) LC 70-18861.
                                                         ML 3557 D362
       Chapters on Indian life, social organization, language, arts and crafts,
ceremonies, dances, games, customs, etc. Types of Indian songs: children's songs,

love songs, and other varieties. Instruments, scales; history of the study of Indian music, with bibliography of early writings.

Densmore, of the Bureau of American Ethnology, was responsible for much of the pioneer field work in music among the Indians. The original studies appeared as official Bulletins of the Bureau, which was a unit of the Smithsonian Institution. Reprints have been published by Da Capo Press with nothing new added.

These are the titles concerning individual tribes and groupings:

0617   Densmore, Frances. **Chippewa Music.** Washington: U.S. Government
En   Printing Office, 1910-13. 2v. (Bureau of American Ethnology, Bulletins
       45 and 53). Reprint—New York: Da Capo Press, 1972. LC 77-164513.
       ISBN 0-306-70459-5. (Da Capo Press Music Reprint Series)
                                                    ML 3557 D355 1972
                                                    (E 51 U6 no. 45, 53)
       Discussion of the cultural setting and folkways of the group; the role of
music, dance and song. Illustrated with 20 photographs. Transcriptions and analyses
of 200 songs.

0618   Densmore, Frances. **Choctaw Music.** Washington: Smithsonian Institution,
En   1943. 101-188p. (Bureau of American Ethnology, Anthropological Paper
       28, p. 101-188 of its Bulletin 136.) Reprint—New York: Da Capo Press,
       1972. (Da Capo Press Music Reprint Series) LC 72-1883. ISBN 0-306-
       70511-7.   ML 3557 D3554
       ARBA 74—1047   (E 51 U6 no. 136)
       As in other volumes of this series, there is a background discussion of
cultural setting and folklore. Detailed account of instruments and their uses.
Transcriptions and analyses of songs, and comparisons of the characteristics of
these songs with those of songs in other tribes. Index.

0619   Densmore, Frances. **Mandan and Hidatsa Music.** Washington: U.S.
En   Government Printing Office, 1923. 192p. (Bureau of American Ethnology.
       Bulletin 80.) Reprint—New York: Da Capo Press, 1972. (Da Capo Press
       Music Reprint Series) LC 72-1886. ISBN 0-306-70514-1.
                                                    ML 3557 D357 1972
       ARBA 74—1048   (E 51 U6 no. 80)
       Same format as others in the series. Transcriptions, with close melodic and
rhythmic analyses, of 110 songs. Nineteen pictures and six diagrams. Comparisons of
songs among the Chippewa, Sioux, Ute, Mandan and Hidatsa.

0620   Densmore, Frances. **Menominee Music.** Washington: U.S. Government
En   Printing Office, 1932. 230p. (Bureau of American Ethnology. Bulletin 102)
       Reprint—New York: Da Capo Press, 1972. (Da Capo Press Music Reprint
       Series) LC 72-1882. ISBN 0-306-70510-9.   ML 3557 D358 1972
       ARBA 74—1049   (E 51 U6 no. 102)
       Similar format to the preceding.

0621 Densmore, Frances. **Music of Acoma, Isleta, Cochiti and Zuñi Pueblos.**
En Washington: U.S. Government Printing Office, 1957. 117p. (Bureau of
American Ethnology. Bulletin 165) Reprint—New York: Da Capo Press,
1972. (Da Capo Press Music Reprint Series) LC 72-1877. ISBN 0-306-
70505-2.   ML 3557 D3583 1972
ARBA 74—1050   (E 51 U6 no. 165)
Similar format. Transcriptions of 82 songs; six plates. No index.

0622 Densmore, Frances. **Nootka and Quileute Music.** Washington: U.S.
En Government Printing Office, 1939. 358p. (Bureau of American Ethnology,
Bulletin 124) Reprint—New York: Da Capo Press, 1972. (Da Capo Press
Music Reprint Series) LC 72-1885. ISBN 0-306-70513-3.
                                                            ML 3557 D3645 1972
ARBA 74—1051   (E 51 U6 no. 124)
Similar format.

0623 Densmore, Frances. **Northern Ute Music.** Washington: U.S. Government
En Printing Office, 1922. 213p. (Bureau of American Ethnology. Bulletin 75)
Reprint—New York: Da Capo Press, 1972. (Da Capo Press Music Reprint
Series) LC 72-1887. ISBN 0-306-70515-X.   ML 3557 D365 1972
ARBA 74—1052   (E 51 U6 no. 75)
Similar format.

0624 Densmore, Frances. **Papago Music.** Washington: U.S. Government Printing
En Office, 1929. 229p. (Bureau of American Ethnology. Bulletin 90)
Reprint—New York: Da Capo Press, 1972. (Da Capo Press Music Reprint
Series) LC 72-1881. ISBN 0-306-70509-5.   ML 3557 D367 1972
ARBA 74—1053   (E 51 U6 no. 90)
Similar format, with 167 musical examples and eight plates. Index.

0625 Densmore, Frances. **Pawnee Music.** Washington: U.S. Government Printing
En Office, 1929. 129p. (Bureau of American Ethnology. Bulletin 93) Reprint—
New York: Da Capo Press, 1972. (Da Capo Press Music Reprint Series)
LC 72-1880. ISBN 0-306-70508-7.   ML 3557 D368 1972
ARBA 74—1054   (E 51 U6 no. 93)
Similar format, with 86 songs transcribed; eight plates. Index.

0626 Densmore, Frances. **Seminole Music.** Washington: Smithsonian Institution,
En 1956. 223p. (Bureau of American Ethnology. Bulletin 161) Reprint—New
York: Da Capo Press, 1972. (Da Capo Press Music Reprint Series) LC 72-
1878. ISBN 0-306-70516-0.   ML 3557 D373 1972
ARBA 74—1055   (E 51 U6 no. 161)
Similar format; 243 songs transcribed and analyzed; 18 plates, diagram,
index.

0627   Densmore, Frances. **Teton Sioux Music.** Washington: Smithsonian Institu-
En   tion, 1918. 561p. (Bureau of American Ethnology. Bulletin 61) Reprint–
       New York: Da Capo Press, 1972. (Da Capo Press Music Reprint Series)
       LC 72-1889. ISBN 0-306-70516-8.   ML 3557 D376 1972
          ARBA 74–1056   (E 51 U6 no. 61)
       Similar format, but a particularly extended study: 240 songs transcribed
and analyzed in great detail; 82 pictures and 43 other illustrations (mostly diagrams).
Index.

0628   Densmore, Frances. **Yuman and Yaqui Music.** Washington: U.S. Government
En   Printing Office, 1932. 216p. (Bureau of American Ethnology, Bulletin 110)
       Reprint–New York: Da Capo Press, 1972. (Da Capo Press Music Reprint
       Series) LC 72-1884. ISBN 0-306-70512-5.   ML 3557 D379 1972
          ARBA 74–1057   (E 51 U6 no. 110)
       Similar format.

0629   Herzog, George. "A Comparison of Pueblo and Pima Musical Styles."
En   **Journal of American Folklore** 49 (1936), 283-417.
       Very technical analysis of vocal technique, tonality, melody, rhythm,
structure, types. Pueblo music found to be "the most complex musical development in aboriginal North America." Pima music is much simpler. Song texts and
comments; list of Pueblo songs and dances. Music examples: pp. 341-407. Bibliography of three pages, not annotated. No index.

0630   Kurath, Gertrude Prokosch. **Iroquois Music and Dance: Ceremonial Arts**
En   **of Two Seneca Longhouses.** Washington: U.S. Government Printing
       Office, 1964. 268p. (Bureau of American Ethnology. Bulletin 187)
       LC 64-61317.   ML 3557 K87
                                                 (E 51 U6 no. 187)
       In the manner of the Densmore series. Rituals, social dances (table of
"dance functions") with all dance patterns diagrammed and analyzed; melodic
and structural examination of songs; 146 pages of musical transcriptions. Name
and topical index. Only three photos.

0631   Kurath, Gettrude Prokosch; Garcia, Antonio. **Music and Dance of the**
En   **Tewa Pueblos.** Santa Fe: Museum of New Mexico Press, 1970. viii, 309p.
       (Museum of New Mexico. Research Records, no. 8) LC 76-113265.
                                                 ML 3557 K875
       Study of musical patterns, choreography, body movements, all in social
contexts. Bibliography of 7 pages. Lists of slides, films, photos and recordings.

0632   McAllester, David Park. **Peyote Music.** New York: [no pub.] 1949. 104p.
En   (Viking Fund Publications in Anthropology, no. 13) LC 50-123 rev.
       (Reprint–New York: Johnson Reprint Corp., 1964)
                                                 ML 3557 M3
       Peyote Comanche ceremonies, music and songs; analysis of style, accompani-
ments, rhythm, tempo, texts. Comparisons with music of other tribes. Bibliography.

0633   Merriam, Alan P. **Ethnomusicology of the Flathead Indians.** Chicago:
En   Aldine Pub. Co., 1967. xvi, 403p. (Viking Fund Publications in
       Anthropology, no. 44) LC 66-23167/MN
       Very detailed study of music in the Flathead culture, describing forty
different kinds of songs in such categories as war songs, personal power songs, life
cycle songs, etc. Attempts to identify the ideas held about music, and the influences
both of other tribes and of modern civilization on Flathead music. A sampling of
the repertoire is given close analysis, with tables of data on technical features. An
appendix glossary (by Susan Houston) gives basic Flathead music terminology.
Bibliography; index.

0634   Stevenson, Robert Murrell. "Written Sources for Indian Music until
En   1882." **Ethnomusicology**, 17-1 (Jan. 1973), 1-40.
                                       ML 1 E77
       Inventory and discussion of basic sources for Indian music of Latin
American and the U.S. Southwest, 1492-1882. Full documentation; musical
examples.

       For discographies of Indian music see Folk Music and Folksong, p. 91.

Anglo-American Folk Music

0635   Abrahams, Roger D.; Foss, George. **Anglo-American Folksong Style.**
En   Englewood Cliffs, N.J.: Prentice-Hall, 1968. 242p. LC 68-11288.
                                       ML 3553 A27
       Texts, verse, tunes, and word-music relationships in songs of white rural
America. A useful presentation at introductory level, with 50 traditional songs
(collected in the field by the authors in the southern Appalachians and the Ozarks)
given in full.

0636   Coffin, Tristam P. **The British Traditional Ballad in North America.**
En   Rev. ed. Philadelphia: The American Folklore Society, 1963. xvii, 186p.
       (Publications of the American Folklore Society: Bibliographical and
       Special Series, vol. 2) LC 63-22101.   ML 3553 C6
       (1st ed. 1950) Most of this book concerns the 305 English and Scottish
popular ballads compiled in the 19th century by Frances James Child and thereafter
known as the "Child Ballads." Coffin indexes published locations of variants for
these ballads, and also discusses previous scholarship for each of them. In the rest
of the book, he gives general information and ideas on ballads and their variations.
The entire work is focused on literary elements of the ballad, with no musical factors
introduced. Bibliography. The discussion of this work in *0790* gives a concise view
of ballad research in the United States since Child.

0637   Bronson, Bertrand Harris. **The Traditional Tunes of the Child Ballads.**
En   Princeton: Princeton University Press, 1959. 4v. LC 57-5468.
                                       ML 3650 B82
       In contrast to Coffin (*1502*), Bronson concentrates on the music of the
Child repertoire; he has endeavored to compile all the actual melodies for Child's

texts, and has gathered 210 of the 305 ballads. Some of the texts are represented by more than a hundred different tunes. Extensive bibliographies and indexes, and scholarly commentaries throughout.

Country and Western Music

The first two items are the major encyclopedic approaches.

0638   Gentry, Linnel. **A History and Encyclopedia of Country, Western and**
En   **Gospel Music.** 2d ed. Nashville, Tenn.: Clairmont Corp., 1969. xiv, 598p.
        LC 70-7208.   ML 200 G4

        Duckles 74–202; Jackson–32; ARBA 73–1059 (for reprint of 1st ed.)
(1st ed. 1961) A collection of 76 articles, originally published 1908-1968, and some 600 biographical sketches. The articles are intended to present an historical perspective. Biographical coverage is good, although virtually limited to living performers. Jackson has noted that "one stunning flaw is the (total?) omission of black gospel performers. Not even Mahalia Jackson, Clara Ward, or Sister Rosetta Tharpe are included."

0639   Shestack, Melvin. **The Country Music Encyclopedia.** New York: T. Y.
En   Crowell Co., 1974. xii, 410p. LC 74-9644. ISBN 0-690-00442-7.
        ARBA 75–1176   ML 102 C7 S5
        Emphasis is on the most prominent performers, i.e., those with the greatest commercial success. Other persons connected with country music are neglected (many can be found in Stambler, *0613*). Lengthy coverage for those who are included, with photographs. Also a discography, list of country music radio stations, and a "sampling of country songs." A popular chatty style and a number of factual errors detract from the value of the presentation.

        See also Stambler, *0613*.

        The next book concentrates on biography:

0640   Malone, Bill C.; McCulloh, Judith. **Stars of Country Music; Uncle Dave**
En   **Macon to Johnny Rodriguez.** Urbana: University of Illinois Press, 1975.
        LC 75-15848.   ML 385 S73
        Individual chapters on 19 leading performers or groups as well as an opening chapter on "early pioneers" and a closing chapter on "country music since World War II." Bibliographies; discographies; index of names, songs, radio stations, and record companies.

        The following entries focus on historical considerations.

0641   Malone, Bill C. **Country Music U.S.A; a Fifty-year History.** Austin, Texas:
En   Published for the American Folklore Society by the University of Texas
        Press, 1968. xii, 422p. (Publications of the American Folklore Society.
        Memoir Series, vol. 54) LC 68-66367. ISBN 292-78377-9.
                                                     GR 1 A5 vol. 54

A fine, scholarly work, proceeding from the early "hillbilly" era (with its first star, Jimmie Rodgers), into cowboy songs, the post-war boom period, country-pop and Nashville sound, honky-tonk, saga song, bluegrass, and urban folk revival. Extensive biographical information throughout. Particularly strong bibliography, which includes unpublished materials such as letters, manuscripts, theses, and reports of interviews. No musical examples; but sixteen photos and a good index. Gilbert Chase says that Malone "has pointed the way for other scholars to follow with a work of exemplary thoroughness and empathetic comprehension" [Review of the book, in *Notes* 26-1 (Sept. 1969), 37-39].

0642   Shelton, Robert. **The Country Music Story; a Picture History of Country**
En   **and Western Music.** Photos by Burt Goldblatt. Indianapolis: Bobbs-Merrill,
       1966. 256p. LC 65-25655.   ML 2811 S5 1966ax
       Jackson—37
       "A superb visual record," Jackson calls it; with a text commentary,
selective discography, and name index.

0643   Price, Steven D. **Take Me Home; the Rise of Country and Western Music.**
En   New York: Praeger Publishers, 1974. 184p. LC 71-189922. ISBN 0-275-
       53610-2.   ML 3561 C69 P7
       Discussion of work songs, love songs, adventure songs. Emphasis on texts;
no music included. About 50 biographies; bibliography of 17 items with brief
comments; discography of some 150 entries, not annotated. Footnotes, pictures,
name index and song title index.

0644   White, John I. **Git Along Little Doggies; Songs and Songmakers of the**
En   **American West.** Urbana: University of Illinois, 1975. 268p. LC 75-6404.
       ISBN 0-252-00327-6.   ML 3551 W48
       History of western and cowboy songs and information about the singers.
Photos, musical examples and song texts. Discography of the author's own recordings.
Index.

The next items deal specifically with the "bluegrass" idiom.

0645   Artis, Bob. **Bluegrass.** New York: Hawthorn Books, 1975. 182p. LC 74-
En   33588. ISBN 0-8015-0758-8.   ML 3561 B62 A7
       ARBA 76—1022
       Biographical data, discography; lists of bluegrass magazines, radio stations
and organizations (with addresses). Good index, but a weak bibliography.

0646   Price, Steven D. **Old as the Hills: the Story of Bluegrass Music.** New York:
En   Viking Press, 1975. x, 110p. LC 74-20637. ISBN 0-670-52204-X.
                                                ML 3561 B62 P7
       A general narrative, emphasizing personalities; much less substantial than
Price's *Take Me Home* (*0643*). Useful annotated discography. No index.

There are two scholarly journals in the field:

0647   **The Journal of Country Music.** v.2, no.4– ; Winter 1971– . Nashville:
En   Country Music Foundation. LC 73-646348.   ML 1 C91774
      Continues the numbering of the earlier *Country Music Foundation News
Letter.* Articles and discographies on country-western, bluegrass, and Anglo-American
folksong. "Museum notes"; book reviews.

0648   **JEMF Quarterly.** v.1– . Oct. 1965– . Los Angeles: John Edwards Memorial
En   Foundation. (quarterly) LC 72-217195.   ML 1 J55
      Formerly the *JEMF Newsletter.* Published by the Folklore and Mythology
Center of the University of California at Los Angeles. The Foundation carries on
studies of country, western, bluegrass, gospel, blues, rock, and other folk/popular
forms. Issues of the *Quarterly* contain discographies, book reviews, articles, news
notes, library inventories, and resumes of taped interviews.

There is also some information value, mostly biographical and/or related
to current hit recordings, in the popular magazines. Four useful titles:

0649   **Bluegrass Music News.** v.1– . 1964– . Lexington, Kentucky: University
En   of Kentucky, Music Dept. Indexed in *Music Article Guide* (*0290*).

0650   **Bluegrass Unlimited.** v.1– . no.1– . July 1966– . Burke, Virginia:
En   Bluegrass Unlimited. (monthly) LC 73-646162. ML 1 B517
      Indexed in *Music Index* (*0289*).

0651   **Muleskinner News.** v.1– . 1969– . Elon College, North Carolina:
En   Muleskinner News. (monthly) LC 73-646203.   ML 1 M 1948

0652   **Pickin'.** v.1– . 1974– . Cedar Knolls, New Jersey: Universal Graphics
En   Corp. (monthly) LC 75-643607.   ML 1 P69202
      Other periodicals carrying material on country-western music are listed
elsewhere: *0754-0759.*

Discographies of country-western music are listed under Discographies
(see p. 91).

Other Folk Music

0653   Cook, Harold E. **Shaker Music: A Manifestation of American Folk
En   Culture.** Lewisburg, Pennsylvania: Bucknell University Press, 1973.
      312p. LC 71-161507.   ML 3178 S5 C6
      The Shakers (United Order of Believers) were a communal, religious
society which flourished in the mid-nineteenth century; it included 18 communities
in New England, New York, Ohio, Kentucky, and Indiana. Cook examines the
history of the movement, and then its musical life. Surviving manuscripts are listed.
One reviewer cautions that the "end result is an incomplete and sometimes
misleading account" (Nicholas Tawa, in *Journal of the American Musicological*

Society 28-1 (Spring 1975): 156-159). This review should be consulted before information is drawn from the book.

0654 Laws, George Malcolm. **Native American Balladry; a Descriptive Study**
En **and a Bibliographical Syllabus.** Philadelphia: American Folklore Society,
1950. xii, 276p. (Publications of the American Folklore Society.
Bibliographical Series, v.1) LC 51-1319 ML 3551 L3
Duckles 74–684
Ballad is defined as a "narrative folk song which dramatizes a memorable event" by Laws, who considers 185 of them. The songs are grouped by type: war, pioneers, lumberjacks, sailors, etc., and analyzed from historical and technical viewpoints. Geographical distribution is noted. Partial texts of the ballads are provided, with references to publications that have the complete texts. Bibliography of four pages, not annotated. Index of songs only.

Popular Music

General

0655 Kinkle, Roger D. **The Complete Encyclopedia of Popular Music and Jazz,**
En **1900-1950.** New Rochelle, N.Y.: Arlington House, 1974. 4v. LC 74-7109.
ISBN 0-87000-229-5. ML 102 P66 K55
ARBA 75–1171
A remarkable and well-organized assemblage of facts. Vol. 1 presents a chronology of events relating to popular music from 1900 to 1950 (including for each year the new Broadway musicals with their casts, dates and songs; other leading songs; filmed musicals and hit records). Vols. 2 and 3 are biographical: 2,105 sketches, with discographies. These are pop/jazz people; country-western and blues performers are omitted. In Vol. 4 there are chronological lists of records issued by nine manufacturers from the mid-20s to the early 40s. Indexed by personal names, song titles (28,000 of them), and films.

0656 Mattfeld, Julius. **Variety Music Cavalcade, 1620-1969; a Chronology of**
En **Vocal and Instrumental Music Popular in the United States.** 3d ed.
Englewood Cliffs, N.J.: Prentice-Hall, 1971. xx, 766p. LC 70-129240.
ISBN 0-13-940718-9. ML 128 V7 M4 1971
Duckles 74–962; Jackson–11
(1st ed. 1952) Annual summary of world events, as background, and list of top songs with some instrumental pieces as well. Index of musical works by title.

0657 Ewen, David. **Panorama of American Popular Music; the Story of Our**
En **National Ballads and Folk Songs, the Songs of Tin Pan Alley, Broadway**
and Hollywood, New Orleans Jazz, Swing, and Symphonic Jazz.
Englewood Cliffs, N.J.: Prentice-Hall, 1957. 365p. LC 57-6173.
ML 2811 E8

That very ambitious title suggests that the subjects will be treated very superficially, but there is a good deal of information in this book. It is in popular style, undocumented and subjective. Chapters on patriotic song, folk song, Negro music, minstrel shows, vaudeville songs, musicals, ragtime, revues, Hollywood, etc. Index to song titles and persons.

0658   Ewen, David. **American Popular Songs from the Revolutionary War to**
En   **the Present.** New York: Random House, 1966. xiii, 507p. LC 66-12843/MN.
          Duckles 74–958   ML 128 N3 E9
Entries for musicals, composers and some topics as well as some 3,600 songs. For songs, gives basic facts and considerable background information. Also lists of all-time best selling records 1919-1966 (about 1,000 titles), and a chronological "all-time hit parade" 1765-1966. Short list of performers and the songs identified with them.

Regarding other lists of songs, see note after *0662.*

0659   Spaeth, Sigmund. **A History of Popular Music in America.** New York:
En   Random House, 1948. xv, 729p. LC 48-8954.   ML 2811 S7
          Jackson—73
A popular-style chronological account of songs, beginning with Yankee Doodle. War songs, hymns, carols, Stephen Foster, minstrel songs, show tunes, blues songs, modern writers. The songs are listed in chronological order, 1770-1948, on pp. 587-657. Much biographical information and miscellaneous data throughout. Indexed by song title and by persons.

0659a   Stambler, Irwin. **Encyclopedia of Popular Music.** New York: St. Martin's,
En   1965. 359p. LC 65-20817.   ML 102 J3 S8
About 600 articles, mostly biographical; some for musicals, and a few for terms. Popular style. Useful lists of award-winning records in many categories, by year from 1958 to 1964. Also awards for musicals, film music (including nominations as well as winners of academy awards) 1934-1964; list of gold records.

0660   Wilder, Alec. **American Popular Song; the Great Innovators, 1900-1950.**
En   New York: Oxford University Press, 1972. xxxix, 536p. LC 70-159643.
          ISBN 0-19-501445-6.   ML 3551 W54
          Jackson—75
A sophisticated study of songs by 23 major writers, 11 of whom are given the greatest attention. There is also a section of individual outstanding songs by other composers. Endeavors to isolate the peculiarly American elements in these songs; discusses verbal characteristics and melodic/harmonic/rhythmic features. Index of song titles, composers, lyricists. Many musical examples.

0661   Edwards, Joseph. **Top 10's and Trivia of Rock & Roll and Rhythm & Blues**
En   **1950-1973.** St. Louis: Blueberry Hill, 1974. 632p. **1974 Supplement** . . .
          1974. 35p. LC 74-171039.   ML 128 N3 E34
          ARBA 76—1023, 1024

Begins with a month-by-month listing of tunes and singers in various categories (popular, rock & roll, rhythm & blues; singles and albums) marked to show which numbers reached the top popularity rankings, as reported by *Billboard* magazine. Indexes follow, by artist. There is also a 70-page chapter of questions and answers about popular music. The supplement continues in the same format, but without the question-answer portion.

0662   **Popular Music Periodicals Index** 1973— . comp. Dean Tudor and Nancy
En   Tudor. Metuchen, N.J.: Scarecrow Press, 1974— . (annual) LC 74-11578.
       ISBN 0-8108-0763-7.   ML 118 P66
       A well-made and useful guide to contents of 47 English-language periodicals (in 1973 edition) of the pop field. Subject arrangement, with author index. Record reviews not indexed (they are covered in Tudor's *Annual Index to Popular Music Record Reviews* (*0489*). Some overlap with *Music Index* (*0289*) and *Music Article Guide* (*0290*).

Note: Lists of popular songs and popular titles are found under Lists of Music (see p. 84). However, certain works that are valuable for other sorts of information as well—in addition to their title lists—are found in the appropriate sections of this unit, under Theatre Music, Songs, Jazz, Ragtime and Blues, and Rock to Soul.

Theatre Music, including Film

0663   Ewen, David. **New Complete Book of the American Musical Theater.**
En   [3d ed.] New York: Holt, Rinehart, and Winston, 1970. 800p. LC 70-
       117257. ISBN 03-085060-6.   ML 1711 E9 1970
           Duckles 74—347; Jackson—62
       (1st ed. 1958, as *Complete Book of the American Musical Theater*)
More than 300 musicals described in detail: plots, box-office data, first performances, songs. Also biographies of composers, lyricists, and librettists. Chronological listing, 1866-1970. Indexes for persons, titles of musicals and song titles. Jackson notices various omissions.

0663a Mates, Julian. **The American Musical Stage before 1800.** New Brunswick,
En   N.J.: Rutgers University Press, 1962. ix, 331p. LC 61-12409.
                                                  ML 1711 .M4
       Ewen (*0663*) and other writers on the American musical theater have traditionally begun their coverage with *The Black Crook*, a production of 1866. Mates digs deeper and uncovers a considerable heritage in the previous century; his "first extant musical performed in American and written by Americans" was *The Archers*, 1796. This is a scholarly history of theatres, orchestras, audiences, companies, artists, repertory and criticism, with 67 pages of notes and 14 pages of bibliography (not annotated). Name and topic index.

Songs

0664　Levy, Lester S. **Flashes of Merriment: a Century of Humorous Song in**
En　　**America, 1805-1905.** Norman, Okla.: University of Oklahoma Press,
　　　1971. 370p. LC 74-108805. ISBN 8061-0914-9.　　ML 2811 L48
　　　ARBA 72–1135
　　　The history of about 100 songs and their composers, with performers
associated with them. Original covers are reproduced, and some of the verses
are given, with melody lines in notation. Name and title index.

0665　Levy, Lester S. **Give Me Yesterday: American History in Song, 1890-1920.**
En　　Norman, Okla.: University of Oklahoma Press, 1975. xii, 420p. LC 74-
　　　18119. ISBN 0-8061-1241-7.　　　　　　　　　ML 3561 P6 L5
　　　ARBA 76–1028
　　　Musical perspectives on the period, illustrated with sheet music covers
and verses. Biographical asides of various singers and other musicians. Good
bibliography and index.

0666　Levy, Lester S. **Grace Notes in American History; Popular Sheet Music**
En　　**from 1820 to 1900.** Norman, Okla.: University of Oklahoma Press, 1967.
　　　xviii, 410p. LC 67-24623/MN.　　　　　　　　ML 2811 L5
　　　Stories of about a hundred songs, about shipwrecks, oil, fashions, presidents,
liquor, etc. Illustrations of covers and musical extracts. Melody lines in notation.

Jazz, Ragtime and Blues

　　　Jazz is a difficult term to define, and the literature using that term is
difficult to classify. We have tried to place in this section books which are primarily
concerned with the improvisatory styles that preceded rock.

　　　The first three titles are general and historical.

0667　Feather, Leonard. **The Encyclopedia of Jazz.** Rev. ed. New York: Horizon
En　　Press, 1960. 527p.　　　　　　　　　　　　ML 3561 J3 E55 1960
　　　Duckles 74–199; Jackson–49
　　　(1st ed. 1955) A number of strong essays on the history and techniques of
jazz, data from international jazz polls, 378 pages of biographies (with fine portraits),
discographies, lists of jazz organizations, agents, record companies. Annotated
bibliography. Useful international list of cities, with names of jazz artists born in
each. The next title is a supplement.

0668　Feather, Leonard. **The Encyclopedia of Jazz in the Sixties.** New York:
En　　Horizon Press, 1966. 312p. LC 66-26705.　　　ML 105 F35
　　　Duckles 74–200
　　　An updating of *0667*, with some new biographies.

0669   Keepnews, Orrin; Grauer, Bill, Jr. **A Pictorial History of Jazz; People and**
En   **Places from New Orleans to Modern Jazz.** Rev. ed. New York: Crown,
        1966. 297p. LC 66-4300.   ML 3561 J3 K4 1966
        Jackson–53
        (1st ed. 1955) A scholarly commentary accompanies this fine collection
of visual material. Indexed.

The next work is the principal essay in technical analysis of the music:

0670   Schuller, Gunther. **Early Jazz; Its Roots and Musical Development.** New
En   York: Oxford University Press, 1968. xii, 389p. LC 68-17610.
                                                     ML 3561 J3 S3295
        First volume of a projected "history of jazz," by the noted composer/
performer. In contrast to the common biographical/narrative approach to jazz
history, Schuller's focus is on the music itself: with numerous musical examples
and perceptive analyses of them. Concludes around 1932. Discography, glossary,
and index.

0671   Russell, Ross. **Jazz Style in Kansas City and the Southwest.** Berkeley:
En   University of California Press, 1971. xviii, 292p. LC 72-138507.
        ISBN 0-520-01853-2.   ML 3561 J3 R848
        A general account; with chapters on blues and folk, ragtime, Jack Teagarden,
Count Basie, Lester Young, Andy Kirk, Charlie Parker, etc. Also sections on bebop,
Kansas City pianists and other instrumentalists. Footnotes: 80 illustrations; seven-
page bibliography (not annotated); seven-page discography, and index.

There is one scholarly journal in the field:

0671a   **Journal of Jazz Studies.** v.1– . 1973– . New Brunswick, N.J.: Rutgers
En   University, Transaction Periodicals Consortium. (semiannual)
        Historical and technical essays; discographies.

A periodical with a more popular point of view is *0564.*

Following are the basic biographical sources:

0672   Chilton, John. **Who's Who of Jazz: Storyville to Swing Street.** London:
En   The Bloomsbury Book Shop, 1970. 447p. Reissued–Philadelphia:
        Chilton Book Co., 1972. 419p. LC 72-554746. ISBN 0-9501290-0-3.
                                                     ML 106 U3 C5
        Duckles 74–197; Jackson–48; ARBA 73–1038
        About a thousand detailed biographies of persons born before 1920 who
were basically active in the United States. Portraits, cross references; partial index
of bandleaders mentioned. Many little-known figures, and facts not found elsewhere.

0673   Blesh, Rudi; Janis, Harriet. **They All Played Ragtime: The True Story of**
En   **an American Music.** 4th ed. New York: Oak Publications; London: Music
        Sales Limited, 1971. xxiv, 347, ixp.
        Jackson–44

(1st ed. 1950) Historical and biographical information on a wide range of topics and persons. List of works, list of player-piano rolls, selective list of phonograph records. A list of cylinder recordings appeared in the second edition (1959) but has not been retained. Many good photographs. The New York edition also prints 16 complete rag pieces.

0674   Charters, Samuel Barclay. **The Bluesmen. The Story and the Music of the**
En   **Men Who Made the Blues.** New York: Oak Publications, 1967. 223p.
        LC 67-24017.   ML 3561 J3 C425
        Jackson—45
The first volume of a projected trilogy which will revise and expand *The Country Blues* (*0675*). This book studies the male singers and styles of Mississippi, Alabama, and Texas during the 1920s and 1930s. Biographies based on interviews. Musical examples and analyses, bibliographic notes and discography; index.

0675   Charters, Samuel Barclay. **The Country Blues.** New York: Rinehart, 1959.
En   288p. (Reprint—New York: Da Capo Press, 1975) LC 75-14122. ISBN
        0-306-80014-4.   ML 3556 C475 C7 1975
        Jackson—46
A pioneer field investigation of the early blues singers; biographical information based on interviews.

0676   Charters, Samuel Barclay. **Jazz: New Orleans 1885-1963; an Index to the**
En   **Negro Musicians of New Orleans.** Rev. ed. New York: Oak Publications,
        1963. 173p. LC 63-23662.   ML 3561 J3 043
        Duckles 74—196; Jackson—47
(1st ed. 1958) Biographical sketches of individuals, and information on bands and groups; arrangement is by chronological periods. Excellent photographs, discographies, indexes.

The books which are listed next concentrate on fewer persons and/or more limited time periods.

0677   Shapiro, Nat; Hentoff, Nat. **The Jazz Makers.** New York: Rinehart, 1957.
En   xiii, 368p. LC 57-11618.   ML 395 S5
        Jackson—57
A collection of 21 essays by ten authors, dealing with the lives and music of major artists (one in each essay). Photographs, discographies, and index.

0678   Stewart, Rex. **Jazz Masters of the Thirties.** New York: Macmillan Co.;
En   London: Collier-Macmillan Ltd., 1972. 223p. (The Macmillan Jazz Masters
        Series) LC 73-169239.   ML 3561 J3 S82
        Jackson—58d
There are six volumes in this series by Macmillan, of which three are cited here. Stewart (himself a stellar performer in the thirties) presents a set of vignettes—originally published in magazines—about the people he knew. Photographs; no index.

0679   Gitler, Ira. **Jazz Masters of the Forties.** New York: Macmillan Co., 1966.
En   290p. (Reissue—New York: Collier Books, 1974. (The Macmillan Jazz
        Masters Series) LC 66-17874.   ML 395 G58
        Jackson—58a; ARBA 75—1162
        In his ARBA review, Nat Shapiro acclaims this work as "probably the best
book thus far on modern jazz and musicians." Detailed biographical and critical
approach to all major performers, composers and arrangers. A scholarly piece of
research, based in part on interviews (e.g., with Charlie Parker, Dizzy Gillespie,
Thelonius Monk, Bud Powell). Bibliography, photographs, and index.

0680   Goldberg, Joe. **Jazz Masters of the Fifties.** New York: Macmillan Co., 1965.
En   246p. (The Macmillan Jazz Masters Series) LC 65-13117.
        Jackson—58b   ML 394-G63
        Twelve essays, containing much unique biographical information based on
interviews and personal acquaintanceships. Discographies.

Rock to Soul

        The next four entries are probably the most informative works on rock.

0681   Stambler, Irwin. **Encyclopedia of Pop, Rock, and Soul.** New York: St.
En   Martin's Press, 1975. 609p. LC 73-87393.   ML 102 P66 S8
        ARBA 76—1030
        About 500 articles, concentrating on rock and soul. Emphasis is on
personalities (performers, producers, promoters) but Stambler also covers terms,
instruments, and historical topics. Lists of various prize winners. Treatment is
popular and informal, but much information is included. Bibliography; no discography and no index.

0682   Belz, Carl. **The Story of Rock.** 2d ed. New York: Oxford University Press,
En   1972. 286p. LC 77-182870. (Paperback reprint—New York: Harper & Row,
        1973 [Harper Colophon Books]) ISBN 06-090344-9.
        ARBA 73—1056   ML 3561 J3 B34
        (1st ed. 1969) A scholarly review of rock's origins and development as an
art form—with less attention to the sociological aspects. Some consideration of rock
in Britain, but this is primarily a book about the United States. Good analyses of
the music and the personalities, based mostly on close study of hit records. Critical
bibliography of 14 books. Selective discography, arranged by year, 1953-71. Index
of titles and persons.

0683   Gillett, Charlie. **The Sound of the City: the Rise of Rock and Roll.** New
En   York: Outerbridge & Dienstfrey (distributed by E. P. Dutton), 1970.
        vii, 375p. LC 79-106611.   ML 3561 J3 G525
        "This is by far the best history of rock and roll . . . " according to Gilbert
Chase in his review [*Notes* 29-1 (Sept. 1972): 39-42]. Particularly strong in defining
and separating the various musical strands; emphasizes the relations between these

strands and background influences at work in the urban environment. Bibliography, discography, and index.

0684   Nite, Norm N. **Rock On: the Illustrated Encyclopedia of Rock 'n Roll,**
En   **the Solid Gold Years.** New York: Thomas Y. Crowell, 1974. 676p.
        LC 74-12247. ISBN 0-690-00583-0.   ML 105 N49
        ARBA 76–1029
        About a thousand entries for individuals and performing groups of the
1950s and 1960s. Information given includes a career summary and names of the
artist's 100 top records. Data carried into the 1970s for persons still active.
Illustrated with 300 photographs.

The next title gives attention to the specifically black music styles:

0685   Morse, David. **Motown & the Arrival of Black Music.** London: Studio
En   Vista; New York: Macmillan Co., 1971. 110p. LC 76-186443. ISBN
        0-289-70131-7.   ML 3556 M7
        A popular survey, emphasizing careers of leading performers such as
Martha Reeves, Smokey Robinson, and the Supremes. No bibliography; no index.

See also *0515a.*

Opera and Vocal Music

In this section we list writing about serious, composed vocal music. The line between serious and popular is elusive, so there is some overlap of content between the present section and the preceding two, Folk Music and Folksong, and Popular Music.

The first three titles are concerned primarily with concert songs.

0686   Yerbury, Grace Helen (Davies). **Song in America, from Early Times to**
En   **About 1850.** Metuchen, N.J.: Scarecrow Press, 1971. 305p. LC 79-
        149993. ISBN 0-8108-0382-8.   ML 3811 Y47
        A general narrative of art song development, beginning in the eighteenth
century. Songs are grouped by period and composer. Imprint data given. Chapter
bibliographies only. Composer index; no title index of the songs.

0687   Upton, William Treat. **Art-Song in America; a Study in the Development**
En   **of American Music.** Boston: Oliver Ditson Co., 1930. 279p. LC 30-33445.
                                                   ML 2811 U7

        A Supplement to Art-Song in America, 1930-1938. Boston: Oliver Ditson
        Co., 1938. 41p.   ML 2811 U7 Suppl.
        An extensive survey of the repertoire, with valuable commentaries.
Particular strength in early twentieth-century works.

0688   Lawrence, Vera Brodsky. **Music for Patriots, Politicians and Presidents;**
En   **Harmonies and Discords of the First Hundred Years.** New York:
        Macmillan Co.; London: Collier Macmillan Publishers, 1975. LC 75-
        28041. ISBN 0-02-569390-5.   ML 3551 L29

A very attractive presentation of the social context of popular song. More than 500 illustrations (of title pages, places, and persons). Song texts, with detailed background information. Indexed.

The national anthem has been subject of several writings, of which this book is the most comprehensive:

0689 Svejda, George J. **History of the Star-Spangled Banner from 1814 to the**
En   **Present.** [Washington:] Division of History, Office of Archeology and
      Historic Preservation, 1969. vii, 525p. LC 76-603542.

      ML 3561 S8 S9

This study is available from the U.S. Government Printing Office (publication 1969/14704). It is a scholarly history, covering the flag itself, background of the anthem (War of 1812), early publications and arrangements, rise of popularity, formal adoptions. Bibliography of 34p., primary and secondary sources; not annotated. No index.

These are the main sources of facts about American opera and operatic history in the United States. Except for one book on Chicago opera (*0689a*) and several on New York (*0692c, 0692d, 0692e, 0694*), they are national in scope. Further information on operatic life in specific cities may be found in the regional histories cited under Regional and Local Histories (see p. 60).

0689a Davis, Ronald. **Opera in Chicago; a Social and Cultural History, 1850-1965.**
En   New York: Appleton-Century, 1966. 393p. LC 65-23018.

       ML 1811.8 C5 D4

A popular survey; although the author states that "the bulk of the material presented here is drawn from contemporary Chicago newspapers . . . " he has not provided footnote references and there is no bibliography. Emphasis on the personal lives of the singers. Useful factual feature is the listing of casts for performances from 1910 to 1965. Illustrations; index.

0690 **Directory of American Contemporary Operas.** Central Opera Service
En   Bulletin, v.10, no. 2 (Dec. 1967). New York: Central Opera Service, 1967.
      79p.
      Duckles 74–345

A composer list of operas by Americans premiered since 1930. Gives name of librettist, characters, number of acts, publisher or other availability, and data on first performance. See also the following entry.

0691 **Directory of American and Foreign Contemporary Operas and American**
En   **Opera Premieres, 1967-1975.** Central Opera Service Bulletin, v.17, no. 2
      (Winter 1975). New York: Central Opera Service, 1975. 66p.

Supplements *2707*. A composer list, with name of librettist, characters, number of acts, story source, instrumentation required, and publisher. Also a list of North American opera premieres since 1968. Title indexes.

0692   Drummond, Andrew H. **American Opera Librettos.** Metuchen, N.J.:
En   Scarecrow Press, 1973. 277p. LC 72-8111. ISBN 0-8108-0553-7.

ARBA 74–1126   ML 1711 D8

An examination of 40 important opera libretti, for works performed at the New York City Opera, 1948-1971. Critical analysis is a focus of the book, but considerable information value is found in the complete list of N.Y.C.O. performances, 1948-1971, plot synopses, and a 16-page bibliography. Name and title index.

0692a   Graf, Herbert. **The Opera and Its Future in America.** New York: W. W.
En   Norton, 1941. 305p. (Reprint—Port Washington, N.Y.: Kennikat Press,
        1973.) LC 78-154712. ISBN 0-8046-1744-9.   ML 1700 G75 07

A popular, speculative survey, with a good review of the historical background and an interesting cross-section of opera life in the United States in 1940. Index.

0692b   Johnson, H. Earle. **Operas on American Subjects.** New York: Coleman-Ross
En   Co., 1964. 125p. LC 64-17352.   ML 128 04 J6
        Duckles 74–349

A composer list of operas having some sort of American subject matter—with "American" here covering all of North or South America (emphasis on United States). Composers may be of any nationality. Plot synopses, critical notices; subject and title indexes. Also a useful inventory of American and British literary works that have formed the basis for opera librettos.

0692c   Kolodin, Irving. **The Metropolitan Opera, 1883-1966: a Candid History.**
En   4th ed. New York: Knopf, 1966. xxi, 762, xiviip. (A Borzoi Book)
        LC 66-19384/MN.   ML 1711.8 N3 M44

(1st ed. 1953) A survey of performances, repertory, conductors, managers, singers; economic and organizational problems. Complete list of operas, ballets, and choral pieces performed from 1883 to 1952, with dates and number of performances. Index.

0692d   Krehbiel, Henry Edward. **Chapters of Opera; Being Historical and Critical**
En   **Observations and Records Concerning the Lyric Drama in New York from**
        Its Earliest Days Down to the Present Time. 3d ed. New York: Holt, 1911.
        xvii, 460p. LC 12-262.   ML 1711.8 N3 K73

Survey of the years before 1825; the early Italian opera performances; the great impresarios; the Metropolitan Opera; 20th-century developments. Author's direct contact with opera over a long period of time (as music critic for the *New York Tribune*) gives immediacy to these accounts. Appendix gives tables of opera seasons 1908-1911. See also next entry.

0692e   Krehbiel, Henry Edward. **More Chapters of Opera; Being Historical and**
En   **Critical Observations and Records Concerning the Lyric Drama in New**
        York from 1908 to 1918. New York: Holt, 1919. xvi, 474p. LC 20-217.
                                                   ML 1711.8 N3 K74

Continues the survey of the preceding entry. Critical commentary emphasized. Tables of performances and singers.

0692f   Lahee, Henry Charles. **Grand Opera in America.** Boston: L. C. Page, 1902.
En   348p. (Reprint—New York: AMS Press, 1973) LC 72-2050.
                                                              ML 1711 L18
        Historical survey; artists, performances. Stresses the influences of England,
Italy, and Germany. Index.

0693   Mattfeld, Julius. **A Handbook of American Operatic Premieres, 1731-1962.**
En   Detroit: Information Service, Inc., 1963. 142p. (Detroit Studies in Music
        Bibliography, 5) LC 64-55003.   ML 128 04 M3
        Duckles 74—355
        A title list of some 2,000 works performed between 1731 and 1962;
includes works by Americans (from the United States) performed in other countries.
Some operettas and musicals are listed. Facts given: number of acts, language, place
of performance, and date. Composer index.

0694   Seltsam, William H. **Metropolitan Opera Annals; a Chronicle of Artists and**
En   **Performances.** New York: H. W. Wilson Co., 1947. 751p. LC 47-11435.
        Duckles 74—976   ML 1711.8 N32 M48
        Supplemented in annual issues of *Opera News*; with two cumulated
supplements publi;hed: *First Supplement 1957* (covering 1947-57) and *Second
Supplement: 1957-1966—a Chronicle of Artists and Performers.* A chronological
record of operas given from the Metropolitan's first season, 1883/84, with casts
and selections from press notices. Photographs; artist and opera indexes.

0695   Sonneck, Oscar G. T. **Early Opera in America.** New York: G. Schirmer,
En   1915. viii, 230p. (Reprint—New York: B. Blom, 1963) (Roots and Sources
        of the American Theatre) LC 63-23189/MN.   ML 1711 S73
        Jackson—81
        A companion study to Sonneck's *Early Concert Life in America* (*0715*),
also based on newspapers and other primary documents. Much detail on productions
and performers, and extended bibliographical references. Emphasis on New York,
Philadelphia, Boston and New England, Baltimore, Charleston; and also the South.
Coverage begins with performances of 1703 and extends through the 18th century.
Later periods are organized by city. An epilogue considers French opera companies
in America. An essential, scholarly work. Indexed.

        The following has been announced for publication:

0696   Northouse, Cameron. **Twentieth-Century Opera in England and the United**
En   **States.** Boston: G. K. Hall. ISBN 0-8161-7896-8.

        For detailed information on operatic history, it is often fruitful to examine
histories of the theater (of "the stage") in particular localities. The chapter on
"Theater Arts" in Winchell is a good starting point for identifying relevant titles.

Church and Religious Music

0697   Ellinwood, Leonard Webster. **The History of American Church Music.**
En   New York: Morehouse-Gorham Co., 1953. 274p. Reprint—New York:
        Da Capo Press, 1970. (Da Capo Press Music Reprint Series) LC 53-13402.
        LC 69-12683.   ML 200 E4
        Divided into three segments: 1) Colonial era 1494-1820 treats metrical
psalmody, singing schools, early choirs, fuguing tune, first organs and bells; 2)
1820-1920 treats subjects of quartet choirs, growth of choir repertory; 3) the
contemporary scene including musicians, hymnals, liturgical matters. Biographies
of American church musicians, notes, bibliography; indexed.

0698   Foote, Henry Wilder. **Three Centuries of American Hymnody.** Cambrdige,
En   Mass.: Harvard University Press, 1940. 418p. Reprints—Hamden, Conn.:
        Shoe String Press, 1961, 1968; Archon Books, 1968. LC 40-34386.
        LC 61-4914. LC 68-156151/MN.   ML 3111 F6T4
        Covers English psalmody, Bay Psalm Book, hymns of the German settlers
in Pennsylvania, hymnody developing from psalmody, hymns of the 20th century.
Indexes: names and subjects, first lines, titles of psalm and hymn books. 1968
edition has *Recent American Hymnody* (Hymn Society of America, 1952) bound
in as an appendix.

0699   Gould, Nathaniel Duren. **Church Music in America. Comprising its History**
En   **and its Peculiarities at Different Periods, with Cursory Remarks on Its**
        Legitimate Use and Its Abuse; with Notices of the Schools, Composers,
        Teachers, and Society. Boston: A. M. Johnson, 1853. 240p. Reprint—
        New York: AMS Press, 1972. LC 78-144620. ISBN 0-404-02888-6.
                                        ML 2911 G69
        Traces our national musical beginnings in psalmody, singing schools, music
in churches, choirs, instruments, societies, academies, concerts; but not well documented. Included a list of song books (sacred and secular) published in the last 20
years (1833-1853).

0700   Stevenson, Robert Murrell. **Protestant Church Music in America: a Short**
En   **Survey of Men and Movements from 1564 to the Present.** New York: W. W.
        Norton, 1966. xiii, 168p. LC 66-15317/MN.   ML 3111 S8 Pt
        Jackson—79
        A "distinguished and highly informative" (Jackson) survey and guide to
the primary sources. Considers the Huguenots in Florida during the 16th century,
the Puritans, singing schools, Pennsylvania Germans, the 17th-century South,
spirituals, recent currents. Bibliography, index.

0701   Wienandt, Elwyn A.; Young, Robert H. **The Anthem in England and**
En   **America.** New York: Free Press, 1970. 495p. LC 76-76225/MN.
                                      ML 3265 W54
        The various influences on the formation of the American anthem: the
English cathedral traditions, gospel songs, Russian liturgical music, etc. Discussion
of composers; the current scene.

The following are representative regional treatments:

0702 Daniel, Ralph T. **The Anthem in New England before 1800**. Evanston,
En   Ill.: Northwestern University Press, 1966. xvi, 282p. (Pi Kappa Lambda
      Studies in American Music) LC 65-24626/MN.   ML 2911 D35
      Jackson—76
      A scholarly historical review, with much detail on individual composers
(including lists of works). Strong bibliography, musical supplement of 14 anthems,
index.

0703 Macdougall, Hamilton Crawford. **Early New England Psalmody; an**
En   **Historical Appreciation, 1620-1820**. Brattleboro, Vermont: Stephen
      Daye Press, 1940. 179p. (Reprint—New York: Da Capo Press, 1969)
      (Da Capo Press Music Reprint Series) LC 41-558; LC 79-87398.
                                       ML 200.3 M23E2
      Finds the origins of New England psalmody in Bohemia, Germany, France,
England, and Scotland during the Reformation. Analyses of melody, rhythm,
meter, etc. Studies of the music in Billings' time, fuguing tunes, singing schools,
performance practice. Well documented, but no bibliography. Index.

Music Theory and Musicology

0704 Harrison, Frank; Hood, Mantle; Palisca, Claude V. **Musicology**. Englewood
En   Cliffs, N.J.: Prentice-Hall, 1963. 337p. (The Princeton Studies: Humanistic
      Scholarship in America)
      Duckles 74—516
      Three essays: "American Musicology and the European Tradition"
(Harrison), "Music, the Unknown" (Hood), and "American Scholarship in Western
Music" (Palisca). Philosophical, bibliographical reviews of the place and progress of
musical research in the United States.

0705 Goldthwaite, Scott. "The Growth and Influence of Musicology in the
En   United States." **Acta musicologica** 33 (1961): 72-79.
      Duckles 74—745

Continued in the same issue:

0706 La Rue, Jan. "Codetta: Some Details of Musicology in the United States."
En   **Acta musicologica** 33 (1961): 79-83.

Historical Studies, Chronologies, Contemporary Narratives

The first eight items are general in scope. They are presented in probable
order of utility in the search for facts.

0707   Howard, John Tasker. **Our American Music; a Comprehensive History**
En   **from 1620 to the Present.** 4th ed. New York: Thomas Y. Crowell,
        1965. xii, 944p. LC 65-18697.   ML 200 H82
        Jackson–18
        (1st ed. 1931) First three editions had title: *Our American Music; Three
Hundred Years of It.* Described by Jackson as "one of the classic histories of the
subject." An encyclopedic range of topics; biographical information, lists of works,
good illustrations. Strong bibliographies: one of histories in chronological arrangement; one of 21 regional and state histories. Indexed.

0708   Howard, John Tasker; Bellows, George Kent. **A Short History of Music**
En   **in America.** New York: Thomas Y. Crowell, 1967. 496p. LC 67-29928.
                                                         ML 200 H82
        A more compressed presentation than that of the preceding entry, conceived
as a textbook or handbook. Good discography, pp. 413-432. Indexed.

0709   Hitchcock, H. Wiley. **Music in the United States: a Historical Introduction.**
En   2d ed. Englewood Cliffs, N.J.: Prentice Hall, 1974. xvii, 286p. LC 73-19751.
        ISBN 0-13-608398-6. (Prentice-Hall History of Music Series)
        Jackson–17   ML 200 H58 1974
        (1st ed. 1969) Part of the series described at *0103.* Best of the brief surveys;
erudite but clear and readable throughout. Good annotated bibliography; footnotes.
Index.

0710   Chase, Gilbert. **America's Music; From the Pilgrims to the Present.** 2d ed.
En   New York: McGraw-Hill, 1966. xxi, 759p. LC 66-23622.
        Jackson–14   ML 200 C5 1966
        (1st ed. 1955) An excellent and influential work; the influence was that of
bringing popular and vernacular styles into the range of scholarly concern—"to
declare that these forms were quite as worthy of study as art music" (Jackson).
The book coordinates a vast amount of data, on composers, trends, works, bibliography, and recordings. Index.

0711   Mellers, Wilfrid Howard. **Music in a New Found Land: Themes and**
En   **Developments in the History of American Music.** New York: A. A. Knopf,
        1965. 543p. LC 64-17706.   ML 200 M44
        A reflective account of the American musical experience, emphasizing
twentieth-century trends. Considerable serious thought given to jazz, ragtime, blues
and other popular forms. Extended discography, pp. 452-519; brief bibliography.
Index.

0712   Elson, Louis Charles. **The History of American Music.** 3d ed. rev. by
En   Arthur Elson. New York: Macmillan Co., 1925. xiii, 423p. (History of
        American Art) (Reprint of 1st ed.—New York: Burt Franklin, 1971)
        (Burt Franklin Research and Source Works Series, 686) LC 79-132809.
        Jackson–15   ML 200 E5 E5
        (1st ed. 1904) Note that the 1904 edition is the one chosen to be reprinted
by Franklin. This is the second major history, following that of Ritter (*0714*). As

the titles of the two works indicate, a different emphasis is favored by each of the two authors: Ritter had looked most closely at musical activity in the United States, while Elson turned his eye toward the music written by Americans. Elson is still useful today for biographical and some critical information on the native forms of folk, patriotic/popular, and art music—particularly of the nineteenth century. Excellent illustrations in the original editions, not so well reproduced in the reprint. Bibliography; index.

0713 Lahee, Henry Charles. **Annals of Music in America; a Chronological Record**
En **of Significant Musical Events, from 1640 to the Present Day with Comments on the Various Periods into Which the Work Is Divided.** Boston: Marshall Jones Co., 1922. 298p. (Reprints—New York: AMS Press, 1969; Freeport, New York: Books and Libraries Press, 1970) LC 78-97889.
ML 200 L14
Each time period has a chronological listing of events, performances, personages. Interesting topical chronological lists (e.g., ballad operas with locations, concerts, debuts of pianists, singers, violinists, choral and orchestral societies).

0714 Ritter, Frederic Louis. **Music in America.** 2d ed. New York: C. Scribner's
En Sons, 1890. xiv, 521p. (Reprint—New York: Burt Franklin, 1972) (Burt Franklin Research and Source Works Series. Music History and Reference Series, 1) LC 79-143650. ISBN 0-8337-3004-5.
Jackson—22   ML 200 R62
(1st ed. 1883) The first attempt at a comprehensive historical treatment of music in the United States. Emphasis is on the transplant of European art music; hence there is great attention to performing organizations with many facts on these groups. Considerable biographical detail on contemporary figures. See comment under Elson (*0712*). Indexed.

The next entries deal with more narrow time periods.

0715 Sonneck, Oscar George Theodore. **Early Concert Life in America (1731-**
En **1800).** Leipzig: Breitkopf & Hättel, 1907. 338p. (Reprints—New York: Musurgia, 1949; Wiesbaden: Martin Sändig, 1969) LC A50-7306; 74-387578.   ML 200.3 S6
Jackson—23
Sonneck, head of the Library of Congress Music Division from 1902 to 1917, was unable to find an American publisher for his book; hence the German imprint. His research was the first methodical examination of primary sources for the period studied: he drew on newspaper accounts, programs, actual music, and other contemporary documents. These are related to one another in a perceptive commentary. Biographical information throughout. Bibliographical notes as well; but repetition with respect to Sonneck's *Bibliography of Early Secular American Music* (*0819*) was avoided. Name, title and subject index.

0716 Lowens, Irving. **Music and Musicians in Early America.** New York: W. W.
En Norton, 1964. 328p. LC 64-17518.   ML 200 L7
Jackson—20

A collection of 18 scholarly articles and papers previously published else-where, revised for the present edition. Of particular interest are the biographical sketches, and the chapter on the "Bay Psalm Book in 17th-century New England." An interesting appendix also: a checklist of writings on music found in American periodicals, 1835-1850 (183 items). Bibliographical notes; index.

0717   Mathews, William S. B. **A Hundred Years of Music in America; an Account**
En   **of Musical Effort in America During the Past Century . . . Together with**
       Historical and Biographical Sketches of Important Personalities. Chicago,
       G. L. Howe, 1889. 715p. (Reprint—New York: AMS Press, 1970). LC 6-
       32339. LC 73-135725. ISBN 0-404-04259-7.   ML 200 M37
       Jackson—21
       An informative work on composers, performers, and musical organizations.
Good supplementary "Dictionary of American Musicians," pp. 703-15; excellent portraits and illustrations (240 plates). Not indexed.

0718   Chase, Gilbert. "United States." Vinton (*0507*), pp. 781-788.
En   A useful brief survey of current trends, which can serve as a supplement
to Chase's *0710*) for very recent developments.

0719   Goldman, Richard Franko. "Music in the United States." **New Oxford**
En   **History of Music** (*0101*; and update in present volume), x, 569-638.
       A good survey of trends in the twentieth century, to 1960.

0720   Thomson, Virgil. **American Music Since 1910.** New York: Holt, Rinehart
En   and Winston, 1971. 204p. (Twentieth-century Composers, 1) LC 77-
       80367. ISBN 03-076465-3.   ML 200.5 T5
       ARBA 72—1087
       A perceptive approach by a leading composer. Includes biographical
sketches and lists of works for 106 composers; portraits, bibliography, and index.

0721   Lang, Paul Henry. **One Hundred Years of Music in America.** New York:
En   G. Schirmer, 1961. 322p. LC 61-65802.   ML 200 L25
       Anecdotal narrative, in topical sections, covering 1861 to 1961. Considers
political and social contexts in particular. No bibliography or index.

0722   Tick, Judith. "Women as Professional Musicians in the United States,
En   1870-1900." **Anuario interamericano de investigación musical** (*0880*)
       9 (1973), 95-133.
       A documented study, including a chronology, musical examples, and a
two-page bibliography (not annotated).

Regional and Local Histories

Titles in this section are grouped alphabetically by locality (following the first, which is general).

0723　Eaton, Quaintance. **Musical U.S.A.** New York: Allen, Towne and Heath,
En　　Inc., 1949. 206p. LC 49-8928.　　　　　　ML 200 E2
　　　　　A collection of historical sketches on individual cities: New York, Boston,
Philadelphia, Chicago, Baltimore, Cincinnati, Minneapolis, St. Louis, New Orleans,
San Francisco, Los Angeles, and Seattle; plus areas of the Pacific Northwest and
Texas. Well illustrated, popular approach. No index.

Baltimore

0723a　Keefer, Lubov. **Baltimore's Music; the Haven of the American Composer.**
En　　Baltimore, [no pub.] 1962. xvii, 343p. LC 62-53630.
　　　　　　　　　　　　　　　　　　　　　　　ML 200.8 B19 K4
　　　　　A well-documented history of musical activity in Baltimore. Opera,
oratorio societies, development of the orchestra, the critics. Bibliography of about
350 entries, not annotated. Index.

Boston

0723b　Johnson, H. Earle. **Musical Interludes in Boston.** New York: Columbia
En　　University Press, 1943. xv, 366p. (Reprint–New York: AMS Press, 1967)
　　　　　NUC 68-18586.　　　　　　　　　　　　ML 200.8 B7 J6
　　　　　A study of musical activity in Boston, 1800-1827: concert life, organiza-
tions, personalities, music industry. List of music teachers. Appendix lists music
of publishers by individual publishers; lists of music by copyright. Index.

0723c　Ayars, Christine Merrick. **Contributions to the Art of Music in America**
En　　**by the Music Industries of Boston, 1640-1936.** New York: H. W.
　　　　　Wilson, 1937. 326p. (Reprint–New York: Johnson Reprint Corp.,
　　　　　1969)　　　　　　　　　　　　　　ML 200.8 B657 A9 1969
　　　　　Detailed history of publishers, instrument makers and others engaged in
the production of music. Much miscellaneous data on musical activity as well.

California

0724　Swan, Howard. **Music in the Southwest, 1825-1950.** San Marino, Calif.:
En　　Huntington Library, 1952. 316p. LC 51-14504.
　　　　　　　　　　　　　　　　　　　　　　ML 200.7 S74 S9
　　　　　Mostly about music in California, but covers also Mormon music, music
in mining camps, mission and pueblo music, cowboy music. Considerable detail
on Lynden Behymer, a leading impresario in California during the late nineteenth
and early twentieth centuries. Prominent professional musicians; the depression
era; music during World War II. A semi-popular style, with some footnotes. Six-
page bibliography, not annotated. Index.

0725   **Music and Dance in California and the West.** 4th ed. Hollywood, Calif.:
En   Bureau of Musical Research, 1953– . LC 34-7462.

Duckles 74–182 (for 3d ed.)   ML 200.7 C2 M8

(1st ed. 1933) Title and editors vary. This and the other "Music and
Dance . . . " titles in this section are a group of regional works of considerable
similarity in format, and of variable quality. They are all useful for biographical
sketches and portraits of local musical figures, and for data on performing organizations and current musical activity. They are also wasteful of space, and weak-
ened in focus, by the inclusion of general articles on musical topics written at
very low popular levels. The California volume is relatively well constructed, with
material on film music, opera, music in schools and universities, and local organizations. Biographies of more than 600 persons. No index.

Central

0726   **Music and Dance in the Central States.** Ed. Richard Drake Saunders.
En   Hollywood, Calif.: Bureau of Musical Research, 1952. 162p.

Duckles 74–183   ML 200.7 C4 M8

Mostly trivial articles on general topics; this is the least valuable book in
the series. It does present biographical information and portraits on about 400
individuals. No index.

Cleveland

0727   Grossman, F. Karl. **A History of Music in Cleveland.** Cleveland: Case
En   Western Reserve University Press, 1972. xii, 201p. LC 74-116383.

ML 200.8 C7 G76

A thorough account of musical activity, including visiting artists and
local performing groups. Opera companies, orchestras (special emphasis on the
Cleveland Orchestra), vocal music societies, ethnic music societies, chamber music
players, schools and conservatories, music in the public schools, clubs, church
music. Pictures of old programs and halls, portraits. Unfortunately, footnotes and
bibliography were not provided. Indexed.

Colorado

0727a   Denver. Public Library. **Music in Denver and Colorado.** Denver: Denver
En   Public Library, 1927. 162p.

A collection of articles that provide an historical survey and also cover
special topics (school and church music, institutions and organizations, etc.).
Biographical section includes lists of works for composers. Bibliography of three
pages, not annotated. Index.

Delaware

0728   **Music and Dance in Pennsylvania, New Jersey, and Delaware.** Ed. Sigmund
En   Spaeth [*et al.*]. New York: Bureau of Musical Research, 1954. 339p.
      LC 54-14250.   ML 200.7 P3 M8
      Useful for review of musical life, city by city, and for biographical section
of about 500 persons.

Denver. See *0727a.*

Hawaii

0729   Hausman, Ruth L. **Hawaii; Music in Its History.** Rutland, Vermont: C. E.
En   Tuttle Co., 1968. 112p. LC 67-15317.   ML 200.7 H4 H4
      Presents the actual music of several old chants and 25 songs (with piano
accompaniment) and endeavors to relate their texts to events in Hawaiian history.
A very popular, almost juvenile, style interferes with a basically good idea. Index.

0730   Roberts, Helen Heffron. **Ancient Hawaiian Music.** Honolulu: Bishop
En   Museum, 1926. 397p. (Reprint—New York: Dover Publications, 1967)
      LC 67-18240.   ML 3560 H3 R67 1967
      Based on a field survey made by Roberts in 1923/24. Examines old and
modern instruments, poetry, song, dance tunes, hulas, geographical distribution
of instruments. A scholarly work; 152 musical examples, 15 pictures, and bibliography of 187 entries (not annotated).

0731   Todaro, Tony. **The Golden Years of Hawaiian Entertainment, 1874-1974.**
En   Honolulu: T. Todaro Pub. Co., 1974. 470p. [plus advertisements]
      LC 75-318165.   ML 106 U4 H37
      An account of popular music, and biographical information on performers.
Discography of 16 pages.

Maine

0731a Edwards, George Thornton. **Music and Musicians of Maine.** Portland,
En   Maine: Southworth Press, 1928. 542p. LC 28-30345.
                                                     ML 200.7 M2 E26
      Comprehensive history of musical life and activity, 1497-1928. Includes
music of the Indians. Biographical chapter with paragraph-length sketches of
1,800 musicians alive in 1928. Illustrations, indexes.

Missouri

0731b Krohn, Ernst C. **Missouri Music.** 2d ed. New York: Da Capo Press, 1971.
En   xliv, 380p. LC 65-23398. ISBN 0-306-70932-5.
                                                     ML 200.7 M691 K72 1970

(1st ed. 1924: *A Century of Missouri Music*) A collection of essays on music history and activity. Lists of musicians, composers, musicologists, organizations. The second edition adds nine studies to the content of the original.

New England

0732   **Music and Dance in the New England States, including Maine, New**
En   **Hampshire, Vermont, Massachusetts, Rhode Island and Connecticut.**
      Ed. Sigmund Spaeth. New York: Bureau of Musical Research, 1953.
      347p. LC 53-3437.   ML 200.7 N3 M8
      Duckles 74–184
      Useful for accounts of musical activity in the different cities, and for about
600 biographical sketches, with portraits. "Classified professional directory" (pp.
311-332) is of some interest.

0733   Hood, George. **A History of Music in New England, with Biographical**
En   **Sketches of Reformers and Psalmists.** Boston: Wilkins, Carter & Co.,
      1846. 252p. (Reprint–New York: Johnson Reprint, 1970.) LC 76-
      107854.   ML 200 H77
      The reprint edition includes a new introduction by Johannes Riedel, who
also wrote this comment in RILM Abstracts: "Special attention is given to music
education in the light of religion, reform, and change. The interaction of theologians,
ministers, composers, and congregations is emphasized."

New Hampshire

0733a Pichierri, Louis. **Music in New Hampshire, 1623-1800.** New York:
En   Columbia University Press, 1960. xv, 297p. LC 60-13940.
                                                    ML 200.7 N4 P5
      A scholarly history, in topical arrangement: instruments, religious music,
music for public occasions, opera, concert life, teachers, academies, individuals,
music theory, etc. Appendixes: teachers' advertisements, selected opera programs.
Bibliography of about 220 entries, not annotated (published and unpublished
writings, plus list of tunebooks). Extensive notes, pp. 245-270. Index.

New Jersey. See *0728.*

New Orleans

0734   Kmen, Henry A. **Music in New Orleans: the Formative Years, 1791-1841.**
En   Baton Rouge, Louisiana: Louisiana State University Press, 1967. 314p.
                                                    ML 200.8 N48 K6
      A scholarly survey of concerts, opera, the balls, Creole and Negro music.
Good bibliography (16 pages) of primary and secondary sources (not annotated).
Footnoted; indexed.

New York City

0735   Aldrich, Richard. **Concert Life in New York, 1902-1923.** New York: G. P.
En   Putnam's Songs, 1941. xvii, 795p. LC 41-26614. (Reprint–Freeport, N.Y.:
       Books for Libraries Press, 1971) LC 78-156603. ISBN 0-8369-2263-8.
                                                    ML 200.8 N5 A6
       This is a collection of concert criticisms by Aldrich, who was music critic
for the *New York Times* from 1902 to 1923. The arrangement is chronological.
See also the next item.

0735a Downes, Olin. **Olin Downes on Music; a Selection from His Writings**
En   **during the Half-century 1906 to 1955.** Ed. Irene Downes. New York:
       Simon & Schuster, 1957. 473p. LC 56-9923.   ML 60 D73
       Downes succeeded Aldrich (see preceding item) on the *Times* in 1924.
This collection of his reviews starts earlier, however, and covers Downes' precocious
career on the *Boston Post* as well. A chronological arrangement of about 150 reviews.
Name and title index.

0736   Redway, Virginia L. **Music Directory of Early New York City; a File of**
En   **Musicians, Music Publishers and Musical Instrument Makers Listed in New**
       York Directories from 1786 through 1835, Together with the Most
       Important New York Music Publishers from 1836 through 1875 . . .
       New York: New York Public Library, 1941. 102p.
       Duckles 74–!701   ML 15 N3 R4
       Data drawn from city directories, copyright records and early New York
music imprints. Lists of musicians and teachers; publishers, printers, lithographers,
dealers; instrument makers and dealers; dancers and dancing teachers. Chronological
list of firms and individuals, 1786-1811; list of musical societies, 1789-1799.

0737   Rogers, Delmer D. "Public Music Performances in New York City from
En/Sp 1800 to 1850." **Anuario interamericano de investigación musical**, 6
       (1970), 5-50.
       Summary in Spanish included. Describes sacred and secular music concerts,
opera performances, variety shows and dance programs. Complete details on the
events–names of artists, works performed, etc.–with commentaries and bibliographic references.

       Other material on New York City is found in the section on opera: *0692,
0692c, 0692d, 0692e, 0694.*

New York State

0738   **Music and Dance in New York State.** Ed. Sigmund Spaeth [*et al.*]. New
En   York: Bureau of Musical Research, 1951. 435p. LC 52-58.
       Duckles 74–185   ML 200.7 N7 M8
       Articles on various localities, and extensive biographical section of about
1,000 names.

Ohio

0738a   Osburn, Mary Hubbell. **Ohio Composers and Musical Authors.** Columbus,
En   Ohio: F. J. Heer Printing Co., 1942. 238p. LC 42-12514.
                                                            ML 200.7 O4
        Primarily a biographical work, with a short historical sketch, and some
miscellaneous information. About 750 musicians included, with one- or two-
paragraph articles and lists of works for composers. Also a list of 38 Ohio songs.
See also *0727*.

Oklahoma. See *0745*.

Pennsylvania

0738b   Rohrer, Gertrude Martin. **Music and Musicians of Pennsylvania.**
En   Philadelphia: Presser, 1940. 121p. LC 41-1275.
                                                            ML 200.7 P3 R6
        Collection of articles including short treatments of folk and school
music and a 40-page survey, "300 Years of Music in Pennsylvania," dealing with
musical life in Pittsburgh and Philadelphia. Appendix is a 25-page biographical
dictionary of musicians, with paragraph-length entries. See also *0728, 0739, 0740*.

Philadelphia

0739   Gerson, Robert A. **Music in Philadelphia.** Philadelphia: Theodore Presser,
En   1940. vii, 422p. (Reprint—Westport, Connecticut: Greenwood Press,
        1970) LC 76-95121. ISBN 8371-3930-9.   ML 200.8 P5 G4
        Jackson—25
        A scholarly history, beginning in colonial times. Consideration of perform-
ing groups, societies, music schools, publishing. Interesting time-chart shows the
life spans of prominent musicians. Index includes brief fact entries for persons not
cited in the text. Bibliography (80 items) of published and unpublished materials;
not annotated. Index.

0740   Madeira, Louis Cephas. **Annals of Music in Philadelphia and History of the
En   Musical Fund Society from Its Organization in 1820 to the Year 1858.**
        Philadelphia: J. B. Lippincott Co., 1896. 202p. LC 6-32332. (Reprint—
        New York: Da Capo Press, 1973) (Da Capo Press Music Reprint Series)
        LC 78-169650. ISBN 0-306-70260-6.   ML 200.8 P5 M94
        Study of early church music, dramatic entertainments, instruments, the
Musical Fund Society, visiting and local artists, performances. Membership lists
of the Society, 1820-1858. Index. See also *0738b*.

Pittsburgh. See *0738b*.

Rhode Island

0741   Mangler, Joyce Ellen. **Rhode Island Music and Musicians, 1733-1850.**
En   Detroit: Information Service, 1965. xix, 90p. (Detroit Studies in Music
         Bibliography, 7) LC 65-8473.   ML 14 R5 M3
         Duckles 74—181
         A biographical directory of about 500 names, with brief data given. The
names are indexed chronologically and by performing instruments. Supplements:
organ builders and their works in Rhode Island; members of the Psallonian Society,
1816-1832. Also a seven-page historical survey. Good bibliography of primary and
secondary sources.

San Francisco

0742   United States. Work Projects Administration. Northern California. **The**
En   **History of Music in San Francisco.** San Francisco: History of Music
         Project, 1939-42. 7v. (Reprint—New York: AMS Press, 1972) LC 74-
         38305. ISBN 0-404-07240-2.   ML 200.8 S2 H4
         Consists of: 1—*Music of the Gold Rush Era* (music of missions and fiestas;
fandangos, Barbary Coast melodeons, firemen's balls, choral societies, orchestras,
instrument makers, minstrels, opera, personalities, milestone events); 2—*A San
Francisco Songster* (anthology of songs and ballads, Gold Rush to 1939); 3—
Letters of Miska Hauser (travel accounts first published in Leipzig, in German,
1859); 4—*Celebrities in El Dorado 1850-1906* (biographies of 111 musicians,
lists of visiting artists); 5—*50 Local Prodigies, 1906-1940* (accounts of precocious
local musicians); 6—*Early Master Teachers* (photos and biographies of 17 persons);
7—*An Anthology of Music Criticism* (extracts from newspapers and magazines,
1850-1940).

The South

0742a   Stoutamire, Albert. **Music of the Old South; Colony to Confederacy.**
En   Rutherford, N.J.: Fairleigh Dickinson University Press, 1972. 349p.
         LC 74-149827. ISBN 0-8386-7910-2.   ML 22.7 V819 S8
         Documented historical survey of musical activity in the South to 1865.
Appendices list concert halls and programs. Index; eight-page unannotated
bibliography.

0743   Harwell, Richard Barksdale. **Confederate Music.** Chapel Hill, North
En   Carolina: University of North Carolina Press, 1950. viii, 184p. LC 50-
         7226.   ML 3551 H3
         A carefully confined study, considering only the music that was published
in Southern cities while they were in the Confederacy. Scholarly history, plus a list
of sheet music published (about 500 items) in title order with bibliographic details.
Appendix information on publishers and music dealers, geographic distributions.
Bibliography of about 100 entries, covering primary and secondary sources; not
annotated. Index.

0744　Music and Dance in the Southeastern States, including Florida, Georgia,
En　Maryland, North & South Carolina, Virginia & the District of Columbia.
　　Ed. Sigmund Spaeth. New York: Bureau of Musical Research, 1952.
　　331p. LC 52-13292.　　　　　　　　　　　ML 200.7 S7 M8
　　Duckles 74—187
　　Useful for state-by-state survey of musical life. Short accounts for
individual cities, colleges, organizations. Biographical section of some 1,000
persons, with portraits. Classified professional directory, pp. 293-317. No index.

Southwest

0745　Whitlock, Ernest Clyde. **Music and Dance in Texas, Oklahoma, and the**
En　**Southwest.** Hollywood, Calif.: Bureau of Musical Research, 1950. 234p.
　　[plus advertisements] LC 51-1022.　　　　ML 200 W5
　　Duckles 74—188
　　Similar format to the preceding.

Texas

0745a　Spell, Lota. **Music in Texas.** (Reprint—New York, AMS Press, 1973)
En　LC 72-1675. ISBN 0-404-09907-6.　　　　ML 200.7 T4 S6
　　History of musical life: folk music, organizations, performances, music
education. List of music by Texans or composed in Texas. Index. See also *0745*.

Music Printing and Publishing

0746　Fisher, William A. **150 Years of Music Publishing in the U.S.; an Historical**
En　**Sketch with Special Reference to the Pioneer Publisher Oliver Ditson Co.,**
　　Inc., 1783-1933. Boston: Oliver Ditson, 1933. 156p. LC 33-12389.
　　　　　　　　　　　　　　　　　　　　ML 112 F53
　　Music shops and publishers of Boston, Philadelphia, New York, Baltimore,
Cincinnati and Chicago, discussion with illustrations (buildings, views, maps). Some
footnotes, but essentially a popular style. Music title pages reproduced; portraits
of leading figures. Index.

0747　Krohn, Ernst C. **Music Publishing in the Middle Western States Before the**
En　**Civil War.** Detroit: Information Coordinators, 1972. 44p. (Detroit Studies
　　in Music Bibliography, 23) LC 70-175173. ISBN 911772-47-2.
　　Duckles 74—1679; ARBA 73—1018　　　ML 112 K74
　　A scholarly introduction to publishing of sheet music in St. Louis,
Cincinnati, Louisville, Detroit, Cleveland and Chicago, from around 1839.
Discussions of the publishing houses, and of their plate number systems.

0748   Krummel, Donald W. "Graphic Analysis; Its Application to Early American
En   Engraved Music." **Notes**, 16 (1959), 213-33.
       Duckles 74—1680
       Detailed study of printing processes in early American music publishing.

       For the names of American music publishers, see the list (of American and
non-American publishers) in Vinton, *0507*.

Directories

0749   American Music Center, New York. **The Contemporary Music Performance**
En   **Directory; a Listing of American Performing Ensembles, Sponsoring Organ-**
       izations, Performing Facilities, Concert Series and Festivals of 20th-Century
       Music. Compiled by Judith Greenberg Finell. New York: American Music
       Center, 1975. xv, 238p. LC 75-24697. ISBN 0-916052-03-6.
                                                       ML 13 C65x 1975
       Entries arranged by state, within categories indicated by the title of the
directory. About 2,500 institutions, organizations, etc., are identified, with notes
of their activities, personnel, and mailing addresses. Name index. See note at *0760a*.

0750   Pavlakis, Christopher. **The American Music Handbook**. New York: Free
En   Press, 1974. xx, 836p. LC 73-2127.   ML 13.P39
       ARBA 75—1150
       More than 5,000 entries arranged in 14 chapters covering the American
music scene: organizations, instrumental ensembles (symphonies, chamber groups,
bands), vocal ensembles, opera, dance companies, music tents and summer theaters,
instrumental performers, composers, musical festivals, contests, awards, grants,
fellowships, music education, radio and television, music industries, American music
periodicals, concert managers, and a supplement of foreign music festivals, competitions, publishers. Indexed.

       See also *0144, 0145, 0146*.

Periodicals

0751   Wunderlich, Charles. "A History and Bibliography of Early American
En   Musical Periodicals, 1782-1852." Doctoral dissertation, University of
       Michigan, 1962. 796p.
       Sixty-nine periodicals carefully described and placed in a detailed historical
context. For each title this information appears: title variants, inclusive volume numbers and dates of the complete run, full publication data, periodicity, subscription
price, related works (mergers, absorptions, etc.), names of editors and biographical
sketches, names of principal contributors, contents notes, complete list of musical
compositions published in the magazine, notes regarding indexes, and indication of
library locations. Appendix of biographical information on more than 800 publishers,
printers, engravers and others associated with musical periodicals before 1852.
Indexes: alphabetical title list; geographical.

0752   Weichlein, William J. **A Checklist of American Music Periodicals, 1850-1900.**
En   Detroit: Information Coordinators, 1970. 103p. (Detroit Studies in Music
        Bibliography, 16)   ML 128 P29 W4
        Duckles 74–641

An alphabetical array of 309 titles, with place and dates of publication,
frequency of issue, and locations of files in libraries. Also chronological and geographical lists, index of editors and publishers, and bibliography. Periodicals which
contained only music compositions were not included.

0752a   Johnson, H. Earle. "Early American Periodicals Devoted to Music."
En   **Musical Quarterly**, 26 (1940), 153-161.

A bibliographic narrative, listing the periodicals preceding Dwight's *Journal*
(1852) and outlining their history. None lasted more than three years.

0753   Davison, Mary Veronica. "American Music Periodicals, 1853-1899."
En   Unpublished doctoral dissertation, University of Minnesota, 1973. 2v.
        730p.

An examination of some 300 journals, with attention to content characteristics as well as facts of publication. Attempts to show the influence of the journals
on the musical audience. Data for each title: publishers, editors, dates, title changes,
and locations in one or more of five major libraries.

There are a number of sources which provide the names of selected American
periodicals, e.g., *The Musicians Guide* (*0146*) or *Music Article Guide* (*0290*); the
latter presents in a recent issue nearly 200 titles of current magazines. Pavlakis (*0750*)
identifies about 100 journals, and gives indication of their coverage. See also the
article "Zeitschriften" in *MGG* (*0058*). For magazines in the pop/folk fields, there
is an annotated list in Sandberg (*0521a*).

Some individual periodicals which carry factual information about American
concert life, operatic activities, and news relating to performing artists:

0754   **High Fidelity/Musical America.** v.1– . 1964– . New York: Billboard
En   Publishing Co. (monthly; twice in December) LC 56-3398 r 602
                                                 ML 1 H45
        Combines *Musical America* (1898-1964) and *High Fidelity* (1951-64).

0755   **Musical Courier.** v.1– . 1962– . Evanston, Ill.: Summy-Birchard Co.
En   (monthly) LC 64-4899.   ML 1 M43
        Started in 1880 as *Musical & Sewing Machine Gazette*.

0756   **Opera News.** v.1– . no.1– . Dec. 1936– . New York: Metropolitan Opera
En   Guild. (weekly, Sept.-June)

In the popular field:

0757   **Billboard.** v.1– . 1894– . New York: Billboard Publishing Co. (weekly)
En   LC 64-36753.   PN 2000 B5

Standard source of news, data and opinion on the commercial aspects of popular genres. Locus of the widely used "top-100" and other charts.

0758 **Crawdaddy.** v.1– . 1966– . New York: Paul Williams. (monthly)
En   Probably the most informative of the slick fan magazines, with much biographical coverage, reviews of rock and soul records.

0759 **Rolling Stone.** v.1– . 1967– . San Francisco: Straight Arrow Publishers.
En   (semi-monthly) LC 73-644466.   ML 1 R65
      Extensive coverage of rock personalities, tours, records. Tabloid format.

See also the country/western magazines cited earlier, items *0647-0652*, and the annotated list in Sandberg, *0521a*.

An informative publication on various facets of American music:

0760 Institute for Studies in American Music. **Newsletter.** v.1– . 1971– .
En   New York: Brooklyn College, Department of Music.
     News of performances, publications, recordings and events involving all sorts of music, but emphasizing serious music.

Another valuable newsletter:

0760a American Music Center. New York. **Music Today . . . Newsletter.** v.1– .
En   1968– . New York: American Music Center. (six times a year)
      The Center was established in 1940 "to foster and encourage the composition of contemporary music and to promote its production, publication, distribution and performance." Since 1962 it has been the official U.S. information center for music. The newsletter gives information about contests, premieres, new publications and recordings, and other news relating to American music. Biographical files are maintained in the Center library, which also has extensive holdings of published and unpublished scores. Inquiries should be addressed to 250 W. 57th St., New York 10019, New York. See also entries *0749* and *0813*.

Instruments

The first three works concern the organ.

0761 Barnes, William Harrison. **The Contemporary American Organ**; Its
En   **Evolution, Design and Construction.** 8th ed. Glen Rock, N.J.: J. Fischer,
     1964. 389p. LC 64-5170/MN.   ML 561 B2
     (1st ed. 1930) Considerable detail on organ building as practiced by leading companies of the United States. Illustrations of unusual mechanical features. History of French, German, English and American design concepts, and a supplement dealing with electronic instruments.

0762   Barnes, William Harrison; Gammons, Edward B. **Two Centuries of American**
En   **Organ Building.** Glen Rock, N.J.: J. Fischer, 1970. 142p. LC 77-14226.
                                                                    ML 561 B18
        Brief histories of leading companies, with many photographs of their
presents; description of a typical organ installation; history of organ action; names
of nineteenth-century organ builders, and a current list of firms.

0763   Ochse, Orpha. **The History of the Organ in the United States.** Bloomington,
En   Ind.: Indiana University Press, 1975. 494p. LC 73-22644. ISBN 0-253-
        32830-6.   ML 561 O3
        Discussion of organ installations from 1524 onward, in all parts of the
country. One chapter on the American classic organ. Well documented; extensive
bibliography of 524 items.

0764   Eliason, Robert E. **Keyed Bugles in the United States.** Washington:
En   Smithsonian Institution Press, 1972. 44p. LC 77-39883.
                                                                    ML 960 E45
        An informative study of the first use of the instrument and its era of
popularity (from 1810 into the Civil War). Development of the smaller E-flat
bugle, the brass band era. Descriptions of outstanding specimens. Documented;
brief bibliography.

Performing Groups

0765   Seltzer, George Albert. **The Professional Symphony Orchestra in the**
En   **United States.** Metuchen, N.J.: Scarecrow Press, 1975. vii, 486p.
        LC 75-19271. ISBN 0-8108-0855-2.   ML 1211 P 76
        An uneven anthology of 89 previously published articles, in popular style.
Some deal with individual orchestras, others concern conductors, the musicians,
audiences, and commercial aspects. Index.

0765a   Mueller, John Henry. **The American Symphony Orchestra; a Social**
En   **History of Musical Taste.** Bloomington; Indiana University Press, 1951.
        xii, 437p.   ML 200 M8
        A scholarly study, comprising a general historical perspective plus profiles
of 17 orchestras, and discussions of the repertoires from the viewpoints of composers
and national sources represented. Also consideration of socioeconomic aspects.
Indexed.

0765b   Hart, Philip. **Orpheus in the New World; the Symphony Orchestra as an**
En   **American Cultural Institution.** New York: W. W. Norton, 1973. xix,
        562p. LC 73-3151. ISBN 0-393-02169-6.   ML 1211 H3
        A documented examination of the past and present condition of the
American symphony orchestra, emphasizing economic aspects. Special attention
to the roles of Theodore Thomas, Henry Higginson, Arthur Judson, James Petrillo,
and Helen Thompson. Six orchestras receive detailed study: Philadelphia, Utah,

Louisville, Buffalo, Albuquerque, and Cincinnati. Data on repertoires, attendance and finance; private and governmental supports. Bibliography (four pages, not annotated); index.

0765c BMI Inc. **BMI Orchestral Programs Survey**. New York: Broadcast Music
En Inc., 1960– . (annual) ML 1200 B7x
The 11th edition gives data on 6,758 concerts by 620 orchestras. Emphasis on identifying composers and works most performed, with special attention to contemporary composition.

Recent factual information about orchestras is available also in items cited in Volume One: *Musical America Directory Issue (0144)*, *Musical Courier Annual Directory (0145)*, *The Musician's Guide (0146)*, and *World Almanac (0155)*. Various retrospective approaches are found in several sources, e.g., *International Who Is Who in Music (0138)*, *International Who's Who . . . (0139)*, and *Pierre Key's Music Year Book (0153)*.

Black-American Music

Until the 1960s there was little writing about the serious concert music of black composers. This topic is now of considerable interest, and it seems useful to assemble several important books in one section.

The most extensive bibliography is Maultsby *(0793a)*, cited under Guides to Other Sources.

The basic historical work is:

0766 Southern, Eileen. **The Music of Black Americans: a History**. New York:
En W. W. Norton, 1971. xviii, 552p. LC 77-98891.
  Jackson—42 ML 3556 S74
A general historical survey of all musical activities of American blacks from 1619. Good biographical data throughout, and meticulous concern for sources of all kinds (including newspapers and court records). Considers folk music, popular and jazz, and concert music; attempts to relate black music to traditional Western styles. Fine bibliography; index.

Three books of composite authorship present some useful perspectives and gatherings of facts:

0767 Southern, Eileen. **Readings in Black American Music**. New York: W. W.
En Norton, 1972. xii, 302p. LC 70-98892. ISBN 0-393-02165-3.
  ML 3556 S75
An anthology of writings from 36 sources, seventeenth to nineteenth centuries. Good sections on slaves and plantation music, and on modern urban music. Most of the authors write in popular style (Ethel Waters, Mahalia Jackson, W. C. Handy, etc.); there is a scholarly essay by William Grant Still. Biographical notes, musical examples; index.

0768   De Lerma, Dominique-René. **Black Music in Our Culture; Curricular Ideas**
En   **on the Subjects, Materials, and Problems.** Kent, Ohio: Kent State University
        Press, 1970. 263p. LC 70-131429. ISBN 0-87338-110-6.

                                                            ML 38 B68 B66
        Based on the proceedings of a 1969 seminar, entitled "Black Music in
College and University Curricula," held at Indiana University. Nineteen major
contributors, including some leading writers on black music (Eileen Southern,
Portia Maultsby, William Grant Still, etc., have presented information and ideas
related to the concept of integrating the black musical experience into college
courses. "Selective list of scores . . . recordings . . . films," pp. 171-222.

0769   De Lerma, Dominique-René. **Reflections on Afro-American Music.** Kent,
En   Ohio: Kent State University Press, 1973. 271p. LC 72-619703.

                                                            ML 3556 D43
        Continues the format and topics of discussion of the preceding, with some
of the same contributors and some new ones.

The next group of works concerns the historical matrix.

0769a   Fisher, Miles Mark. **Negro Slave Songs in the United States.** Ithaca, N.Y.:
En   Published for the American Historical Association. Cornell University
        Press, 1953. xv, 223p. LC 53-13501.   M 1670 F35 N4
        A scholarly narrative of African antecedents and the emergence of
American Negro song, emphasizing spirituals. Many song texts, with their back-
grounds, but no music. Bibliography of 20 pages, not annotated. Index, which
includes song titles.

0770   Courlander, Harold. **Negro Folk Music U.S.A.** New York: Columbia
En   University Press, 1963. 324p. (Paperback reprint—1970)

                                                            ML 3556 C7
        A dependable survey of anthems, spirituals, and other religious music;
work songs; blues; creole songs; ballads; dances; instruments and other topics.
Well documented, with bibliography, discography, musical examples and index.

0771   **The Social Implications of Early Negro Music in the United States.** Ed.
En   by Bernard Katz. New York: Arno Press, 1969. xlii, 146p. LC 68-29005.

                                                            ML 3556 K28
        An anthology which reprints articles and portions of monographs, mostly
from the nineteenth century, predominantly on the spiritual. Music examples, a
selective bibliography, and song index are included.

0772   Jones, LeRoi. **Blues People; Negro Music in White America.** New York:
En   William Morrow, 1963. 244p. LC 63-17688.   ML 3556 J73
        An important, objective historical study. Considers slave music, Afro-
Christian music, primitive blues and jazz, music in middle-class life, and swing.
Index. There are translations into French and Italian.

0773   Heilbut, Tony. **The Gospel Sound; Good News and Bad Times.** New York:
En   Simon and Schuster, 1971. 350p. LC 76-156151. ISBN 0-671-20983-3.
       Jackson–40   ML 3556 H37
       A popular historical survey, emphasizing personalities. Good discography
of ten pages. Name index.

0774   Keil, Charles. **Urban Blues.** Chicago: University of Chicago Press, 1966.
En   ix, 231p. LC 66-13876.   ML 3356 K43
       Serious sociological study of the blues–and black music in related
idioms–considering historical, musical, and commercial aspects. Well documented.
Good chapter on soul; annotated outline of blues styles. Index.

0775   Hare, Maude Cuney. **Negro Musicians and Their Music.** Washington:
En   Associated Publishers, Inc., 1936. xii, 439p. LC 34-11223. (Reprint–New
       York: Da Capo Press, 1974) (Da Capo Press Music Reprint Series) LC 74-
       4108. ISBN 0-306-70652-0.   ML 3556 H27 N3
       Jackson–39
       Extensive coverage of history and idioms: African influences, Negro folk
song, musical comedy, folk themes in art music (with list of works), music in war
service (bands, soldier songs), biographical notes. Subjective comments. Footnotes
and five-page bibliography (citations incomplete); index. See note at *0776.*

       The remaining items offer some valuable perspectives.

0776   Trotter, James M. **Music and Some Highly Musical People.** Boston: Lee
En   and Shepard; New York: Charles T. Dillingham, 1878. 353, 152p.
       (Reprint–New York: Johnson Reprint Corp., 1968.) LC 70-55613.
                                                ML 385 T76
       The first history of Negro music, a landmark which remains useful today
for unique information on black musicians. Much data gathered by personal
correspondence. Some errors to be found, most of them resulting from unreliable
secondary sources consulted. Robert Stevenson has written a definitive study of
this book and its author: "America's First Black Music Historian," *Journal of the
American Musicological Society*, 26-3 (Fall 1973), 383-404. Stevenson points out
the dependence of Hare (*0775*) on Trotter, and notes that she made numerous
mistakes in extracting material from his book. An appendix of 152 pages presents
13 complete compositions.

0777   Lovell, John. **Black Song: the Forge and the Flame; the Story of How the
En   Afro-American Spiritual Was Hammered Out.** New York: Macmillan, 1972.
       xviii, 686p. LC 71-150067.   ML 3556 L69
       Evaluates research on the spiritual, examines the social history of the form,
and interprets black song as philosophy and literature. Bibliographic notes; index.
List of spirituals (about 500) referred to in the text. Index.

There is a useful scholarly journal:

0777a **The Black Perspective in Music.** v.1— . Spring 1973— . New York:
En   Foundation for Research in the Afro-American Creative Arts.
       (Editor, Eileen Southern, Spring 1973—) Fine, serious journal with
historical and ethnomusicological studies. Articles on musicians, book and record
reviews. Lists of new books, dissertations, music and recordings. Also lists "research
in progress." Annual index.

       For lists of music by black composers, see entries *0814-0816*.

BIOGRAPHICAL SOURCES

       Many works cited in Volume I are useful for direct information about
Americans connected with music, or as guides to such information. Among these
are *Biography Index (0169)*, Bull's *Index . . . (0170)*, Baker's *(0175)*, *Current
Biography (0184*; and see Jackson, *0786c*, for musicians included, 1940-1970),
Portraits . . . (0188), Ewen's *Composers Since 1900 (0189)*, and Ewen's *Great
Composers (0190)*.

       A number of general biographical works on Americans are of value in
the search for facts about musicians; these are cited next.

0778 **Dictionary of American Biography.** Published under the auspices of the
En   American Council of Learned Societies. New York: Charles Scribner's
      Sons, 1928-37. 20v. and Index. LC 28-28500. (Reprint—New York:
      Scribner, 1943, 21v.; 1946, 11v. on thin paper) Supplements 1-4. New
      York: Scribner, 1944-74.   E 176 D56
      Sheehy 76—AJ41; Jackson—5
      The most important national biography for the United States, with long
scholarly articles on more than 13,000 persons in the basic set and about 2,400
more in the supplements. Only deceased persons (through 1950, in the fourth
supplement) are included. Musicians can be found via the occupations index
(basic set only), or most conveniently in Jackson (basic set plus first two supplements), where 131 names are listed.

0778a **National Cyclopaedia of American Biography.** New York: White, 1892— .
En   Sheehy 76—AJ43   E 176-N27
       53v. published through 1971, plus volumes in a "current series" and index
volumes. A complex work, the most comprehensive for Americans, although below
the editorial standards of DAB *(0778)*. No occupational index, but some musicians
can be traced through various topical indexes and lists (award winners, presidents
of societies, etc.) given in two companion volumes: *White's Conspectus of American
Biography* (New York: White, 1937), and *Notable Names in American History*
(Clifton, N.J.: James T. White, 1973). For details on these, see Winchell 76—AJ45.

0778b **Who's Who in America; a Biographical Dictionary of Notable Living Men**
En **and Women.** Chicago: Marquis, 1899– . (biennial)
Sheehy 76–AJ57   E663 W58
A reliable collection of sketches, with high standards for inclusion; some
73,000 persons in the 1974/75 volume. A vocational-geographical index was
published only for issues of the 1950s. Deceased persons are transferred to *Who
Was Who in America* (1942–); cf. Sheehy 76–AJ51, AJ52. Other Marquis
publications of value are the various sectional lists—*Who's Who in the East, Who's
Who in the Midwest, Who's Who in the South and Southwest,* and *Who's Who in
the West* (Sheehy 76–AJ58-61)—and *Who's Who of American Women* (Sheehy
76–AJ68). None of these have occupational indexing.

The following sources are concerned entirely with persons in the field
of music.

0779 American Society of Composers, Authors and Publishers. **The ASCAP**
En **Biographical Dictionary of Composers, Authors and Publishers.** 3d ed.
New York: ASCAP, 1966. 845p. LC 66-20214.
Duckles 74–176; Jackson–59   ML 106 U3 A5
(1st ed. 1948) Brief entries for 5,238 persons; mailing address included,
and some representative works. Popular and concert composers both covered.
Useful feature of the first edition, grouping of names by place of birth, date of
birth and residence, has not been continued.

0780 Chase, Gilbert. **The American Composer Speaks: a Historical Anthology,**
En **1770-1965.** Baton Rouge: Louisiana State University Press, 1966. 318p.
LC 66-14661/MN.   ML 90 C55
Letters and other documents. Each composer entry is prefaced with a
biographical sketch. Indexed. Bibliography. Composers: Billings, Hopkinson,
Heinrich, Fry, Foster, Gottschalk, Waler, Hewitt, MacDowell, Farwell, Gilbert,
Ives, Mason, Cowell, Gershwin, Harris, Morton, Copland, Thomson, Varèse,
Partch, Berger, Schuller, Cage, Babbitt, Carter, Flanagan, Sessions, Hann, Brown.

0781 Claghorn, Charles Eugene. **Biographical Dictionary of American Music.**
En West Nyack, New York: Parker Pub. Co., 1973. 491p. LC 73-5534.
ISBN 0-13-076331-4.   ML 106 U3C6
ARBA 75–1155
About 5,000 very brief notices on native Americans and immigrants who
have settled in the United States. Includes popular, folk, jazz, and serious artists.
Criteria for inclusion not stated, and appear vague; many important omissions,
especially among orchestra players and writers on music. Black musicians are so
identified.

0782 Contemporary Music Project for Creativity in Music Education. **The CMP**
En **Library.** 2d ed. Washington: Music Educators National Conference, 1969.
3v. LC 68-2963.   ML 128 S25 C62
Jackson–84
(1st ed. 1967/68) This *Library* is a collection of works for school-
level performing groups written by 73 composers-in-residence sponsored by

the Project over a ten-year period. Listed here are all those works, plus biographical information on each composer. The names of composers included are listed in Jackson, pp. 59-60.

0783　Edmunds, John; Boelzner, Gordon.**Some Twentieth-Century American**
En　　**Composers; a Selective Bibliography.** New York: New York Public
　　　Library, 1959. 2v. LC 59-15435.　　　　ML 120 U5 E3
　　　Duckles 74–649; Jackson–86
　　　A list of writings by, and about, 32 composers; plus brief citations on
others. Composers' names are listed by Jackson.

0784　Ewen, David. **Popular American Composers from Revolutionary Times**
En　　**to the Present: a Biographical and Critical Guide.** New York: H. W. Wilson
　　　Co., 1962. 217p. Supplement, 1972. LC 62-9024.
　　　Duckles 74–198　　　　　　　　　　　ML 390 E845
　　　Past and present composers in the popular idioms; biographical information
and portraits. Chronological index of names, and index to about 3,500 so.igs cited.

0784a　Fisher, Suzanne M. "An Index to Biographical Information on Rock
En　　Musicians." Unpublished Master's research paper, Kent State University,
　　　School of Library Science, 1973. 57p.
　　　Provides access to writings in 27 books and six magazines dated 1965 or
later. Refers to biographical material only; reviews and critical studies omitted.
Both individual performers and groups covered, and cross references connect
individuals with their present or former group affiliations.

0785　Goss, Madeleine Binkley. **Modern Music Makers; Contemporary American**
En　　**Composers.** New York: E. P. Dutton & Co., 1952. 499p. LC 52-5304.
　　　(Reprint–Westport, Conn.: Greenwood Press, 1970)
　　　Jackson–87　　　　　　　　　　　　ML 390 G69
　　　Detailed accounts of 37 composers (their names are listed in Jackson,
p. 87), with photos, facsimiles, lists of works, and chronologies.

0786　Historical Records Survey. District of Columbia. **Bio-bibliographical Index**
En/Sp/　**of Musicians in the United States of America Since Colonial Times.** 2d ed.
Pr　　　Washington: Pan American Union, Music Section, 1956. xxiii, 439p.
　　　LC P A 57-4. (Reprints–New York: Da Capo Press, 1971 [Da Capo Press
　　　Music Reprint Series]; St. Clair Shores, Mich.: Scholarly Press, 1972; New
　　　York: AMS, 1972) LC 76-159677. (Da Capo); 76-1662 (Scholarly)
　　　　　　　　　　　　　　　　　　　ML 106 U3 H6
　　　Duckles 74–179; Jackson–1; ARBA 72–1090
　　　(1st ed. 1941) Jackson notes that the "second edition" is merely a reprint
of the 1941 edition. More than 10,000 entries, which include dates, profession, and
citations to further information in any of 66 books. Coverage is almost entirely
limited to concert composers and serious music performers active before 1939;
only slight representation of popular, jazz, and folk artists.

0786a　Howard, John Tasker; Mendel, Arthur. **Our Contemporary Composers:**
En　　**American Music in the Twentieth Century.** New York: Thomas Y. Crowell,
　　　1941. 447p. LC 41-6742.　　　　　　ML 200 H82

A complementary volume to *Our American Music* (*0707*). Considerable detail, and portraits, of composers from diverse fields: folk, Broadway, jazz, concert music. Indexed.

0786b   Hughes, Rupert. **American Composers; a Study of the Music of This**
En   **Country and of Its Future, With Biographies of the Leading Composers**
        of the Present Time. 2d ed., with added chapters by Arthur Elson.
        Boston: Page, 1914. 582p. LC 14-20511. (Reprint—New York: AMS
        Press, 1973) LC 72-1618.   ML 390 H89
        (1st ed. 1900: *Contemporary American Composers*) A good view of the
prominent artists of the time, with both biographical data and critical comments
offered.

0786c   Jackson, Richard. **United States Music; Sources of Bibliography and**
En   **Collective Biography.** New York: Institute for Studies in American
        Music, Department of Music, Brooklyn College of the City University
        of New York, 1973. 80p. (I.S.A.M. Monographs, 1) LC 73-80637.
        ARBA 75–1128   ML 120 U5 J2
        This is the "Jackson" cited throughout the present chapter. A very useful
guide to the contents of 90 books of biography, history, or bibliography, with some
topical studies. Full imprint data, reference to some reviews, evaluative annotation,
and content summary given for each entry. A valuable feature is the listing of
persons covered in particular collective biographies: Simeon Cheney, *The American
Singing Book*; *Current Biography*; *Dictionary of American Biography*; Tony Heilbut,
The Gospel Sound; Stanley Green, *The World of Musical Comedy*; Contemporary
Music Project . . . *CMP Library*; Edmunds and Boelzner, *Some Twentieth-century
American Composers*; Madeleine Goss, *Modern Music Makers*; and *Compositores
de America*. Furthermore, all the names of all those persons are interfiled in one
index. The same index contains the names of authors of the books themselves;
an infelicitous feature—there is no separate index to authors and titles.

0787   Jones, F. O. **A Handbook of American Music and Musicians, Containing**
En   **Biographies of American Musicians, and Histories of the Principal**
        Institutions, Firms and Societies. New ed. Buffalo: C. W. Moulton, 1887.
        182p. (Reprint—New York: Da Capo Press, 1971) (Da Capo Press Music
        Reprint Series) LC 76-155355. ISBN 0-306-70163-4.
        Jackson—10; ARBA 72–1139   ML 106 U3 J7
        (1st ed. Canaseraga, N.Y.: F. O. Jones, 1886) Jackson notes that the two
editions are identical. Still useful despite its age, this is a wide-ranging dictionary
of American musical life based largely on information gained from personal
correspondence. Entries for personal names, with some lists of works. Also topical
entries, for concert halls, opera houses, periodicals, tune books, songs and other
compositions, publishers, instrument makers, performing groups and music of
major cities.

0788   Lloyd, Frederic E. J. **Lloyd's Church Musicians' Directory: the Blue Book**
En   **of Church Musicians in America.** Chicago: Ritzmann, Brookes, 1910. 176p.
      (Reprint—New York: AMS Press, 1974) LC 72-1733.
                             ML 17 L5
      Brief data on choir directors, organists, teachers, etc., with their affiliations
and years of experience.

0788a   Marks, Edward Bennet. **They All Had Glamour; From the Swedish Night-**
En   **ingale to the Naked Lady.** New York: J. Messner, Inc., 1944. 448p.
      LC 44-4384. (Reprint—Westport, Conn.: Greenwood Press, 1972) LC
      79-154104.   ML 3551 M3
      Biographical information mixed with gossip, in very casual style. But does
give some facts not available elsewhere, on about 200 women of the stage and
film—many of them singers or dancers. Index of names.

0788b   Metcalf, Frank Johnson. **American Writers and Compilers of Sacred Music.**
En   2d ed. New York: Russell & Russell, 1967. 373p. LC 66-24731.
                             ML 106 U3 M3
      (1st ed. 1925) About 100 short biographies, useful for many persons not
covered in other sources. Lists of works not included.

0788c   Reis, Claire R. **Composers in America; Biographical Sketches of Living**
En   **Composers with a Record of Their Works.** 2d ed. New York: Macmillan,
      1947. xvi, 339p. LC 47-31210.   ML 390 R38
        Duckles 74—190; Jackson—90
      (1st ed. 1938) Stems from an earlier work by the author, *American
Composers* (1930). A valuable, authoritative collection of biographical data on
332 composers of serious music, with detailed lists of works (published and
unpublished). Information about the compositions includes dates, publishers,
durations, instrumentation. Some persons who died between the first and second
editions were omitted in the second; hence the two editions need to be checked
for complete coverage.

0789   Smith, Julia. **Directory of American Women Composers.** Chicago: National
En   Federation of Music Clubs, 1970. 51p. LC 73-645158.
       Duckles 74—191   ML 19 S5
      Identifies more than 600 composers of serious music and teaching pieces.
Gives type of music associated with each person but does not give lists of titles.
Publishers or distributors cited.

      The following title has been announced for publication:

0789a   Anderson, E. Ruth. **Contemporary American Composers: a Biographical**
En   **Dictionary.** Boston: G. K. Hall. ISBN 0-8161-1117-0.

      There are many other sources of biographical facts in the present volume,
especially under Folk Music and Folksong (see p. 36), Popular Music (see p. 45),
and Black-American Music (see p. 73).

GUIDES TO OTHER SOURCES

Bibliographies of Bibliographies

See Jackson, *0786c.*

Selective and Critical Guides

General

0790   United States. Library of Congress. General Reference and Bibliography
En   Division. **A Guide to the Study of the United States of America; Representative Books Reflecting the Development of American Life and
Thought.** Washington: Government Printing Office, 1960. 1,193p.
LC 60-60009. **Supplement 1956-1965,** 1976. 526p.
                                                          Z 1215 U53
     A fine list of titles in 32 fields, with extended descriptive and evaluative
comments. About 6,500 works covered, 82 of them in the Music chapter. Other
books of musical interest are found in the Folklore chapter. The supplement adds
35 music titles.

Folk Music and Folksong

0791   United States. Department of the Interior. **Biographical and Historical
En   Index of American Indians and Persons Involved in Indian Affairs.**
Boston: G. K. Hall, 1966. 8v.   Z 1209 U494
     Entries, with bibliographic and imprint data, for 79 works in the main
Music and Musical Instrument heading, plus other material scattered under various
headings.

Church and Religious Music

0791a Eskew, Harry. "Using Early American Hymnals and Tunebooks." **Notes,**
En   27-1 (Sept. 1970), 19-23.
     A useful brief survey of major writings on hymnals (in the original sense,
a book of hymn texts without music) and tunebooks (originally books of melodies,
with texts perhaps incomplete).

0792   Metcalf, Frank Johnson. **American Psalmody; Or, Titles of Books
En   Containing Tunes Printed in America from 1721 to 1820.** New York:
Charles F. Heartman, 1917. 54p. (Reprint, with new introduction by
Harry Eskew–New York: Da Capo Press, 1968) LC 68-13274.
    Duckles 74–1128   ML 120 U5 M3
     An author list of 724 titles, with full bibliographic information on all
editions, and library locations. Excellent facsimile illustrations. Eskew warns in
the introduction to the reprint edition about the need for caution in accepting

certain facts presented. He also notes that Britton (0793) has more or less superseded Metcalf, except for the difference in cutoff dates for inclusion. See also the review by Richard A. Crawford, in *Notes*, 26-1 (Sept. 1969), 42-43.

0793   Britton, Allen. "Theoretical Introductions in American Tune-books to
En   1800." Doctoral dissertation, University of Michigan, 1949.
                                                            Mic A 50-48
         Considers the history of psalmody in America, the development of
vocal music instruction, and the publication of tune books. A comprehensive
bibliography of tune-books (all books containing religious music) for the United
States up to the year 1800 is an extremely valuable feature (see note at *0792*).
This bibliography gives pagination, dimensions, content, number of editions, and
library locations. It complements the secular list of Sonneck-Upton (*0819*). There
is also a bibliography of eighteenth century sermons and pamphlets relating to
music, and another of articles and books.

         A selective list of tune-books appears in Grove's American supplement,
0610.

Other Topics: Black Music

0793a   Maultsby, Portia K. "Selective Bibliography: U. S. Black Music."
En   **Ethnomusicology**, 19-3 (Sept. 1975), 422-449.
         About 550 entries, grouped by subject (minstrels, blues, jazz, art music,
etc.); also works about individuals. Appears to be the most comprehensive listing.
Not annotated.

Dissertations and Theses

0794   Mead, Rita H. **Doctoral Dissertations in American Music; a Classified**
En   **Bibliography.** New York: Institute for Studies in American Music,
        Department of Music, Brooklyn College of the City University of New
        York, 1974. xiv, 155p. (I.S.A.M. Monographs, 3) LC 74-18893.
        ISBN 0-914678-02-7.   ML 128 M8
          ARBA 76-990
         A thorough list of 1,226 numbered entries for doctoral dissertations
produced in American (and a few foreign) universities from the 1890s to December
1973. Subject order, with author and subject indexes; occasional brief notes to
clarify contents. These titles also appear in the *Comprehensive Dissertation Index*
(*0335*) and its supplements, but CDI has rather limited "keyword" access, while
Mead has far more convenient and detailed access through extensive subject
approaches.

LISTS OF MUSIC

Bibliographies of Lists of Music

0795 Krummel, D. W. "American Music Bibliography: Four Titles in Three
En Acts." **Anuario interamericano de investigación musical. Yearbook for
Inter-American Music Research**, 8 (1972), 137-146.
  A lucid state-of-the art review on works relating to early American music
imprints, based on a critique of Hixon (*0818*) and Tanselle (*0796*).

0796 Tanselle, George Thomas. **Guide to the Study of United States Imprints.**
En Cambridge, Mass.: Belknap Press of Harvard University Press, 1971. 2v.
   Winchell 76—AA442   Z 1215 A2 T35
  A guide to the published research concerning material published in the
United States. Lists about 10,000 works, in nine categories (regional lists, copy-
right catalogs, book-trade directories, etc.). Krummel has counted 100 works on
music (cf. *0795*); his article is a necessary supplement for anyone checking
Tanselle for musical aides.

Selective and Critical Lists

General

0797 Music Educators National Conference. Bicentennial Commission. "Selective
En List of American Music for the Bicentennial Celebration . . . " **Music
Educators Journal** 61/62 (1975/76.
  A series of bibliographies by various authors. The topics and *MEJ* dates:
Choral—April 1975, pp. 54-61; about 300 works. Band—May 1975, pp. 48-52;
about 400 works. Orchestra—October 1975, pp. 66-73; about 600 works.
Opera—February 1976, pp. 55-63; about 180 works. The Journal also published
a double article of interest: "Directions in American Composition Since the
Second World War. Part I—1945-1960" (February 1975, pp. 29-39, by Elliott
Schwartz); " . . . Part II—1960-1975" (March 1975, pp. 35-45, by Barney Childs).
This is a survey of names, works and trends, emphasizing electronic processes,
with portraits and illustrations. Another article worth noting is Eileen Southern's
"America's Black Composers of Classical Music," November 1975.

0798 Eagon, Angelo. **Catalog of Published Concert Music by American
En Composers.** 2d ed. Metuchen, N.J.: Scarecrow Press, 1969. 348p.
  LC 68-9327. Supplement, 1971. 150p.   ML 120 U5 E23 1969
   Duckles 74—864; ARBA 70—v.2, p.26
   (1st ed. 1964) The first edition was an official government document:
Catalog of Published Concert Music by American Composers, selected, compiled
and prepared by Music Branch, Information Center Service, under the direction
and supervision of the Music Advisor, United States Information Agency
(Washington: U.S. Government Printing Office, September 1964; 175p.).

Duckles observes that "the Scarecrow Press publication is an unacknowledged descendant." It is a classified list of solo songs, choral works, instrumental solos and ensembles, orchestral pieces, opera, band (concert works), with instrumentation, publisher, and miscellaneous information about the works. More than 500 composers, native and naturalized citizens, plus Menotti (not a citizen). List of publishers; composer index.

Popular Music

General Lists

The first four items are best seen as a group:

0799   Burton, Jack. **The Blue Book of Broadway Musicals.** Rev. ed. Watkins
En   Glen, N.Y.: Century House, 1969. 327p.   ML 200.5 B88
        Duckles 74–340; Jackson–60a
        (1st ed. 1952) A list of operettas and musical revues, by decade, and
within each decade by composer; presents more than 1,500 works dating from
the 1890s to 1969. Identifies librettists, lyricists, original cast principals, and the
major songs for each one. Although "stained by sins of omission and commission"
(Jackson) this is a useful compilation. For access, the separate index is necessary
(*0802*).

0800   Burton, Jack. **The Blue Book of Hollywood Musicals.** Watkins Glen,
En   N.Y.: Century House, 1953. 296p. LC 53-6568.
        Duckles 74–341; Jackson–60b   ML 128 M7 B8
        A film chronology, with information on their principal songs. Composers,
lyricists, singers all identified. Also lists of award-winning songs and a discography.
Index of film titles, but for other indexing it is necessary to have *0802*.

0801   Burton, Jack. **The Blue Book of Tin Pan Alley; a Human Interest**
En   **Encyclopedia of American Popular Music.** Expanded new ed. Watkins
        Glen, N.Y.: Century House, 1962-65. 2v. LC 62-16426 (rev./MN)
                                            ML 390 B963
        Duckles 74–955; Jackson–60c (1st ed. only)
        (1st ed. 1951) A chronological and composer arrangement of songs,
1776-1965. Biographical sketches, discographies. Indexes of composers and
lyricists. For a song index, however, it is necessary to have the following item
(*0802*):

0802   Burton, Jack. **The Index of American Popular Music.** Watkins Glen,
En   N.Y.: Century House, 1957. (unpaged) LC 57-3788 rev.
        Duckles 74–956; Jackson–60d   ML 120 U5 B92
        This is the title index to songs in items *0799*, *0800*, and *0801*. For *0799*
and *0801* only the first editions are covered.

Lists of Theatre Music

0803   Lewine, Richard; Simon, Alfred. **Encyclopedia of Theatre Music; a**
En   **Comprehensive Listing of More Than 4,000 Songs from Broadway and**
       Hollywood, 1900-1960. New York: Random House, 1961. vii, 248p.
       LC 61-13837.   ML 128 S3 L5
       Duckles 74—352; Jackson—66
       Title lists of theatre and film songs, giving composer, lyricist, show, and
date for each; also a show chronology, 1925-1960. Published vocal scores for
musicals are listed. Index of shows.

0804   Lewine, Richard; Simon, Alfred. **Songs of the American Theater: a**
En   **Comprehensive Listing of More Than 12,000 Songs Including Selected**
       Titles from Film and Television Productions. New York: Dodd, Mead,
       1973. 820p. LC 72-3931. ISBN 0-396-06657-7.
       ARBA 74—1072   ML 128 S3 L53
       This complementary work to *5610* concentrates on the period from
1925 to 1971, aiming for comprehensiveness. Earlier songs are listed selectively.
Arrangement is by title of song; information given for each is composer, lyricist,
show title and year. The songs are also arrayed chronologically, in a second
section. Indexed by composer and lyricists.

Lists of Songs

0805   Chipman, John H. **Index to Top-Hit Tunes, 1900-1950.** Boston: B.
En   Humphries, 1962. 249p. LC 61-11711.   ML 128V7 C54
       Duckles 74—957
       An alphabetical title list of some 3,000 songs. All songs included have
sold at least 100,000 copies in sheet music or recorded form. Facts given for each
song: key, composer, lyricist, publication date, film or show in which the song
appeared. Chronological index.

0806   Dichter, Harry; Shapiro, Elliott. **Early American Sheet Music; Its Lure**
En   **and Its Lore, 1768-1889.** New York: R. R. Bowker, 1941. xxvii, 287p.
       Duckles 74—1059; Jackson—4   ML 112 D53
       A subject-ordered list of titles, with composers, publishers and dates
given. Many illustrations of covers. Directory of publishers from the eighteenth
and nineteenth centuries; lists of "lithographers and artists working on American
sheet music before 1870." Song title index.

0807   Fuld, James J. **American Popular Music (Reference Book) 1875-1950.**
En   Philadelphia: Musical Americana, 1955. 94p. Supplement, 1956. 9p.
       LC 55-5415.   ML 120 U5 F9
       Duckles 74—959; Jackson—64
       A descriptive inventory of about 250 first editions of popular songs,
giving dates and details of appearance. List of pseudonyms of composers; 20
plates illustrating the covers; index. The Supplement was bound into a second
printing.

0808   Havlice, Patricia Pate. **Popular Song Index.** Metuchen, N.J.: Scarecrow
En   Press, 1975. 933p. LC 75-9896. ISBN 0-8108-0820-X.

ARBA 76—1026   ML 128 S3 H4

An index to the songs found in 301 collections which were published
between 1940 and 1972. All but 13 of the collections are American. Contents
cover folk songs, children's songs, popular tunes, show music and many other
types. Title, first line, and first line of chorus are indexed in one alphabet; with
index of composers and lyricists. About 30,000 songs altogether.

0809   Shapiro, Nat. **Popular Music; an Annotated Index of American Popular**
En   **Songs.** New York: Adrian Press, 1964— . LC 64-23761.

ML 120 U5 S5

Duckles 74—963; Jackson—71; ARBA 75—1175

Published so far: v.1, 1950-59 (1964); v.2, 1940-49 (1965); v.3, 1960-64
(1967); v.4, 1930-39 (1968); v.5, 1920-29 (1969); v.6, 1965-69 (1973). A selective
list of principal songs, arranged by year; gives composer, lyricist, publisher, film or
musical show if appropriate, best-selling recordings, and miscellaneous facts. Title
index in each volume. An invaluable work of solid scholarship.

0810   Stecheson, Anthony; Stecheson, Anne. **The Stecheson Classified Song**
En   **Directory.** Hollywood, Calif.: Music Industry Press, 1961. ix, 503p.
LC 62-753.   ML 128 V7 S83

A list of about 60,000 popular songs, grouped in some 450 categories.
Most of the categories are subject classes, informal but effective: Jail, Jealous,
Jewelry, Jewish, Judge, Jungle, Kiss, etc. There are some form groupings too,
such as Adaptations (pop tunes taken from classical works). Information given
is minimal: composer (not every time) and publisher. A casual work, but clearly
unique and definitely entertaining.

See also Ewen, *American Popular Songs (0658)*; Mattfeld, *Variety Music
Cavalcade (0656)*; Kinkle, *Complete Encyclopedia (0655)*; Burton, *Index of
American Popular Music (0802)* and the Lewine entries cited above (see p. 85).

Instrumental Music

0811   American Society of Composers, Authors and Publishers. **ASCAP**
En   **Symphonic Catalog.** 2d ed. New York: American Society of Composers,
Authors and Publishers, 1966. 369p. LC 67-4434.

Duckles 74—862   ML 128.05 A55

A composer list of works by members of ASCAP. Facts given: instrumentation, duration, publisher. A third edition has been announced for late 1976 publication by Bowker.

0812   Broadcast Music Inc. **Symphonic Catalogue.** New York: Broadcast Music
En   Inc., 1963. 132p. LC 64-55150.   ML 128 I65 B7
Duckles 74—863

A composer list of works controlled by BMI. Instrumentation, duration and publisher are given for each entry.

0812a Ferris, Sharon Paugh. "American Piano Music in Print." Unpublished
En   Master's thesis, Kent State University, School of Library Science, 1971.
       189p.
       A classified list of about 1,500 works located in current publishers'
catalogs; all separately published compositions for piano or pianos, alone or with orchestra, are cited—except elementary teaching pieces. Native and naturalized citizens are included among the approximately 500 composers; their birth and death dates are mentioned, and sources of further biographical data are identified. Available recordings given. List of the 47 publishers whose catalogs were searched; composer index.

Opera and Vocal Music

See also items under Opera and Vocal Music, p. 52.

0813 American Music Center, New York. **American Music Center Library**
En   **Catalog of Choral and Vocal Works.** Compiled by Judith Greenberg Finell.
      New York: American Music Center, 1975. viii, 198p. LC 75-24698.
      ISBN 0-916052-02-8.   ML 120 V5 A47
      See note on the Center at *0760a*. About 5,000 works, arranged by
composer, with facts about voicing, accompaniment, and publisher; information on manuscripts. No indexes.

Lists of Music by Black Composers

0814 George, Zelma Watson. **A Guide to Negro Music: an Annotated**
En   **Bibliography of Negro Folk Music, and Art Music by Negro Composers**
      or Based on Negro Thematic Material. Doctoral dissertation, New York
      University, 1953. 302p. Ann Arbor: University Microfilms, 1954.
      Publication No. 8021.   Microfilm AC-1 No. 8021
      The actual bibliography on which this study is based exists only as a card
file of 12,163 titles, located in the Howard University Library, Washington, D.C. In the dissertation, there is an extended discussion of terms and problems involved in Negro music research, plus a critical review of the literature about Negro music. Thorough bibliography of references.

0815 White, Evelyn Davidson. **Selected Bibliography of Published Choral Music**
En   **by Black Composers.** Washington: Howard University Bookstore, 1976.
      87p. LC 75-312252.   ML 128 V7 W5
      Lists some 700 works by 63 composers. Copyright date, number of pages,
voicing and solo requirements given, with vocal ranges, difficulty, accompaniment and publisher.

See also entries under Black-American Music (see p. 73).

0816   De Lerma, Dominique-René. **Black Concert and Recital Music; a**
En   **Provisional Repertoire List.** Bloomington, Indiana University, 1975– .
       ML 128 N4 D4

An extensive bibliography, issued in fascicles, designed as a preliminary
draft of a comprehensive listing to be published subsequently. Full bibliographic
citations are provided for each title (including plate numbers and selected locations
in libraries), grouped alphabetically by composer. Sole distributor: Theodore Front
Musical Literature (115 North San Vicente Boulevard, Beverly Hills CA 90211).

Lists of Early Music (to 1800)

The best record of American publication from colonial times to 1800 was
compiled by Charles Evans:

0817   Evans, Charles. **American Bibliography; a Chronological Dictionary of All**
En   **Books, Pamphlets and Periodical Publications Printed in the United States**
   of America from the Genesis of Printing in 1639 down to and Including
   the Year 1800; with Bibliographical and Biographical Notes. Chicago:
   printed for the author, 1903-59. 14v. (Publisher varies) (Reprint–New
   York: Peter Smith, 1941-1967)   Z1215 E92
   Sheehy 76–AA445

Various supplements, corrections and indexes have appeared; these are
noted in Sheehy 76, p. 40. See also comments in Krummel (*0795*). The next item
is of interest to musical research:

0818   Hixon, Donald L. **Music in Early America: a Bibliography of Music in**
En   **Evans.** Metuchen, N.J.: Scarecrow Press, 1970. 607p. LC 74-16407.
   ISBN 8108-0374-7.   ML 120 U5 H6
   Duckles 74–1076; Jackson–9; ARBA 72–1103

Extracts all publications from the Evans list which contain actual music,
and lists them by name of composer. Title index; index of Evans serial numbers;
biographical sketches. Indispensable for the study of this period in American music
history; but note criticisms in Krummel (*0795*).

0818a   Heard, Priscilla S. **American Music, 1698-1800: An Annotated Bibliog-**
En   **raphy.** Waco, Texas: Baylor University Press, 1975. 246p.
   LC 75-14907   ML 120 U5 H4

This is a list of "all entries pertaining to music from the *American Bibliography* by Evans" presented in date order. Includes most of what Hixon covered
(0818), adding items about music. Extensive bibliographic descriptions, commentaries, references to literature and to later printings, etc. Title and author index.

There is also a valuable list of more limited scope:

0819   Sonneck, Oscar G. T. **A Bibliography of Early Secular American Music**
En   **(18th Century).** Rev. and enlarged by William Treat Upton. Washington:
   Library of Congress, Music Division, 1945. xvi, 616p. (Reprint, with a
   new preface by Irving Lowens–New York: Da Capo Press, 1964) LC
   64-18992.   ML 120 U586
   Duckles 74–1107; Jackson–12

(1st ed. 1905) A title list of music and writings about music issued to
1800, with full bibliographic descriptions. The Upton expansion was considerable,
bringing the number of titles from about 500 to some 3,000 (Wolfe, *0824*, adds 33

more). Upton also provided new indexes: to articles and essays on music; composers (with biographical sketches), first lines, patriotic songs, opera librettos, publishers, printers and engravers. See comments in Krummel (*0795*), and see also Dichter (*0806*). For sacred music of the same period, see Britton (*0793*).

0820 Gombosi, Marilyn. **Catalog of the Johannes Herbst Collection.** Chapel
En   Hill: University of North Carolina Press, 1970. xix, 255p. LC 72-97011.
      ISBN 0-8078-1124-6.   ML 97 H375
      Duckles 74–1541
      This collection, housed in the Moravian Archives, Salem, North Carolina,
consists of about 1,000 vocal works used in worship services. The Gombosi inventory covers 464 manuscripts that were assembled by Herbst (1735-1812), a minister and musician. These works are considered to be representative of the Moravian sacred tradition.

A microfiche edition of the collection itself has been announced:

0821 **The Johannes Herbst Collection; the Complete Collection of Manuscripts**
En   **as Found in the Archives of the Moravian Music Foundation** . . . New
      York: University Music Editions, 1976 (in preparation). (microfiche of
      11,300 pages)

0822 Rau, Albert George; David, Hans T. **A Catalogue of Music by American**
En   **Moravians, 1742-1842, from the Archives of the Moravian Church at**
      Bethlehem, Pa. Bethelehm, Pa.: Moravian Seminary and College for
      Women, 1938. 118, A-X p. (Reprint–New York: AMS Press, 1970)
      LC 76-134383. ISBN 0-404-07206-2.   ML 120 U5 R14
      Short biographies and lists of compositions for 17 persons. Selection of
pieces and other pages from the manuscripts reproduced in plates.

Lists of 19th and 20th Century Music

0823 Kuceyeski, Mary Jo. "Music Titles in **Bibliotheca Americana 1852-1861**:
En   a Preliminary Checklist." Unpublished paper, Kent State University,
      School of Library Science, 1975. 26p.
      A continuation of Dempsey (*0265*). Lists all works containing music or
about music which appeared in Roorbach. Title arrangement only, and no verification of bibliographic data attempted. Decision to include was made on the basis of information given in Roorbach only. About 500 entries.

0824 Wolfe, Richard J. **Secular Music in America, 1801-1825; a Bibliography.**
En   New York: New York Public Library, 1964. 3v. LC 64-25006.
      Duckles 74–1114   ML 120 U5 W57
      A major bibliographic contribution, giving some 10,000 titles and editions
of musical imprints. Includes some sacred music, when printed in secular collections or series. Composer arrangement, with title, first-line and publisher indexes, plus a general index. Library locations of copies provided. Short biographical notes on lesser-known composers.

0825   Board of Music Trade of the United States of America. **Complete Catalogue**
En   **of Sheet Music and Musical Works . . . 1870.** New York: Board of Music
    Trade, 1870. 575p. (Reprint–New York: Da Capo Press, 1973) (Da Capo
    Press Music Reprint Series) LC 69-1666. ISBN 0-306-71401-9.

ARBA 75–1121   ML 120 U5 B6

    Classified list of music and some books about music published by 20
publishers (members of the "Board") and still in print in 1870. Don Hixon has
noted, in his ARBA review, that at least 45 non-member firms were excluded–so
this is hardly a complete picture. Nevertheless, it is the principal aid in bridging
the gap between Wolfe (*0824*) and the *Catalog of Copyright Entries* (*0826*).
Material grouped in 56 categories, with no indexes. Publisher and price are the
only facts supplied for each entry.

Annual and Periodic Lists

    There is no national bibliography for publications of the United States,
although *CBI* (*0267*) serves the general purpose in many ways, and *Publishers'
Weekly* (*0268/69*) provides valuable coverage. For issues of actual music, one
must turn to individual publisher announcements and catalogs (music publishers
are not included in the *Publishers' Trade List Annual*, (*0269*), to *Music, Books
on Music, and Sound Recordings* (*0387*), and as a last resort to the next item:

0826   United States. Copyright Office. **Catalog of Copyright Entries**, 1891– .
En   Washington: Government Printing Office, 1891– . (semi-annual)
    LC 6-35347.   Z 1219 U58 C
      Duckles 74–834; Sheehy 76–AA478; BH 52
    Title and issuing agency vary. See Winchell for the complex publishing
history of this massive work. Musical compositions submitted for copyright were
included from the beginning of this catalog, in various ways; 1891-1906, mingled
with other materials; 1906-1946, in a separate series by title; 1946, subdivided
into published and unpublished, and renewal registrations; 1957, regrouped into
current and renewals, with name index–this format is still in use (identified as
Part 5). Name index locates composers, editors, compilers, arrangers, librettists,
and lyricists. Scope of this work reaches to foreign materials deposited for copyright under international agreements, as well as all published and unpublished
music of every genre originating in the United States. No cumulations or cumulative
indexes, so a thorough search of this bibliography is very laborious.

DISCOGRAPHIES

General

See discographies in *0708, 0710, 0711.*

Folk Music and Folksong

Three catalogs issued by the Library of Congress are of particular value. They are listed here in chronological order.

0827   U.S. Library of Congress. Archive of American Folk Song. **Check-list of**
En   **Recorded Songs in the English Language in the Library of Congress**
       Archive of American Folk Song to July, 1940. Alphabetical List with
       Geographical Index. Washington: Library of Congress, 1942. 3v.
       LC 42-15513. (Reprint–New York: Arno Press, 1971) LC 78-151055.
       ISBN 0-405-03420-2. [Also available in electrostatic print of original
       edition from University Microfilms, Ann Arbor]
       Duckles 74–1795; Jackson–30   ML 156.4 F6 U5
       Songs are given by title in the first two volumes (with name of singer,
collector, place and date of recording) and arranged by state and county in the
third volume. Ordering information is provided. (Note that LC imprint and
cataloging titles for the Archive vary somewhat: "Folk Song," "Folksong.")
See note for *0829*.

0828   U.S. Library of Congress. Archive of American Folksong. **A List of**
En   **American Folksongs Currently Available on Records.** Washington:
       Library of Congress, 1953. 176p. LC 53-60046.
       Jackson–35   ML 156.4 F6 U54
       Approximately 1,700 songs in title order, with name of singer and album
or collection in which it appears. These are field recordings and commercial discs.
Index of album titles and singers.

0829   U.S. Library of Congress. Archive of American Folk Song. **Folk Music;**
En   **a Catalog of Folk Songs, Ballads, Dances, Instrumental Pieces, and Folk**
       Tales of the United States and Latin America on Phonograph Records.
       [5th ed.] Washington: Library of Congress, 1964. 107p. LC 58-60095.
       Duckles 74–1796; Jackson–31   ML 156.4 F5 U5
       (1st ed. 1943-45; 2d ed. 1948; 3d ed. 1958; 4th ed. 1959; title varies)
A list of 1,240 pieces on 107 78rpm discs and 59 LP discs. Arrangement by album
or composite LP, with title index to individual selections and a geographical index.
An introductory note from the "Head, Archive of Folk Song" (cf. comment at
0827).

The following work was prepared by two staff members in the Archive:

0830   Hickerson, Joseph C.; Korson, Rae. "The Willard Rhodes Collection of
En   American Indian Music in the Archive of Folk Song." **Ethnomusicology**,
       13-2 (May 1969), 196-304.
       Rhodes made field recordings for the U.S. Department of the Interior
between 1940 and 1952. Ten LP discs, offering a selection of his work, have been
issued by the Library of Congress. Contents are given in this article. Represented:

Kiowa, Sioux, Navaho, Apache; groups from Oklahoma, the Northwest, the Great Basin, and the Southwest.

Popular Music

General

0831 Rust, Brian. **The American Dance Band Discography 1917-1942.** New
En   Rochelle, N.Y.: Arlington House, 1975. 2v. LC 75-33689. ISBN 0-87000-
      248-1.   ML 156.4 P6 R87
      ARBA 76—994
      Another monumental effort by Rust (see *0465, 0496, 0832*). This time
he names 2,373 dance orchestras and cites all their recordings on 78 rpm. For each
disc, facts given include matrix and label numbers, dates of recording, arrangers,
vocalists, and miscellaneous data. Personnel for each band are identified, with their
instruments. About 50,000 records are included, with their instruments. About
50,000 records are included, with an artist index of 8,000 names. Glenn Miller
and Benny Goodman, for whom discographies have already been published, are
omitted. And Negro bands are left out, since Rust covered them in *Jazz Records*
(*0496*). There is no title index to compositions.

0832 Rust, Brian. **The Complete Entertainment Discography from the Mid-1890s**
En   **to 1942.** New Rochelle, N.Y.: Arlington House, 1973. 677p. LC 73-13239.
      ISBN 0-87000-150-7.   ML 156.4 P6 R88
      ARBA 74—1100
      This production is a kind of supplement to Rust's *Jazz Records* (*0496*)
and *American Dance Band Discography* (*0831*). It lists the recordings of 457
artists and groups, arranged by artist with discs in chronological sequence. Persons
included are American (U.S.) by birth or otherwise associated with the United
States. They are from diverse categories: minstrels, vaudevillians, film and stage
actors and actresses, radio performers and other show-business personalities such
as comedians. Facts given: recording dates, matrix and catalog numbers, take
numbers, accompanists, and some biographical data. No indexes.

0833 Whitburn, Joel. **Top Pop Records 1955-70.** Detroit: Gale Research Co.,
En   1972. 1v. (unpaged) LC 76-183555.   ML 156.4 P6 W49
      Duckles 74—1784; ARBA 73—1060
      An index of more than 2,500 artists, with lists of their most popular
recordings (according to *Billboard* magazine charts); 9,800 discs (singles) covered.
A valuable compilation, but its utility is reduced by a lack of indexing; performer
name is the only access.

0834 Propes, Steve. **Those Oldies But Goodies: a Guide to 50's Record Collecting.**
En   New York: Macmillan, 1973. 192p. LC 72-93630.
      ARBA 74—1133   ML 156.4 P6 P76
      An inventory of 2,284 records issued between 1946 and 1959 by 123
"rhythm and blues" groups, seven rhythm and blues duos, 55 rhythm and blues

solo vocalists, and 20 rock groups. Discs are in chronological order, with label and number, release year, and names of pieces on both sides. There are discussions of the groups and of the collecting value of the records. Access is awkward, since various clusters are presented, and there is no index.

0835   Propes, Steve. **Golden Oldies; a Guide to 60's Record Collecting.** Radnor,
En   Pa.: Chilton Book Co., 1974. xii, 240p. LC 74-4102. ISBN 0-8019-6062-2.
        ARBA 75–1173   ML 156.4 P6 P75
        About 3,600 single discs, mostly of rock groups, but with folk and other
styles also covered. Similar in content and approach to preceding entry (*0834*).
No index.

Jazz, Ragtime and Blues

0836   Godrich, John; Dixon, Robert M. W. **Blues and Gospel Records, 1902-1942.**
En   Rev. ed. London: Storyville Publications, 1969. 912p. LC 68-58241.
        Duckles 74–1771; Jackson–50   ML 156.2 D63 1969
        An attempt to cite "every distinctively Negroid folk music record made up
to the end of 1942," in performer order. Discographical facts given; indexes of
accompanists, labels and companies.

0837   Jasen, David A. **Recorded Ragtime, 1897-1958.** Hamden, Conn.: Archon
En   Books, 1973. viii, 155p. LC 73-301. ISBN 0-208-01327-X.
        ARBA 74–1124   ML 156.4 R25 J4
        Consists of two sections: entries by title (with composer, performer, record
number, year and month of recording), and entries by composer (with title and date
of copyright). Bibliography, list of private record collections, and performer index.
About 1,200 compositions altogether.

Rock to Soul

0838   Propes, Steve. **Golden Goodies: a Guide to 50's and 60's Popular Rock &**
En   **Roll Record Collecting.** Radnor, Pa.: Chilton Book Co., 1975. xi, 185p.
        LC 75-6900. ISBN 0-801-96220-X.   ML 156.4 P6 P745
        Supplements *0834* and *0835*. Discographies of Pat Boone, Brenda
Lee, the Crew Cuts, Chipmunks, and their contemporaries. Price information
and advice on collecting. No index.

CHAPTER 3

LATIN AMERICA

GENERAL

Publications listed in this chapter pertain to all, or a large part of, the Western Hemisphere south of the United States: Mexico, Central and South America, and the Caribbean. Most writings that concern two countries, or more than two countries, are presented here, with cross references later under the individual countries. Some material on Mexico is also found in the North American chapter. The index can be used to locate any national material quickly.

In this unit and others concerned with Latin American countries, references are made to entries in Chase's bibliography, *A Guide to the Music of Latin America (0891).*

THE LANGUAGE OF MUSIC

0839   Mayer-Serra, Otto. **Música y músicos de latinoamérica**. México: Editorial
Sp   Atlante, 1947. 2v. LC 49-48553.   ML 199 M3
       Duckles 74–155; Chase–94a
       An encyclopedia of terms, topics, and biography. Entries for theatres
and concert halls, and musical organizations. Musical examples (e.g., for national anthems). Lists of works for some composers, apparently comprehensive in certain cases. Some bibliographical citations. Portraits, no index.

A brief glossary, including song and dance forms and names of instruments is found in Slonimsky (*0840*). For Spanish musical terms, see the dictionaries entered in Volume I, *0040-0043*. Vannes (*0009*) includes many Portuguese terms.

DIRECT INFORMATION SOURCES

Introductions and General Surveys

0840   Slonimsky, Nicolas. **Music of Latin America**. New foreword and addenda
En   by the author. New York: Da Capo Press, 1972. 374p. (Da Capo Press
       Music Reprint Series) LC 69-11288.   ML 199 S55 1972
       (1st ed. 1945) General discussion of music and composers in society;
then essays on musical life in each of 20 countries, which emphasize biographical information. Some portraits and musical examples. No lists of works. Useful appendix, "Dictionary of Latin American Musicians, Songs and Dances, and Musical Instruments," pp. 295-325. General index. This reprint edition carries a new foreword and a two-page addendum of death dates; otherwise it is unchanged from the original edition.

0841   Pahlen, Kurt. "Südamerika." **MGG** (*0058*), XII, columns 1674-95.
Ge   Survey of the Indian and colonial eras, then short studies of each country;
stress on historical questions. Bibliography: two-thirds of a column.

0842   Pahlen, Kurt; Mendoza, Vicente T. "Mittelamerika." **MGG** (*0058*), IX,
Ge   columns 373-386.
      General historical survey (with four-column section on pre-conquest era,
by Vicente T. Mendoza) followed by paragraphs on individual countries. Fullest
treatment of Mexico (three columns), Cuba (two columns), and Costa Rica (one
column). Covered more briefly: Dominican Republic, Guatemala, Haiti, Honduras.
Bibliography: two-thirds of a column.

      Latin America is covered in *The History of Western Music* series (*0511*)
edited by Frederic Sternfeld. Chapters by Robert Stevenson comprise a documented, historical survey for periods covered. Classified discographies and
bibliographies are an additional reference feature of this series.

0843   Pan American Union. **Music of Latin America.** 3d ed. Washington: Pan
En   American Union, 1953. 57p. (Club and Study Fine Art Series) Reprinted
      1963. LC 54-61936.   ML 199 P2 M8 1953
      Chase—59 (1st ed.)
      (1st ed. 1942, *Music in Latin America; a Brief Survey*.) Popular history of
pre-Columbian and colonial periods, nineteenth century and twentieth century,
covering Mexico, Central America, South America, and the Antilles. Appendices
include a 77-item bibliography (with short annotations) of publications in English;
an annotated list of 25 song collections; and a partly annotated list of 49 phonograph record albums, mostly 78 rpm. First edition had personal and place name
indexes, but the third has none. Photographs and musical examples.

0844   Mayer-Serra, Otto. "Panorama de la música hispanoamericana." in
Sp   **Enciclopedia de la música; traducción y adaptación españolas** . . . México:
      Editorial Atlante, 1943. v.2, pp. 379-440.   MT 6 A885
      Chase—54
      Documented historical survey from pre-conquest era to early 1940s. Well
illustrated with many excellent portraits and photos of composers, performers.
Drawings, musical examples. Chase's entry refers to its publication as a separate.
The *Enciclopedia* is a Spanish translation of:
      Hamel, Fred; Hürlemann, Martin. *Atlantisbuch der Musik.*
      Berlin: 1934 etc. 8th ed., Zürich, Atlantis Verlage, 1953.
A Spanish translation of the eighth edition:
      Hamel, Fred; Hürlemann, Martin. *Enciclopedia de la música.* . . .
      Barcelona: Ediciones Grijalbo, 1970.

0845   Corrêa de Azevedo, Luiz Heitor. **La musique en Amérique Latine.** Paris:
Fr   Centre de Documentation Universitaire, 1957. 64p.
      Based on lectures given at the Sorbonne. Includes bibliographic survey;
composers Villa-Lobos, Chávez, and Santa Cruz; Brazilian folk music.

0846 Subirá, José; Cherbuliez, Antoine-E. **Musikgeschichte von Spanien,**
Ge **Portugal, Lateinamerika.** Zürich: Pan Verlag, 1957. 312p. LC A 58-2295.
ML 160 S9414
This work includes a translation of Subirá's original title, *Historia de la
música española e hispano-americana* (Barcelona: Salvat, 1953) with a new section
on Latin America by Cherbuliez, pp. 201-290. (Original work had only a 27-page
summary.) General historical narrative, pre-colonial era to the twentieth century.
Name index, geographic name index, no bibliography.

0847 García, Rolando V.; Croatto, Luciana C.; Martín, Alfredo. **Historia de la**
Sp **música latinoamericana.** Buenos Aires: Librería "Perlado," 1938. 231p.
LC 41-14563.   ML 199 G3 H5
Chase—42, 236
General survey of folk music and dance, instruments, general musical
culture and composers of Brazil, Bolivia, Chile, Cuba, Mexico, Peru, Uruguay, and
Venezuela. Designed as a school text; illustrations and musical examples; no
bibliography or index.

A comprehensive survey of Central American music:

0848 Sider, Ronald Ray. "The Art Music of Central America—its Development
En and Present State." Doctoral dissertation, Eastman School of Music,
University of Rochester, 1967. xiv, 375p. **Dissertation Abstracts,** 28/03-A,
(September 1967), p. 1,097. Ann Arbor: University Microfilms, order
number 67-11084.
Organized by country, giving for each: survey of musical organizations
and institutions, followed by a section on individual composers—biographies and
analyses of works. Folk music is treated briefly, also by country, in an appendix.
Other appendices present lists of works, concert programs and program notes,
musical texts of national anthems, maps and photographs. Musical examples, five-
page bibliography (unannotated) of books and music. No index.

Two sources for twentieth century developments:

0850 Vega, Aurelio de la. "La música artística latinoamericana." **Boletín**
Sp **interamericano de música,** 82 (Nov. 1971-Feb. 1972), 3-33.
Survey of composers (mentioning specific works, with description) and
trends, organized in sections by country. Covers Argentina, Brazil, Chile, Colombia,
Cuba, Mexico, Uruguay, and Venezuela most thoroughly; paragraph treatment for
other countries.

0851 Paz, Juan Carlos. **Introducción a la música de nuestro tiempo.** 2d ed.
Sp Buenos Aires: Editorial Sudamericana, 1971. 659p. LC 73-221430.
ML 197 P36 1971
(1st ed. 1955) General work on contemporary music. Chapter 8,
"Problematica y creación musical en Latinoamerica y en los Estados Unidos,"
deals with Latin America, pp. 462-496. Sections on Brazil, Mexico, Cuba, Chile,
Argentina, Uruguay.

Collections of Essays, Articles, Etc.

0852   *Ethnomusicology*, 10 (Jan. 1966).   ML 1 E77
En   An entire issue on Latin America; contains seven articles and five brief
contributions.

0853   **Inter-American Conference on Ethnomusicology. 1st. Cartagena, Colombia,**
Sp/Pr   **1963. Primera Conferencia Interamericana de Etnomusicología** . . .
        Washington: Pan American Union, 1965. 224p. LC PA 65-40.
        Very brief articles with musical examples and illustrations. Entries *1035*
and *1150* are articles from this volume.

0854   List, George; Orrego-Salas, Juan, eds. **Music in the Americas.** Papers read
En/Sp/ at the First Inter-American Seminar of Composers and the Second Inter-
Pr   American Conference on Ethnomusicology, Bloomington, Indiana, April
        24-28, 1965. Bloomington: Indiana University, Research Center in
        Anthropology, Folklore, and Linguistics, 1967. 257p. (Inter-American
        Music Monograph Series, 1) NUC 69-7298.
        Includes 27 papers on a wide range of topics; among the authors are Luis
Heitor Corrêa de Azevedo, Frank Gillis, Charles Haywood, George List, Alan P.
Merriam, Bruno Nettl, Carlos Vega, and Charles Seeger. Abstracts of these papers
are found in RILM (*0260*), II/2 (May-August 1968.)

Folk Music and Folksong

0855   Nettl, Bruno. **Folk and Traditional Music of the Western Continents.**
En   (*0103*) Chapter 9, "Latin American Folk Music," by Gerard Béhague,
        pp. 179-206; Chapter 10, "Afro-American Folk Music in North and
        Latin America," by Bruno Nettl and Gerard Béhague, pp. 207-249.
                                                      ML 3545 N285
        Types and structures of folk melodies (Hispanic, Mestizo, Indian-Hispanic,
Afro-Hispanic, Afro-American genres). Central America and Caribbean included.
Fifteen musical examples in these two chapters; each chapter has short bibliographical
guide and discography.

0856   Nettl, Bruno. "Lateinamerikanische Volksmusik." **MGG** (*0058*), VIII,
Ge   columns 292-304.
        Hispanic and Mestizo styles; instruments. Nine musical examples, five
other illustrations; bibliography, one and one-fifth columns.

0857   Friedenthal, Albert. **Musik, Tanz und Dichtung bei den Kreolen Amerikas.**
Ge   Berlin-Wilmersdorf: Schnippel, 1913. 328p. LC 13-10971.
           Chase—158   ML 3575 F7
        Survey of song and dance forms organized by country and region. Musical
examples, index.

Although entered in the discography section, Durán (*0917*) is a comprehensive survey of folk song and dance forms of Latin America. Directory-type arrangement, by country in alphabetical order. Includes South America, Central America, and Caribbean.

The remaining entries in this section pertain to specific ethnic groups or particular regions.

Four studies of Afro-Latin American music:

0858 Roberts, John Storm. **Black Music of Two Worlds.** New York: Praeger,
En   1972. LC 77-184031. (Morrow Paperback Edition, 1974; ISBN 0-688-
      05278-9.)   ML 3556 R6
      Studies the development of an Afro-American musical culture. Coverage
of North America, South America, Central America, and the Caribbean. Unannotated
six-page bibliography, classified by region; 11-page discography, classified by region
and topic. Index.

0859 Almeida, Renato. **Danses africaines en Amérique Latine.** Rio de Janeiro:
Fr   Ministério da Educacão e Cultura, Campanha de Defesa do Folclore
      Brasileiro, 1969. 35p. LC 74-526095.   GV 1626 A67
      Brief survey of Latin American dance forms of African origin. Unannotated,
one-page bibliography.

0860 Stevenson, Robert. "The Afro-American Legacy (to 1800)." **Musical**
En   **Quarterly**, 54 (Oct. 1968), 475-502.   ML 1 M725
      Survey of pre-1800 primary source references to black music and musicians
in Latin America. Also one paragraph on the United States. Musical examples.

0861 Epstein, Dena J. "African Music in British and French America." **Musical**
En   **Quarterly**, 59 (Jan. 1973), 61-91.   ML 1 M725
      Survey of primary sources to black music (song and dance forms, instruments)
in the United States and West Indies, 1640-1864. Three illustrations.

Two studies of Caribbean music:

0862 Lekis, Lisa. "The Origin and Development of Ethnic Caribbean Dance
En   and Music." Doctoral dissertation, University of Florida, 1956. 294p.
      Dissertation Abstracts 16 (1956), pp. 1,126-1,127. Ann Arbor: University
      Microfilms, order number 00-16360.
      Comprehensive study of dance music in all of the Caribbean islands.
Extensive bibliographies.

0863 Lekis, Lisa. **Dancing Gods.** New York: Scarecrow Press, 1960. 220p.
En   LC 60-7272.   GV 1631 L45
      Comprehensive survey of Caribbean folk dance, with information on
musical aspects and instruments. Chapters on specific ethnic groups and individual
islands. Annotated 22-page bibliography, classified arrangement by country. Index.

The following two items deal with Argentina and Paraguay:

0864 Baccay, Dalmidio Alberto. **Música regional y método (nordeste argentino**
Sp **y paraguayo).** Buenos Aires: L. Laserre, 1967. 96p. LC 72-245557.
ML 3575 A7 B3
Survey of folk music forms in northeast Argentina and Paraguay. Unanno-
tated three-page bibliography; index; musical examples.

0865 Baccay, Dalmido Alberto. **Vitalidad expresiva de la música guaraní.**
Sp Buenos Aires: Fondo Nacional de las Artes, 1961. 108p. LC 64-1732.
ML 3575 A2 B33
A documented, analytical and descriptive study of music and dance of
the Guaraní Indians (of Argentina and Paraguay). Unannotated two-page bibliog-
raphy; no index. Numerous musical examples.

A study of the Andean region:

0866 Harcourt, Raoul d'; Harcourt, Marguerite d'. "La musique dans la sierra
Fr andine de La Paz à Quito." **Journal de la Société des américanistes de**
Paris, n.s. 12 (1920), 21-53.   E51 S68
Chase—655
Folk music of Bolivia and Ecuador. Contains 22 musical examples and
eight melodies. Two other studies by the d'Harcourts (*0873* and *0874*) include
extensive coverage of Andean folk music. See also items *0852, 0854, 0892.*

Church and Religious Music

0867 Pardo Tovar, Andrés. "L'Amérique latine jusqu'à la fin du XVIIIe siècle."
Fr **Encyclopédie des musiques sacrées.** (*0510*), II, 510-521.
Brief historical survey with illustrations and musical examples.

0868 Pardo Tovar, Andrés. "L'Amérique latine, de la fin du XVIIIe siècle à
Fr nos jours." **Encyclopédie des musiques sacrées.** (*0510*), III, 253-265.
Includes biographical information, illustrations, musical examples, and
unannotated bibliography of 21 entries.

Other articles in the **Encyclopédie des musiques sacrées:**
Stevenson, Robert. "Les musiques incas et aztèques, et leurs survivances,"
I, 105-110; Boulton, Laura. "Le culte *Vaudou*," I, 111-117.

Music Theory and Musicology

0869 Corrêa de Azevedo, Luis Heitor. "The Present State and Potential of
En Music Research in Latin America." In **Perspectives in Musicology,** ed.
Barry Brook, Edward Downes, and Sherman Van Solkema. New York:
W. W. Norton, 1972. pp. 249-269.   ML 55 B77

Informative survey of musicological and ethnomusicological research and publications in Latin America. A bibliographic essay, including music periodicals. Also mentions research institutes, names of scholars.

Historical Studies, Chronologies, Contemporary Narratives

0872
Ge
Martí, Samuel; Besseler, Heinrich; Bachmann, Werner. **Alt-Amerika. Musik der Indianer in präkolumbischer Zeit.** Musikgeschichte in Bildern (*0119*), II-7. 193p. LC 70-547702.   ML 89 M9
Duckles 74-484
A picture history, based on original sources, fully documented. Considers music of the Indians in North, South, and Central America, ca. 1000-1500. Chronology, bibliography.

0873
Fr
Harcourt, Raoul d'; Harcourt, Marguerite d'. "La musique indienne chez les anciens civilisés d'Amérique." In Lavignac, **Encyclopédie de la musique** . . . (*0061*), partie I, pp. 3,337-3,371.
Chase—210, 653, 1564, 2339, 2405
Part one: musical instruments of ancient Mexico and Peru; part two: folk music of the Andean region—Ecuador, Bolivia, Peru. Musical examples; illustrations.

0874
Fr
Harcourt, Raoul d'; Harcourt, Marguerite d'. **La musique des Incas et ses survivances.** Paris: P. Guenther, 1925. 2v. (v.1, 575p., v.2, 39 plates.)
LC 26-12490.   ML 3575 P4 H3
Chase—2349, 2406
Reconstructs music of the Incas, in part through study of Andean folk music. Covers instruments, music, dance of Bolivia, Ecuador, and Peru. A classic work. Many photos, illustrations, musical examples and transcriptions. Unannotated bibliography of 230 entries; synoptic table of contents.

0875
En
Stevenson, Robert. **Music in Aztec and Inca Territory.** 2d ed. Berkeley: University of California Press, 1976. xi, 378p.   ML 3549 S84
(1st ed. 1968) An introduction to the era in which the high musical culture of the Mexican and Peruvian regions was confronted with the musical perspectives of Europe, via Spanish colonization. Coverage to the beginning of the nineteenth century. Stevenson is primarily concerned with identification and description of sources, including contemporary accounts, extant instruments, pertinent documents. Musical examples (native and colonial), unannotated bibliography of about 750 entries, and strong index. The next entry serves as a supplementary notice:

0876
En
Stevenson, Robert. "The First New World Composers: Fresh Data from Peninsular Archives." **Journal of the American Musicological Society**, 23 (Spring 1970), 95-106.   ML 27 U5 A83363
Newly discovered archival facts about certain composers active in the sixteenth and seventeenth centuries.

0877 Mendoza, Vicente T. "Música precolombina en América." **Boletín**
Sp   **latino-americano de música**, 4 (1938), 235-257.

    Chase—212   ML 199 B64

    General summary, covering instruments and musical elements (e.g., scales,
rhythm, melody). Photos, drawings, musical examples.

0878 Hammond, Norman. "Classic Maya Music." **Archeology**, 25 (April 1972),
En   124-131, (June 1972), 222-228.   GN 700 A725

    Part one, "Maya Drums" is descriptive article illustrated with photos and
drawings. Unannotated bibliography of eight entries. Part two is "Rattles, Shakers,
Raspers, Wind and String Instruments," also with illustrations and photos; unannotated one-page bibliography.

0878a **Revista musical chilena**, 16 (jul.-dic. 1962), 225p.
Sp   ML 5 R238

    Entire issue devoted to studies of music in the colonial era. Includes articles
by leading scholars of Latin American music: Lauro Ayestarán, Pablo Hernández
Balaguer, José Antonio Calcaño, Luis Heitor Corrêa de Azevedo, Vicente Gesualdo,
Andrés Sás, Robert Stevenson, Carlos Vega.

Directories

0879   Pan American Union. Music Section. **Conservatorios, academias y escuelas**
Sp/En **de música, y orquestas sinfónicas. Conservatories, Academies and Music**
       Schools, and Symphony Orchestras. Washington: Pan American Union,
       1954. 27p. LC PA 55-218.   ML 21 P23

    Chase—100a

    Directory information by country and city. Data given are variable, from
mere street address in some cases to an extended coverage with names of individuals,
library data, etc.

Periodicals and Yearbooks

    The article ' Zeitschriften" in *MGG* (*0058*), XIII-XIV, includes a list of
Latin American music periodicals, classified by country of publication, columns
1171-1173.

0880   **Anuario interamericano de investigación musical. Yearbook for Inter-**
En/Sp/ **American Musical Research.** v.1– . 1965– . Austin, Tex.: University of
Pr   Texas, Department of Music and Institute for Latin American Studies,
       1970– . [Tulane University, Inter-American Institute for Musical
       Research, 1965-1969] LC 72-620658.   ML 1 T842

    Editor (1965–) Gilbert Chase. A fine, scholarly journal containing articles,
reports, and long book reviews. An index to volumes 1-5 appeared with volume 6.

0881   **Boletín latino-americano de música.** año 1-6, 1935-1946. Montevideo [etc.]:
Sp/Pr   Instituto Interamericano de Musicología, Montevideo, 1941-1946.
"Suplemento musical" issued with v.1, 3-6. LC 40-5410 rev.2.

Chase—35   ML 199 B64

A pioneer publication, edited by Francisco Curt Lange. During its short life
span, it published some 4,000 pages of text and 500 pages of music. Lange cam-
paigned for the serious study of American music, and for cooperation among the
nations concerned. Volume 5 was devoted to the music of the United States; volume
6 to Brazil (see entry *0984*). An interesting article about the *Boletín* appeared in the
initial volume of the *Anuario* (*0880*), by editor Gilbert Chase.

0882   **Boletín interamericano de música.** 1-87, sept. 1957-july-oct. 1973.
Sp   Washington: Organization of American States. (bimonthly to 1970,
quarterly, 1970-1973)

Highly informative publication, including music news of North and South
America; lists of new books, recordings, and music. Feature articles often reprinted
from other journals. Periodic summaries of music periodical contents throughout the
world. Some articles are from *Compositores de América . . .* (*0182*) series, others
deal with folk music, music education, and historical topics. Articles through
March-June 1972 are indexed in *0887*.

0883   **Inter-American Music Bulletin.** no. 1-87, Sept. 1957-July-Oct. 1973.
En   Washington: Organization of American States. (bimonthly to 1970,
quarterly, 1970-1973)

Parallel, English edition of *0882*. Contents are not identical; some articles
appear in both editions, some do not. Shorter, includes fewer news features. Issues
through 1971 are indexed in *0887*.

The *Revista de estudios musicales* (*0953*) and *Revista musical chilena*
(*1068*) include articles on a variety of Latin American topics and countries.

0884   **Enciclopedia universal ilustrada europeo-americana.** Barcelona: Espasa,
Sp   1905-1933. 80v. in 81.

Suplemento anual, 1934— .   AE 61 E6

Sheehy 76—AC82

The basic set of this encyclopedia, which is usually cited as "Espasa," is
not of much value for music information. However, the supplements carry reports
on events of the year under the heading "*Música*," both for Spain and for Spanish
America (arranged by country). Premieres, opera seasons, contests, prominent
personalities in popular music.

Instruments

0885   Izkowitz, Karl Gustav. **Musical and Other Sound Instruments of the South
En   American Indians; a Comparative Ethnographical Study.** Reprint ed. East
Ardsley, England: S. R. Publishers, 1970. 433p. LC 73-158482. ISBN
0-85409-505-5.   ML 3575 A2 I97

(1st ed. 1934) Scholarly, comprehensive study, based on instruments in museums of America and Europe (especially Göteborg, Sweden) and the writings of travellers, historians, anthropologists, and ethnologists. Arrangement of materials is by instrument classification (e.g., ideophones, membranophones, etc.). Unannotated, 16-page bibliography; photos, drawings, tables. No index.

0886   Howard, Joseph H. **Drums in the Americas.** New York: Oak Publications,
En   1967. xv, 319p. LC 67-15826.   ML 1035 H69
       Comprehensive, detailed study of drums in the Western hemisphere.
Includes construction and drum music. Coverage of North, South, and Central America, Caribbean islands. Copiously illustrated with drawings, musical examples, and 77 photos. Glossary of drum names and terms. Extensive, 18-page unannotated bibliography; index.

Miscellaneous

0887   "La OEA y la música." **Boletín interamericano de música,** 83, (marzo-junio,
Sp   1972), 1-120.
       Includes lists of scores and publications by the Organization of American States, and a comprehensive index of articles in the *Boletín interamericano de música* and *Inter-American Music Bulletin.*

BIOGRAPHICAL SOURCES

Major works of international scope are *Compositores de América . . . (0182)* and *Música y músicos . . . (0839).* More recent (albeit very brief) information can be found in *0850.* Vinton, *Dictionary of Contemporary Music (0506)* includes many contemporary composers from Latin America.

0888   Giordano, Alberto. **Cien músicos de América.** Buenos Aires: Ediciones
Sp   Morán, 1946. 347p. LC A48-689.   ML 385 G56
       Popular style, one- to three-page biographies of 100 musicians (mostly composers, some scholars) of North and South America. Argentina, Uruguay, and Brazil account for 67 of the 100 entries. Some lists of works, no pictures. Name index.

GUIDES TO OTHER SOURCES

Bibliographies of Bibliographies

0889   Gropp, Arthur Eric. **A Bibliography of Latin American Bibliographies.**
En   Metuchen, N.J.: Scarecrow Press, 1968. 515p. LC 68-9330. Supplement:
       1971, 277p.   Z1601 A2 G76
       Sheehy 76—AA60

Repeats most entries of earlier compilation of the same title by C. K. Jones (2d ed., 1942) adding bibliographies that were published in monographs to 1964. Supplement brings coverage to 1969. Subject arrangement. Music, pp. 335-337 of base volume; music entries in supplement also.

A companion volume:

0889a Gropp, Arthur Eric. **A Bibliography of Latin American Bibliographies**
En   **Published in Periodicals.** Scarecrow, 1976. 2v. LC 75-32442.
                                                    Z 1601 A2 G76 1975
       Bibliography of bibliographies pertaining to Latin America published in periodicals, 1929-1965 (although also includes some earlier ones.) Subject arrangement; 55 music entries under general heading and individual countries. Index.

0890   Zimmerman, Irene. **Current National Bibliographies of Latin America;**
En   **a State of the Art Study.** Gainesville: Center for Latin American Studies, University of Florida, 1971. x, 139p. LC 73-632969.

       Sheehy 76—AA434   Z 1602.5 Z55

       Information about lists of new publications issued by the various nations of Latin America. No mention of inclusion or exclusion of musical scores and discs.

Selective and Critical Guides

0891   Chase, Gilbert. **A Guide to the Music of Latin America.** 2d ed. A joint
En   publication of the Pan American Union and the Library of Congress. Washington: Pan American Union, 1962. xi, 411p. LC 62-64926.
       (Reprint—New York: AMS Press, 1972)   ML 120 S7 C47 1962
          Duckles 74—749
       (1st ed. 1945, with title *Guide to Latin American Music*) The standard bibliography, including about 3,700 items, both books and articles (or parts of books). Most are briefly annotated. A general section, pp. 26-62, is followed by chapters for 29 geographical divisions. List of periodicals cited; index to authors. Items added in second edition are in separate supplementary groupings. Of fundamental importance, although much of the material listed is extremely brief and of inconsequential research value. Some errors and inconsistencies of an editorial nature. A new edition is in preparation.

0892   Lekis, Lisa. **Folk Dances of Latin America.** New York: Scarecrow Press,
En   1958. 309p. LC 58-7802.   GV 1626 L4
       Comprehensive bibliographic guide to the literature of Latin American folk music and dance. Organization by country, with general survey of each country's folk dance preceding the bibliography section. Lists 611 items (books, articles, parts of books); entries are briefly annotated. Good coverage of the Caribbean islands. Includes a 10-page classified discography (by region) with brief descriptive comments. List of periodicals cited; index.

Corrêa de Azevedo's "The Present State and Potential of Music Research in Latin America" (*0869*) is a bibliographic essay reviewing significant publications. The next item is a similar review:

0893 Devoto, Daniel. "Panorama de la musicología latinoamericana." **Acta**
Sp   **musicologica**, 31 (1959), 91-109.   ML 5 I6
Bibliographic essay with some critical commentary. General section is followed by coverage of individual countries. Includes Hispanic music in the United States. Doesn't cover European publications; doesn't give full bibliographic information. Mentions some periodicals and lexicographical publications.

0894 New York (City). Public Library. **The Folk Music of the Western Hemisphere,**
En   **a List of References in the New York Public Library**. Compiled by Julius
Mattfeld, Music Division. New York: 1925. 74p. LC 25-10473.
      Chase–17   ML 136 N5 M2
Also published in *Bulletin of the New York Public Library*, 28 (1924), 799-830, 864-889. Entries for books, articles and song collections. Classified arrangement, some entries with brief descriptive annotations. Section on Latin America; further coverage of Latin America in sections on Indian and Negro music. Appendix on musical instruments. Index.

0895 Davis, Martha Ellen. **Music and Dance in Latin American Urban Contexts:**
En   **a Selective Bibliography**. Brockport, N.Y.: State University of New York,
Department of Anthropology, 1973. 20p. (Urban Anthropology Bibliographies, 1) LC 74-173557.   ML 120 S7 D35
Consists of 42 annotated entries, with 25 on Brazil and the rest on Spanish American countries. The focus is on popular and folk music "which takes place in population clusters of several thousand or more, or that which is . . . influenced by urban centers." Citations are no more than 10 years old.

0896 Stevenson, Robert. **A Guide to Caribbean Music History**. Lima: Ediciones
En   CULTURA, 1975. 101p. LC 76-352572.   ML 120 C25 S7
Selective list of about 200 titles (books, articles, theses; encyclopedia articles not included) with generous content summaries given for non-English works. Emphasis is on pre-1900 topics. Valuable coverage of primary source material in general historical works. Author arrangement with name and topic index. Musical examples.

The Organization of American States (formerly Pan American Union) has produced much valuable literature on music. For a list of publications to 1972, see item *0887*. See also Stevenson, *Renaissance and Baroque Musical Sources in the Americas* (*0914*) which includes some treatise materials.

General Lists and Library Catalogs

Thanks to G. K. Hall, there is a strong selection of printed catalogs for major libraries in this field:

0897   Florida. University. Gainesville. Libraries. **Catalog of the Latin American**
En   **Collection.** Boston: G. K. Hall, 1973. 13v. LC 73-175215; ISBN 0-8161-
        1041-7.   Z 1610 F6 1973
        Sheehy 76–DB158
        A dictionary catalog of 201,600 cards (for about 120,000 volumes).
Particular strength in Cuba, Haiti, and Dominican Republic. Periodicals included;
analytics often provided.

0898   Hispanic and Luso-Brazilian Councils. Canning House Library. **Canning**
En   **House Libraries, Hispanic Council, London: Author and Subject Catalogues.**
        Boston: G. K. Hall, 1967. 5v. plus 2v. of supplements. LC 67-7666.
                                                           Z 921 L55883 1967
        Coverage of Spain, Portugal, and Latin America. About 30,000 volumes,
mainly on nineteenth and twentieth centuries. Base set includes about 150 books
on music, and about 350 scores–scores are classed by genre with subdivisions for
country. There are also about 50 musical works and 50 books in a supplementary
Brazilian catalog.

0899   Hispanic Society of America. Library. **Catalog of the Library.** Boston:
En   G. K. Hall, 1962. 10v. 1st supplement, 1970. 4v. LC 62-52682.
                                                           Z 881 N639
        More than 100,000 volumes listed, on some 270,000 cards. Music is one
of the subjects emphasized. Spain, Portugal, and all of Latin America are covered.
About 400 books on music listed in the base set and first supplement, under "Music
and Musicians," with country subdivisions. No musical scores included.

0900   Texas. University at Austin. Library. Latin American Collection. **Catalog**
En   **of the Latin American Collection.** Boston: G. K. Hall, 1969. 31v. 1st
        supplement, 1971. 5v. 2d supplement, 1973, 3v. LC 70-10540.
        Sheehy 76–DB161   Z 1610 T48
        A dictionary catalog of 160,000 volumes in about 600,000 card entries.
Non-book material and manuscripts are covered. Base set has about 600 entries
under music, by topic and by country.

0901   Tulane University of Louisiana. Latin American Library. **Catalog of the**
En   **Latin American Library.** Boston: G. K. Hall, 1970. 9v. 1st supplement,
        1973, 2v. 2d supplement in preparation. LC 74-26732.
                                                           Z 1610 T9
        Mexico, Central America, and the West Indies are special strengths of this
collection, which does cover all of Latin America. Social sciences and humanities
form the bulk of the collection. This catalog is in dictionary form; it registers
nearly 200,000 card entries.

Annual and Periodic Lists

        There are two good sources for information on new books issued in
Latin America:

0902   **Fichero bibliográfico hispanoamericano**, v.1– . Oct. 1961– . New York,
Sp   Buenos Aires: Bowker. (quarterly; monthly, Oct. 1964–) LC 65-4139.
     ISSN 0015-0592   Z 1201 F5
     Sheehy 76–AA759
     Since October 1964, a monthly publication listing Spanish language books
published in the Americas and Spain. Classed Dewey arrangement. Occasionally
includes printed music and song collections. According to Zimmerman (*0890*,
p. 11) in the March-June issue of 1969, 24 percent of the entries were from Spain,
26 percent from Argentina, 22 percent from Mexico, and 28 percent from all the
rest of Spanish America. Publications from Chile and Peru are not well represented.
(For its first three years this publication was prepared at the New York Public
Library under a Rockefeller Foundation grant. During this period it did not cover
Spain.)

0903   **Libros en venta en Hispanoamérica y España.** New York: Bowker, 1964– .
Sp   Supplements to 1st ed., for 1964-66, 1967-68, 1969-70, 1971; 2d ed.,
     1974 (coverage through 1972); supplement to 2d ed., 1975 (covers 1973).
     LC 64-3492. ISBN 0-8352-0682-3.   Z 1601 L59
     Sheehy 76–AA760
     A work which combines features of the U.S. *Books in Print* (*0269*) and
Cumulative Book Index (*0267*). The 1964 base volume listed more than 87,000
titles available in Spain, the United States and Latin countries; the first two supplements added 53,000 titles. A revised base volume appeared in 1974, presenting
120,000 titles available at the end of 1972. Arrangement by author, title, and
subject classification, with subject index. The 1975 supplement provides coverage
of 1973 publications. Information given in each entry is publisher, pagination,
illustrations, editions, and price.

     A regional bibliography:

0904   **Bibliografía actual del Caribe, Current Caribbean Bibliography**, v.1– .
Sp/Fr/ June 1951– . Hato Rey, Puerto Rico: Caribbean Regional Library.
En   (annual, irregular; bimonthly issues for 1971 with cumulative 1971
     volume published in 1973)   Z 1595 C8
     Sheehy 76–AA533
     Title and publisher vary; originally titled *Current Caribbean Bibliography*
Useful for music since volume 9-11 (1956-1961), when changed to a classed Dewey
arrangement. Earlier format included some music materials and folksongs under
"folklore." Volume 20, for 1970, had five music entries—books and song collections.
With volume 21, for 1971, arrangement is alphabetical by subject heading; music
is included in "Art and Recreation." Format is reproduction of catalog cards
from contributing libraries—Cuba is not a participant.

     The next two items cover writing about Latin America; the first also
covered Latin American publications:

0905   Pan American Union. Columbus Memorial Library. **List of Books**
En   **Accessioned and Periodical Articles Indexed** . . . Sept. 1950-1969.
        Washington: Pan American Union, 1950-1969. (monthly) LC 53-
        20747.   Z881 W3254
            Winchell 67—AA584
        Title varies. Selective listing of books and index of periodical literature.
Includes Latin American publications and materials about Latin America published
elsewhere.

0906   **Handbook of Latin American Studies.** v.1— . 1935— . Gainesville:
En   University of Florida Press, 1936— . (annual) LC 36-32633.
                                                          Z 1605 H26
            Sheehy 76—DB157; Chase—1, 3, 5, 6, 11, 12, 13
        Publisher varies. A selective, annotated guide to new materials on Latin
America, prepared by a group of experts. Alternate years deal with social sciences
and humanities (beginning with 1964). Books, articles—earlier volumes also
included music scores and discs. Valuable and informative coverage of music;
music editors have included Richard Waterman, Gilbert Chase, Bruno Nettl,
Charles Seeger, and Gérard Béhague.

0907   Florida. University. Gainesville. Libraries. Technical Processes Department.
En   **Caribbean Acquisitions; Materials Acquired by the University of Florida.**
        1957/58— . Gainesville: University of Florida, 1959— . (annual) LC 59-
        9692   Z 1601 F55
            Sheehy 76—AA535
        Lists publications issued in, or concerning, the West Indies, Bermuda,
Colombia, Venezuela, the Guianas, Central America and Mexico. (Mexico not
included after 1964.) Writings on music—not numerous—appear under the heading
"Arts." Music scores not included. Succeeds an earlier author list: Winchell 67—
AA405.

        The current bibliography section of the journal *Ethnomusicology* (*0510a*)
includes full bibliographical citations for new publications on Latin American music
under the general heading "Americas".

Periodical Indexes

        In addition to the Pan American Union List (*0905*) there are two important
works already cited in Volume One: *Index to Latin American Periodical Literature*
(*0308*) and its continuation, the *Indice general.* . . . (*0309*).

LISTS OF MUSIC

        There is only one modern bibliography of scores which can claim any kind
of general scope:

0908   Indiana. University. School of Music. Latin-American Music Center. **Music**
En   **from Latin America Available at Indiana University: Scores, Tapes, and**
         Records. 2d ed. Compiled by Juan A. Orrego-Salas. Bloomington: Indiana
         University School of Music, 1971. xi, 412p. NUC 72-115852.
         Duckles 74–1173 (for 1st ed.)   ML 113 I5 L4 1971
         Revision of *Latin American Music Available at Indiana University . . .*
(1964). It lists some 1,600 scores, composer order, with instrumentation, publisher,
and LC number; some 200 popular songs, by country and composer; some 2,000
tapes, by composer; some 250 folk music recordings, by country. Coverage: Mexico,
Cuba, Central and South America. No index.

The following items touch on special fields:

0909   Esterhazy String Quartet of the University of Missouri-Columbia. **Catalog**
En   **of String Quartets of Latin America.** Columbia: University of Missouri-
         Columbia, Department of Music. [1969?] [19p.]
         List of 51 published quartets, with dates and publishers. Annotated list of
21 unpublished quartets, with musical examples, descriptions, and background
information.

0910   Pan American Union. Music Section. **Latin American Orchestral Music**
En   **Available in the United States.** 2d ed. Washington: Pan American Union,
         1956. 79p. LC PA 56-139.   ML 128 O5 P3
         Duckles 74–855
         (1st ed. 1955) An in-print list, classified order; and a guide to Latin American
scores in the Edwin A. Fleisher Collection, Free Library of Philadelphia.

0911   Thompson, Leila Fern. **Partial List of Latin American Music Obtainable**
En   **in the U.S., and Supplement.** 3d ed. Washington: Pan American Union,
         Division of Music and Visual Arts, Dept. of Cultural Affairs, 1948. 57p.
         (Music Series, 1) LC 49-17861.   ML 120 S7 T47
         Duckles 74–856; Chase—128a
         (1st ed. 1941) Serious music only; arranged by form and then geographically.
Orchestration indicated, and publisher. Composer index, country index.

0912   Phillips, Charles P. "Latin American Art Music for the Piano: a Catalog of
En   Representative Graded Teaching Materials." **Inter-American Music Bulletin**,
         no. 85-86 (Nov. 1972-June 1973), 1-11.   ML 1 I717
         Arranged by country and composer. Includes works by 58 composers,
as well as eight anthologies. Gives publisher and price. Appendix lists 20 works for
piano ensemble. Unannotated bibliography of 11 items; discography of 10 items.

0913   Thompson, Leila Fern. **Selected List of Latin American Song Books and**
En   **References for Guidance in Planning Programs of Music and Dance.** 7th
         ed. Washington: Pan American Union, 1949. 11p.
         Chase—21a   ML 120 S7 T5 1949

(1st ed. 1942) Annotated list of song books, annotated list of miscellaneous reference sources pertaining to fiesta music and dance. (Original title, *Selected List . . . Guidance in Planning Fiestas.*)

A monumental listing of early music and manuscripts in Latin America:

0914 Stevenson, Robert. **Renaissance and Baroque Musical Sources in the**
En **Americas.** Washington: Organization of American States, 1970. 346p.
+ 69p. mus. ex. LC 70-31248.   ML 136 Al S8
Detailed descriptions of musical archives and library holdings in Bogotá, Colombia; Buenos Aires, Argentina; Cuzco and Lima, Peru; La Paz and Sucre, Bolivia; Mexico City, Morelia, Oaxaca, and Puebla, Mexico; Montevideo, Uruguay; Rio de Janeiro, Brazil; Santiago, Chile. Both European and Latin American composers are represented. Nearly all works cited are scores, but some treatises are included. No index. Acclaimed by Gérard Béhague as the "most valuable catalogue ever to appear . . . the most comprehensive listing ever assembled" [*Handbook of Latin American Studies*, 36 (1974), p. 480].

For a list of scores and song collections published by the Organization of American States (formerly Pan American Union) to 1972, see item *0887*. Lists of works by individual composers are found in *Compositores de América (0182)*. Item *0898* includes about 400 scores (base volumes and supplements).

DISCOGRAPHIES

The principal modern discography is the catalog of a major collection:

0915 New Mexico. University. Fine Arts Library. **A Discography of Hispanic**
En **Music in the Fine Arts Library.** . . . compiled by Ned Sublette. Albuquerque:
University of New Mexico, 1973. viii, 110p. LC 73-620024. ISBN 0-913630-
00-4.   ML 156.4 N3 H6
An inventory of some 12,000 recordings, disc and tape. Covers Spain and Spanish composers in the United States, and all of Central America, South America, and Mexico. Portugal not included. Sections for art music, flamenco, and folk music.

0916 "Discos latinoamericanos de larga duración que pueden obtenerse en los
Sp/En Estados Unidos." **Boletín interamericano de música,** 71 (mayo 1969),
21-26.

"Latin American Long-playing Records Available in the United States."
Inter-American Music Bulletin, no. 71 (May 1969), 42-46.
          ML 1 I717
Discography of art music, arranged by composer. Entry identifies his country, date of composition, and label number. Covers 25 composers, usually several entries for each.

These older compilations are strongest in 78 rpm discs:

0917 Durán, Gustavo. **Recordings of Latin American Songs and Dances; an**
En   **Annotated Selective List of Popular and Folk-popular Music.** 2d ed.,
      rev. and enlarged by Gilbert Chase. Washington: Pan American Union,
      1950. xii, 92p. (Pan American Union. Division of Music and Visual
      Arts. Music Series, 3) LC 51-60330.   ML 156.4 F5 D8 1950
      Chase—6a
      (1st ed. 1942) In format, a directory of song and dance forms arranged
by country. In addition to discographical entries, a generous paragraph of descriptive
and historical background for each form, most with rhythmic illustrations. General
material on each country's folk music as well. Five-page bibliography consisting of
the original, four-page unannotated list, and the second edition addenda with brief
descriptive notes. Index of song types.

0918 Lumpkin, Ben G.; McNeil, N. L. **Folksongs on Records** . . . Issue three,
En   cumulative, including essential material in issues one and two. Boulder,
      Colorado: Folksongs on Records, and Allan Swallow, 1950. 98p. LC A
      52-7962.
      Duckles 74—1792
      About 700 titles, albums and singles; contents given. Index to Mexican
and Latin American songs. Also indexes to English and Scottish ballads, Irish songs,
spirituals, and work songs.

See also item *0541*, Archives of Recorded Music, Series C. volume 4:
International Catalogue of Recorded Folk Music. The "Americas" section includes
entries for the Bahamas, Brazil, Chile, Colombia, Cuba, Haiti, Honduras, Mexico,
Puerto Rico, Uruguay, Venezuela. Separate sections for commercial records and
institution-held recordings.

New recordings of Latin American folk and ethnic music are listed in the
current discography section of the journal *Ethnomusicology* (*0510a*), under the
general heading "Americas."

Reviews of Latin American popular music records are included in the
"ethnic" section of *Annual Index to Popular Music Record Reviews*, 1972–
(*0489*).

Discographies of Latin American music are also included in these previously
cited entries: *0511, 0531, 0829, 0843, 0855, 0858, 0892, 0908, 0912.*

ARGENTINA

THE LANGUAGE OF MUSIC

Names of song forms, dances, and instruments are included in three
dictionary-format works: *0919, 0927, 0928*. See also Latin America, p. 94.

DIRECT INFORMATION SOURCES

Introductions and General Surveys

0919   Arizaga, Rodolfo. **Enciclopedia de la música argentina.** Buenos Aires:
Sp   Fondo Nacional de las Artes, 1971. 371p. LC 73-301220.

Duckles 74–103   ML 106 A74 A7

Useful reference work. Dictionary format, with paragraph-length entries
on musicians (performers, critics, composers—with lists of major works, scholars—
with bibliographies), organizations, institutions, song and dance forms, musical
instruments. Prefatory matter is a chronology, 1536-1865, followed by a six-page
historical summary. Appendix includes list of Argentine operas; unannotated,
classified bibliography of about 75 titles; three-page discography; and chronology
of events, 1901-1970. No illustrations.

0920   Gesualdo, Vicente. **Historia de la música en la Argentina.** Buenos Aires:
Sp   Editorial Beta S.R.L., 1961. 2v. (1,085p.) LC 62-2326.

ML 231 G48

Comprehensive, scholarly work with coverage of composers, musical life,
popular music, musical theatre. Much information on opera and musical events in
Buenos Aires; coverage of other cities also. Biographical sketches, information on
musical societies and orchestras, some portraits. List of musical scores published
in Argentina, 1830-1900. Personal name index, subject index. Volume 1: 1536-
1851, with seven-page unannotated bibliography, 127 figures. Volume 2: 1852-
1900, with nine-page unannotated bibliography, 437 figures.

0921   García Acevedo, Mario. **La música argentina durante el período de la**
Sp   **organización nacional.** Buenos Aires: Ediciones Culturales Argentinas,
Ministerio de Educación y Justicia, Dirección General de Cultura, 1961.
115p. LC 62-1837.   ML 231 G37

General, popular survey of the period 1852-1910. Biographical information,
chapters on opera and musical education. Photos; no index.

0922   García Acevedo, Mario. **La música argentina contemporánea.** Buenos Aires:
Sp   Ediciones Culturales Argentinas, Ministerio de Educación y Justicia,
Direcctión General de Cultura, 1963. 196p. LC 65-593.

ML 231.5 G37

Popular survey, covering the period since 1910. Includes chamber and
symphonic music, opera, ballet, lyric theatre. Photos, no index.

Other surveys:

0923   Fúrlong Cardiff, Guillermo. **Músicos argentinos durante la dominación**
Sp   **hispánica.** Buenos Aires: Editorial "Huarpes," 1945. 203p. LC 47-28416.

Chase–214a   ML 231 F87

Scholarly history of music and musical life in the Spanish colonial period,
sixteenth to nineteen centuries. Includes biographical information, traditional music
and dance (Indian, Negro) and instruments. Illustrations, musical examples, four-
page unannotated bibliography.

0924   Luper, Albert T. **The Music of Argentina.** Washington: Pan American
En   Union, 1942. 30p. (Pan American Union Music Series, 5) LC 42-38790
       rev.   ML 231 L8 M8
       Chase—334
       Brief historical survey (pre-Columbian music to the twentieth century)
of 10 pages, followed by a four-page unannotated bibliography, 10-page classified
list of Argentine music available in the United States (with publisher), one-page
discography, and index of composers.

0925   **Artes y artesanías argentinas,** por Luis Ordoz *et al.* Buenos Aires: Centro
Sp   Editor de América Latina, 1969. 120p. LC 77-513945.
                                                  NN 531 A85
       Handsomely printed, popular survey with three chapters on music, p. 41-
100. Information on folk music and dance, instruments, performers, music history.
Many color photos of concert halls, instruments, musicians. Music chapters prepared
by Jorge Novati, Irma Ruiz, and Miguel Angel Rondano.

0926   Dianda, Hilda. **Música en la Argentina de hoy.** Buenos Aires: Edición
Sp   PROARTEL, Producciones Argentinos de Televisión, 1966. 46p. LC 67-
       59481.   ML 231.5 D5
       Survey of musical institutions, organizations, performing groups, festivals.
Eight pages of photos; no bibliography or index.

       Vinton, *Dictionary of Contemporary Music (0507)* includes a brief survey
of contemporary Agentine musical developments (composers, institutions, trends),
pp. 16-19. See also miscellaneous information on musical organizations and musical
activity in *0957.*

Folk Music and Folksong

       Two dictionary-format works:

0927   Coluccio, Felix. **Diccionari folklórico argentino.** 2d ed. Buenos Aires:
Sp   Librería "El Ateneo" editorial, 1950. 503p. LC 52-15628.
                                                  GR 133 A7 C58 1950
       (1st ed. 1948) Includes song and dance forms, instruments, illustrations,
and musical examples. Unannotated bibliography of 1,477 entries.

0928   Serrano Redonnet, Ana. **Cancionero musical argentino.** Buenos Aires:
Sp   Ediciones Culturales Argentinas, Ministerio de Educación y Justicia,
       1964. 83p. LC 66-53399.   ML 3575 A7 S47
       A glossary, with brief identifications of terms relating to song, dance,
instruments. Broad subject arrangement. Unannotated bibliography of 10 entries;
photos; 30-page musical supplement.

Four general treatments:

0929   Aretz de Ramón y Rivera, Isabel. **El folklore musical argentino.** Buenos
Sp   Aires: Ricordi Americana, 1952. 271p. LC 54-24931.

Chase—144a   ML 3575 A7 A669

Comprehensive historical and analytical study covering song, dance,
instruments; 91 musical examples, 8 photos, bibliography for each section.

0930   Vega, Carlos. **Danzas y canciones argentinas; teorías e investigaciones;**
Sp   **un ensayo sobre el tango.** Buenos Aires: Ricordi, 1936. 309p. LC 38-
9556.   ML 3575 V4 D2

Chase—568

Consists of a 60-page introduction on general aspects of Argentine folk
music, followed by chapters on individual song and dance forms. Unannotated
three-page bibliography; 29 illustrations; 25 musical examples; two-page list of
song and dance names. Index of melodies, index of illustrations. Separate two-page
bibliography of Vega's previous publications.

0931   Vega, Carlos. **Panorama de la música popular argentina, con un ensayo**
Sp   **sobre la ciencia del folklore.** Buenos Aires: Editorial Losada, 1944. 361p.
LC A45-5526.   ML 3575 A7 V44

Chase—30a

Analytic, descriptive, and historical study of Argentine folksong, with
general material on the science of folklore and folksong classification. Illustrated
with 150 musical examples, eight plates, and six maps. Index of song-types, authors
cited, melodies, and illustrations. Unannotated, five-page bibliography of the
author's publications.

Other folk music studies by Vega are listed in his **MGG** (*0058*) biography,
volume 12, column 1358, and in item *0960*.

0932   Pichugin, Pavel Alekseevich. **Narodnaya muzika argentinii.** Moscow:
Ru   Muzyka, 1971. 208p. LC 74-876369.   ML 3575 A7 P5

Historical, scholarly narrative with technical analyses, musical examples,
maps, some photos. Includes pre-colonial Indian music. Unannotated four-page
bibliography; no index.

Regional and ethnic studies:

0933   Aretz de Ramón y Rivera, Isabel. **Música tradicional argentina: Tucumán,**
Sp   **historia y folklore.** Buenos Aires: Universidad Nacional de Tucumán,
1946. 743p. LC 48-1175 rev.   ML 3575 A7 A67

Chase—146a

Comprehensive study of traditional music in the province of Tucumán.
Includes pre-colonial and colonial periods, instruments, popular music, dance,
religious songs, children's songs, and musical analyses. Copiously illustrated with
795 musical examples, as well as many photos and drawings. Eighty-one page
appendix of songs and music; unannotated bibliography of 200 items. No index
of names or topics; index of illustrations.

0934   Wilkes, Josué Teófilo; Guerrero Carpeña, Ismael. **Formas musicales**
Sp   **tioplatenses (cifras, estilos y milongas); su génesis hispánica.** Buenos
        Aires: Publicaciones de Estudios Hispánicos, 1946. 312p. LC A48-
        3827.   ML 3575 A7 W42
        Chase–199a
        Documented study–historical, analytical and descriptive, of folk music
forms in the Rio de la Plata region; two-page unannotated bibliography; 90 musical
examples; no index.

0935   Rodríguez Molas, Ricardo. **La música y la danza de los negros en el Buenos**
Sp   **Aires de los siglos XVIII y XIX.** Buenos Aires: Clïo, 1957. 28p. Reprinted
        from **Historia**, 7 (enero-marzo, 1957), 103-126.
        Classification number for *Historia:* F2801 H5
        Brief, scholarly documented study of Negro musical culture in eighteenth
and nineteenth century Buenos Aires.

        Two works by Dalmido Alberto Baccay deal with folk music of north-
eastern Argentina and Paraguay. See items *0864* and *0865*. See also general coverage
of folk music in *0923*.

Popular Music

        General coverage of this topic is included in entries *0920, 0933, 0935*.
The tango claims an extensive bibliography of its own. The following titles have
been selected for their reference features:

0936   Ferrer, Horacio Arturo. **El libro del tango, historia e imágenes.** Buenos
Sp   Aires: Ediciones Ossario-Vargas, 1970. 2v. (379p., 384p.) LC 75-505958.
                                                        GV 1796 T3 F39
        A comprehensive "tango encyclopedia." Dictionary format; average entry
is of paragraph-length but there are also many longer articles. Coverage of musicians,
tango terms, names of instruments, cafes, titles of tangos. Copiously illustrated–
photographs, full-page color plates, glossy, color facsimiles of sheet music covers.
In addition to the encyclopedia material (called "ordenamiento alfabético de
temas"), each volume has popular-style historical chapters tracing tango history
from 1850 to 1970.

0937   Ulla, Noemi. **Tango, rebelión y nostalgia.** Buenos Aires: J. Álvarez,1967.
Sp   223p. LC 67-49296.   ML 3465 U4
        Carefully documented study of aspects of the tango; 236 footnotes to
editions and recordings. Unannotated, four-page bibliography, 23-page list of
composers and their tangos; interviews with composers and performers.

0938   Bozzarelli, Oscar. **Ochenta años de tango platense.** La Plata: Editorial
Sp   Osboz, 1972. 244p. LC 73-329745.   ML 3417 B7
        Text is a 180-page historical survey of the tango, 1890-1970. Balance of
the book is a 111-page biographical dictionary of composers, musicians, singers,
dancers. Many photographs; name index; no bibliography.

0939   Caro, Julio de. **El tango en mis recuerdos: su evolución en la historia.**
Sp   Buenos Aires: Ediciones Centurión, 1964. 470p. LC 65-50211.
                                     GV 1796 T3 C33
      Autobiography and reminiscences of a prominent tango composer and
performer. Sections on tango history; biographies of 11 other tango personalities.
Large, handsome volume with numerous photos. Name index, discography of
author's recordings.

0940   Sierra, Luis Adolfo. **Historia de la orquesta típica; evolución instrumental**
Sp   **del tango.** Buenos Aires: A Peña Editor, 1966. 141p. (Col. La siringa, 36)
      LC 67-96408.   ML 1200 S53
      Studies instrumental evolution of the tango. Appendix is classified list of
tango performers by type of instruments. Considers the tango outside of Argentina
also. No musical examples, bibliography, or index.

See also *0515a.*

Opera and Vocal Music

0941   Caamaño, Roberto. **La historia del Teatro Colón. 1908-1968.** Buenos Aires:
Sp   Editorial Cinetea, 1969. 3v. (349p., 613p., 503p.) LC 71-236845.
                                     ML 1717.8 B9 C3
      Sumptuous, three-volume coffee table book, lavishly illustrated with color
photos and plates of artists, scenes, costume and stage designs. Actual text is mostly
in part one (approximately 200 pages), a collection of essays by several contributors.
Coverage includes the building, repertories, artists, administration, critics, casts of
all operatic performances, symphonic programs, archives, library, etc. Composer
and performer indexes.

      A brief account by this author appeared in article form:

0942   Caamaño, Roberto. "El Teatro Colón de Buenos Aires." **Boletín**
Sp   **interamericano de música,** 43 (sept. 1964), 3-12.

0942a   _____. "The Colón Theater in Buenos Aires." **Inter-American**
En   **Music Bulletin,** no. 54 (July 1966), 1-10.   ML 1 I717
      Description and history, with four illustrations.

0942b   _____. "Templo del arte lírico." **Américas,** 23 (2 feb. 1971),
Sp   17-24.   F 1401 A57
      Adaptation and update of preceding article. Illustrations.

0943   Guardia, Ernesto de la; Herrera, Roberto. **El arte lírico en el Teatro**
Sp   **Colón (1908-1933).** Buenos Aires: Zea y Tejero, 1933. 513p.
      LC 42-12402.   ML 1717.8 B9 G9
      Chase—408
      A precursor to *0941.* A compendium of various documents and types of
information, rather than a unified historical narrative. Bulk of the work is chronological listing of the cast, plot summary, and critics' reviews for each opera performed,

1908-1933. Other sections are a biographical dictionary of singers, biographical sketches of opera composers, lists of ballets and their personnel, lists of concert works by composer, and information on the building. Valuable collection of source material, copiously illustrated with photos, facsimiles, plates.

0944   Bosch, Mariano. **Historia del teatro en Buenos Aires, desde el virreinato**
Sp   **hasta el estreno de "Juan Moreira" (1884).** Buenos Aires: El Comercio,
        1910. 518p. LC 17-10130 rev.   PN 2452 B8 B6
        Chase—405
        Coverage from 1747. Scholarly historical narrative with extensive coverage
of opera in Buenos Aires. Name and topic index, no illustrations.

0945   Fiorda Kelly, Alfredo. **Cronología de las óperas, dramas líricos, oratorios,**
Sp   **himnos, etc., cantados en Buenos Aires.** Buenos Aires: Imp. Riera y Cia.,
        1934. 83p. LC 35-17710.   ML 1717.8 B9 F5
        Chase—407
        Comprehensive chronological listing of musical performances in Buenos
Aires, 1825-1933: mostly operas, some ballet, oratorios, and musical theatre. Also
a list of performances in alphabetical order by composer, and another title list,
including cast and performer information.

        See also coverage of opera in *0919, 0920, 0921, 0922.*

Church and Religious Music

0946   Lange, Francisco Curt. **La música eclesiástica argentina en el período de la**
Sp   **dominación hispánica.** Mendoza: Universidad Nacional de Cuyo, 1954.
        156p. LC 56-37094.   ML 3017 L3
        Chase—227a
        also published in **Revista de estudios musicales**, 3 (dic. 1954), 15-171.
                                        ML 5 R203
        Scholarly study of colonial era church music; mostly documents. Includes
100 pages of plates—photos, facsimiles.

Historical Studies, Chronologies, Contemporary Narratives

0947   Grenón, Pedro. **Nuestra primera música instrumental, datos históricos.**
Sp   2d ed. Mendoza: Universidad Nacional de Cuyo, 1951 and 1954.
        Chase—360, 600, 224a   ML 231 G7
        also published in **Revista de estudios musicales**, 2 (dic. 1950-abril 1951),
        11-96; 3 (dic. 1954), 173-220.   ML 5 R203
        (1st ed. 1929, 106p.) A chronology, 1585-1888, tracing history of
instrumental music, with documentation from primary sources. Compositions
performed and published. No illustrations in second edition.

0948   Barbacci, Rodolfo. "Documentación para la historia de la música
Sp   argentina, 1801-1885." **Revista de estudios musicales**, 1 (dic. 1949),
        11-63.   ML 5 R203
        Chase—201a
A collection of newspaper notices pertaining to musical activity.
Chronology-type format, with some commentary by the author interspersed.
Coverage to 1855.

See entries *0941, 0943, 0945* for chronologies of opera and concerts
in Buenos Aires.

0949   Franze, Juan Pedro. **La participación de la mujer argentina en el campo**
Sp   **de la música.** Buenos Aires: Centro Nacional de Documentacion e
        Información Educativa, 1972. 16 l. LC 73-323877.
                                                              ML 82 F72
        Typescript paper describing the participation of women in Argentine
musical life as composers, educators, patrons. Emphasis is statistical, not
biographical. No bibliography or index.

Entry *0878a* includes an article by Vicente Gesualdo, "La música en la
Argentina durante el período colonial," pp. 125-134.

Regional and Local Histories

Entries *0941, 0943, 0944, 0945* document the history of musical
performance in Buenos Aires.

0950   Epstein, Ernesto. "Buenos Aires." **MGG** (*0058*), Supplement A-Dy,
Ge   columns 1172-1177.
        Historical survey, with unannotated bibliography of paragraph length.

0951   Moyand López, Rafael. **La cultura musical cordobesa.** Córdoba: Imprenta
Sp   de la Universidad, 1941. 212p.   ML 231.8 C6 M6
        Chase—330
        History of musical life in Córdoba since 1860. Classified lists of prominent
musicians (pianists, cellists, guitarists, music historians) and classified appendix of
visiting artists. No index or bibliography.

0952   Otero, Higinio. **Música y músicos de Mendoza, desde sus orígenes hasta**
Sp   **nuestros días.** Buenos Aires: Ministerio de Cultura y Educación, 1970.
        197p. LC 79-875767.   ML 231.8 M523 O8
        Fully documented historical survey covering pre-colonial era to the
twentieth century. Information on folk and art music, musical institutions and
organizations, biographical information on musicians. Photos, illustrations,
musical examples; lists of orchestra personnel; two-page unannotated bibliography;
no index.

See also *0933.*

Periodicals and Yearbooks

0953   **Revista de estudios musicales.** v.1-3, agosto 1949– dic. 1954. Mendoza,
Sp   Argentina: Universidad Nacional de Cuyo. Escuela Superior de Música.
Departamento de Musicología.   ML 5 R203
Edited by Francisco Curt Lange, a successor to *0881*. Scholarly articles
on Argentine and Latin American music, general musical topics, and musical news
of major Argentine cities. Indexed by item *0962*.

0954   **Buenos Aires musical.** Buenos Aires: 1946– . (14 issues per year) LC 59-
Sp   40730. ISSN 0007-3113.   ML 5 B8
Opera and concert reviews, musical news, concert schedules, articles on
musical personalities and organizations. Indexed by *The Music Index* (*0289*).

Instruments

0955   Vega, Carlos. **Los instrumentos musicales aborígenes y criollos de la**
Sp   **Argentina.** Buenos Aires: Ediciones Centurión, 1946. 331p. LC 47-23157.
Chase–190a   ML 486 A7 V4
Organized by instrument classification (e.g., idiofonos, cordofons, etc.)
Introductory matter on instrument classification, and 36-page pictorial survey of
Latin American instruments. Copiously illustrated–214 drawings, 56 photographs,
42 musical examples. Index of instruments under regional, country, and ethnic
groupings. Index of illustrations and musical examples. Unannotated bibliography
of three pages.

See also *0923, 0929, 0933, 0959*.

BIOGRAPHICAL SOURCES

The *Enciclopedia de la música argentina* (*0919*) is an excellent source of
biographical information. See also entries *0920, 0921, 0923, 0936, 0938, 0943,
0951, 0952*.

0956   Senillosa, Mabel. **Compositores argentinos.** 2d ed. Buenos Aires: Casa
Sp   Lottermosser, 1956. 455p. NUC 67-13358.   ML 106 A7 S4 1956
(1st ed. 1948) Biographies of 79 composers, with photos and lists of
works. Alphabetical arrangement. Average length is five pages. Name index, no
bibliography.

0957   Schiuma, Oreste. **Cien años de música argentina: precursores, fundadores,**
Sp   **contemporáneos, directores, concertistas, escritores.** Buenos Aires:
Asociación Cristiana de Jóvenes, 1956. 379p. LC 57-47529.
ML 385 S38
Loosely organized collection of biographical sketches (one paragraph to
three pages in length) and occasionally, other miscellaneous information on musical

organizations and musical life. Covers approximately 600 musicians, colonial era through the twentieth century. No bibliography or index; must use table of contents to locate information. (Entries are grouped in chapters by chronology and topic.)

0958   Argentine Republic. Dirección General de Relaciones Culturales y Difusión.
Sp   **Música de compositores argentinos (grabada en disco).** Buenos Aires, 1955.
       54p. LC 58-40804.   ML 156.4 N3 A7
       Biographical sketches of 26 composers, with descriptions of one or more
major compositions that were recorded in a government-sponsored recording project.
Also a section on popular and folk music forms recorded for the series.

0959   Prat Marsal, Domingo. **Diccionario biográfico, bibliográfico, histórico,**
Sp   **crítico, de guitarras (instrumentos afines), guitarristas (profesores—**
       compositores—concertistas—lahudistas—amateurs), guitarreros (luthiers),
       danzas y cantos—terminología. Buenos Aires: Romero y Fernández,
       1934. 468p. LC 38-35529.   ML 128 G8 P7
       Chase—392, 559, 106, 241, 265; Duckles 74—255
       Biographical sketches of guitarists and composers for the guitar. Also
information on song and dance forms; glossary of musical instruments. "Contains
many biographical sketches of Argentine guitarists and composers for the guitar"
(Chase).

GUIDES TO OTHER SOURCES

See also Latin America, pp. 103-108.

Selective and Critical Guides

0960   "Contribución a la bibliografía de Carlos Vega." **Revista musical chilena,**
Sp   21 (jul.-sept. 1967), 73-86.   ML 5 R238
       Bibliography of Vega's writings; 349 entries.

       Chase, *A Guide to the Music of Latin America* (*0891*) contains approx-
imately 450 entries, pp. 63-99.

Annual and Periodic Lists

0961   **Bibliografía argentina de artes y letras,** 1— . enero-marzo 1959— . Buenos
Sp   Aires: Fondo Nacional de las Artes. (quarterly to 1964, semi-annual
       1965—) LC 66-50285.   Z 1611 B5
       Sheehy 76—AA490
       Classed Dewey arrangement with name and title index. Includes books,
scores, articles, and analyses parts of books. Issue for enero-junio 1969 contained
27 music entries; that of junio-enero 1971 contained 44 music entries.

Periodical Indexes

0962   Suarez Urtubey, Pola. **La música en revistas argentinas.** Buenos Aires:
Sp   Fondo Nacional de las Artes, 1970. 70p. (Bibliografía argentina de artes y
letras compilación especial, 38) LC 74-297620.

ML 128 P24 S9

Index of articles in four musical journals, 1837-1954: *La gaceta musical,
La moda, Revista de estudios musicales* (entry *0953*), *La revista de música.* Classified
arrangement, 652 entries. Form and topic headings: bibliography, biography,
commentary, book reviews, musical criticism (abroad and in Argentina), dance,
musical editions, education, letters, esthetics, photos and portraits, institutions,
instruments, folk music investigation, popular music, music history, news, scores.
Name index.

LISTS OF MUSIC

See entries *0919, 0920, 0924, 0947, 0958, 0961.* Stevenson, *Renaissance
and Baroque Musical Sources in the Americas* (*0914*) lists holdings of the Buenos
Aires Biblioteca Nacional and Ricardo Rojas Museum. See also Latin America,
pp. 108-110.

DISCOGRAPHIES

See *0919, 0924, 0937, 0939, 0958.* See also the discography section
under Latin America (pp. 110-111).

BARBADOS

0963   Handler, Jerome S.; Frisbie, Charlotte J. "Aspects of Slave Life in
En   Barbados: Music and its Cultural Context." **Caribbean Studies,** 11
(Jan. 1972), 5-46. (Rio Piedras: University of Puerto Rico, Institute
of Caribbean Studies.)   F 2161 C29

Scholarly documented article describing musical forms and activity of
Barbados slaves. Includes social contexts, African and European influences,
instruments, vocal music, dance. Unannotated six-page bibliography, one musical
example, one illustration.

Stevenson, *A Guide to Caribbean Music History* (*0896*) includes five
index entries for Barbados.

BELIZE

0964   Whipple, Emory Clark. **Music of the Black Caribs of British Honduras.**
En   Master's thesis, University of Texas at Austin, 1971. 151p.

Descriptive and analytical study based on field work undertaken in 1969.
Musical examples.

BOLIVIA

THE LANGUAGE OF MUSIC

See this section under Latin America–General (p. 94).

DIRECT INFORMATION SOURCES

Introductions and General Surveys

0965   Auza León, Atiliano. **Dinámica musical en Bolivia.** La Paz: Cooperativa de
Sp   Artes Gráficas E. Burillo, 1967. 116p. LC 68-85866.
ML 239 B6 A9
General survey of art and folk music; information on organizations and
institutions; biographical sketches of composers, musicians, scholars, and educators.
Illustrations and musical examples. Unannotated two-page bibliography on general
music topics; no index.

Folk Music and Folksong

Three studies of Andean folk music by Raoul and Marguerite d'Harcourt
include Bolivia: *0866, 0873, 0874.*

0966   Paredes, Manuel Rigoberto. **El arte folklórico de Bolivia.** 2d ed. La Paz:
Sp   Gamarra, 1949. 151p. LC 51-40815.   ML 3575 B6 P3 1949
Survey of folk music, including native instruments, song and dance forms,
dramatic and religious folk music. No bibliography or index. Song texts; no musical
examples.

0967   Paredes Candia, Antonio. **La danza folklórica en Bolivia.** La Paz: Ediciones
Sp   Isla, 1966. 253p. LC 67-76433.   GV 1641 B6 P3
Survey of folk dance forms. Emphasis is choreographic and descriptive, but
each chapter also includes information on music and instruments. Bibliography of
one-half page to four pages at the end of each chapter; bibliographic footnotes.

0968   Vargas, Teófilo. **Aires nacionales de Bolivia.** Cochabamba, Bolivia; Santiago
Sp   de Chile: "Casa Amarilla," 1940. 3v. LC 46-29589.
       Chase–266a   M 1687 B6 V3
Folk song collection with six-page introductory text. "Relación histórica
del orígen de la música 'Incaica' y 'criolla' con demostración sintética de la nomen-
clatura de los instrumentos típicos." Musical examples, drawings of instruments.

A study of the Aymara Indians:

0969   Harcourt, Raoul d'; Harcourt, Marguerite d'. "La musique des Aymara sur
Fr   les hauts plateaux boliviens." **Journal de la Société des Américanistes de
       Paris,** 48 new series (1959), 5-133.   E51 S68

Thorough study of instruments, musical forms, rhythm, dances. Detailed musical analyses of songs; numerous musical examples. Photos, map, detailed table of contents; no bibliography or index.

Historical Studies

Studies of Inca musical culture are entered under Latin America; see items *0873, 0874, 0875.*

0970   Díaz Gaínza, José. **Historia musical de Bolivia: época precolonial.** Potosí:
Sp   Universidad Tomás Frias, 1962. 224p. LC 63-37980.
                                                              ML 239 B6 D5
        Indian musical culture of the pre-colonial era. Deals with musical forms,
Indian terms, scales. No index or bibliography.

0971   Stevenson, Robert. "Music in 'High' Peru." In **The Music of Peru** (*1256*),
En   175-206.
        Thoroughly documented study of art music in colonial Bolivia, then a part
of the Peruvian viceroyalty. Pertains largely to church music, mid-sixteenth century
to late eighteenth century. Sections on Sucre and La Paz. Musical examples: bibliography for this study included in that of the entire book.

Instruments

0972   Fortún, Julia Elena. "Aerófonos prehispánicos andinos." **Folklore americano.**
Sp   17-18 (1969-1970), 49-77.   GR 1 F327
        Based on examination of instruments in museums and archeological collections. Musical examples (showing pitches), photos, bibliographic references.

BIOGRAPHICAL SOURCES

0973   Vásquez Messmer, Peter. **Compositores bolivianos.** La Paz, 1975. 96p.
Sp   LC 76-451055.   ML 106 B6 V4
        Short, popular sketches of 36 persons, grouped by locality. Selected
works identified. Some portraits; no index.

See also *0965*, and the biographical sources listed under Latin America—General (p. 103).

GUIDES TO OTHER SOURCES

See also the Guides to Other Sources section under Latin America—General (pp. 103-108).

Selective and Critical Guides

Chase, *A Guide to the Music of Latin America* (*0891*) includes 69 entries for Bolivia, pp. 100-106.

Annual and Periodic Lists

0974   **Bibliografía boliviana**, v.1– . 1962– . Cochabamba, Bolivia: Los Amigos
Sp   del Libro, 1963– . (annual) LC 66-50678.   Z 1641 B5
       Sheehy 76–AA510
Werner Guttentag Tichauer, ed. Author and title arrangement, with subject index. Issue for 1971 contained one music item; that of 1972 contained five (including song collections). In 1973 there were no music items.

LISTS OF MUSIC

Stevenson, *Baroque and Renaissance Sources of the Americas* (*0914*) describes the holdings of musical archives in La Paz and Sucre. See also the Lists of Music section under Latin America–General (pp. 108-110).

DISCOGRAPHIES

See the discographies listed under Latin America–General (p. 110).

BRAZIL

The Language of Music

Portuguese musical terms are found in Vannes (*0009*) and in the *New Michaelis Illustrated Dictionary, English-Portuguese, Portuguese-English* (Wiesbaden: F. A. Brockhaus, 1961.) The latter includes brief identifications for the names of Brazilian musical forms, and explains idiomatic musical expressions.

Names of folk-song forms, dance forms, and instruments are included in two dictionary-format folklore works, *0993* and *0996*.

For further information on Brazilian music dictionaries, see item *1042*.

DIRECT INFORMATION SOURCES

Introductions and General Surveys

A reliable and comprehensive history:

0975 Almeida, Renato. **História da música brasileira.** 2d ed. Rio de Janeiro:
Pr F. Briquiet, 1942. xxxii, 529p. LC 42-20979. ML 232 A62
   Chase–704, 959x, 1165
   (1st ed. 1926) Scholarly, documented survey covering folk music (song and dance forms, Indian music and instruments) and the history of art music from the sixteenth century to 1940. Biographical sketches of composers and musicians; eight photos (mostly instruments); 151 musical examples; unannotated 13-page bibliography; name and subject index.

   A later imprint with more coverage of the twentieth century:

0976 Corrêa de Azevedo, Luiz Heitor. **150 anos de música no Brasil, 1800-1950.**
Pr Rio de Janeiro: J. Olympio, 1956. 423p. LC 57-30275.
   Chase–327a   ML 232 C65
   Narrative history of the nineteenth and twentieth centuries. Some documentation in text. Chapter on opera, biographical chapters on Villa Lobos, Luciano Gallet, Oscar Lorenzo Fernandez, and Camargo Guarnieri. Note on musicology in Brazil. Index of persons and topics; unannotated bibliography of five pages. No pictures or musical examples.

   Three brief surveys in English:

0977 Corrêa de Azevedo, Luiz Heitor. **A música brasileira e seus fundamentos.**
En/Pr **Brief history of Music in Brazil.** Translated into English by Elizabeth M.
   Tylor and Mercedes de Moura Reis. Washington: Divisao de Música e
   Artes Visuais, Departamento de Assuntos Culturais, União Pan Americana,
   1948. 92p. LC PA 55-30.   ML 232 C75
   Complete text of 42 pages is given in both English and Portuguese. Good historical, documented survey. Sources of traditional music; biographical information on 19 composers. Bibliography of 19 entries, in part with brief annotations; no index.

0978 Luper, Albert T. **The Music of Brazil.** Washington: Music Division, Pan
En American Union, 1943. (Music Series, 9.) iii, 40p. LC 43-52325.
   Chase–771x, 360a   ML 232 L8
   Consists of a short, general survey (12 pages) followed by an 88-entry, unannotated bibliography (articles, books, periodicals); a partial list of Brazilian music obtainable in the United States (16 pages, classified by instrumental category; publisher information), and selected list of recordings (16 entries). Name index.

0979 de Jong, Gerrit, Jr. "Music in Brazil." **Inter-American Music Bulletin,**
En no. 13 (Sept. 1962), 1-15.   ML 1 I717
   General historical overview tracing major composers (with mention of their works), trends, and ethnic influences.

A classic work on the national musical idom:

0980   Andrade, Mario de. **Ensaio sôbre a música brasileira.** 3d ed. São Paulo:
Pr   Livraria Martins, 1972. 188p. (Obras completas, 6)
       Chase—711   ML 232 A7 E6 1972
(1st ed. 1928) Analysis of the characteristic elements of Brazilian music
(rhythm, melody, harmony, instrumentation, forms) and its relation to art music.
The following comment is made of it by Luper in entry *1043*, p. 44-45:

> As most usually happened in those of this works that were closest
> to his heart, this one displays the famed Andradean style of language;
> one which is direct, frequently "James Joycean" in syntax, depleted
> of inner punctuation, spelled phonetically, and sounding as though it
> is the refined transcription of one side of a heated debate.

Text includes numerous musical examples; separate section of folk melodies and
commentary. Classified, two-page discography; classified, 17-page, annotated
bibliography.

0981   Andrade, Mario de. **Pequena história da música.** 6th ed. São Paulo:
Pr   Livraria Martins, 1967. 245p. (Obras completas, 8)
       Chase—326a   ML 160 A6 P3 1967
(1st ed. 1935) A general history of music with two chapters on Brazil,
pp. 163-193. Covers art, folk, and popular music. Musical examples; many Brazilian
photos throughout the book. Index; no bibliography.

An early work, informative but not wholly reliable:

0982   Cernicchiaro, Vincenzo. **Storia della musica nel Brasile, dai tempi coloniali**
It   **sino ai nostri giorni (1549-1925).** Milano: Fratelli Riccioni, 1926. 617p.
       LC 29-28729.   ML 232 C42
       Chase—733
Detailed historical narrative covering native Indian, popular, and art music;
composers and performers. Separate chapters on instrumentalists by category (piano,
violin, cello, harp, etc.) and singers. Other topics are operetta and conservatories.
No index or bibliography. The following comment is made on it by Corrêa de
Azevedo in item *0869*, p. 257:

> This is a book to read with caution, since accuracy is not its major
> virtue, and the author, who as a professional musician took an
> active part in many of the events he describes, was unable to avoid
> a subjective point of view.

0983   Acquarone, Francisco. **História da música brasileira.** Rio de Janeiro:
Pr   F. Alves, [194_]. 300p. LC 49-53371   ML 232 A2
Popular-style historical survey. Coverage of popular and Afro-Brazilian
music. Long biographies of three composers (Villa-Lobos, Lorenzo Fernández,
Francisco Mignone). Many illustrations: photos (poor quality) of popular artists,
drawings of instruments. No index, notes, or bibliography.

See also *0987*.

For a brief survey of contemporary musical developments (composers, institutions, trends) see Vinton, *Dictionary of Contemporary Music (0507)*, pp. 99-102.

Collections of Essays, Articles, etc.

Two issues of important Latin American music journals have been devoted to Brazilian musical studies:

0984   **Boletín latino-americano de música,** *(0881)* 6 (1946), 606p.
Pr/Sp   Twenty-four articles by distinguished contributors on a variety of topics.
Four are separate entries: *0997, 0999, 1027, 1036*. Editor's prologue (in Spanish) gives overview of mid-1940s musical life—organizations, folk music research, conservatories, orchestras, music industry, radio, libraries. Other topics are Brazilian-U.S. musical relations (Chase–384a), Brazilian chamber music (Chase–342a), sacred music (Chase–338a), Villa-Lobos (by Oscar Lorenzo Fernández, Chase–343a), and Fernández (by Villa-Lobos). Many illustrations—photos of instruments and musicians, musical examples. Musical supplement volume.

0985   **Anuario interamericano de investigación musical. Yearbook for Inter-**
En/Pr   **american Musical Research,** *(0880)*, 4 (1968).
Contains six articles, two in English, four in Portuguese with English summaries. (Two are entries *1002, 1023*.) Article by Gérard Béhague has background information on the *modinha*. Other topics are music in colonial Brazil (with a list of manuscripts in the Brasilia library) and musicians in colonial Vila Rica.

0986   Corrêa de Azevedo, Luis Heitor. **Música e músicos do Brasil; história,**
Pr   **crítica, comentários.** Rio de Janeiro: Livraria-Editoria da Casa do
       Estudante do Brasil, 1950. 410p.   ML 232 C67 M8
       Chase–329a
       Consists of 20 biographical chapters on Brazilian composers and articles on a variety of Brazilian topics, including music periodicals, music education, religious music, and opera. No index or bibliography.

0987   Mariz, Vasco. **Música brasileña contemporánea**, por Andrade Muricy *et al.*
Sp   Versión castellano de Marta Casablanca. Rosario: Editorial "Apis," 1952.
       211p. LC 53-38542.   ML 232 M3
       Chase–372a
       Twelve articles by different authors. Historical survey of art music, concert life, and composers of the nineteenth and twentieth centuries; popular music; 10 biographical chapters on composers. Unannotated bibliography of 24 items.

0988   Andrade, Mario de. **Aspectos da música brasileira**. São Paulo: Livraria
Pr   Martins Editôra, 1965. 247p. (Obras completas, 11) LC 66-56975.
ML 232 A2
Collection of five articles originally published 1936-1941. Topics include
the social evolution of Brazilian music, modern Brazilian art song (Chase–710),
and the samba (Chase–971). The samba article is a 90-page study with musical
examples, choreographic diagrams, and photos. No bibliography, no index.

0989   Andrade, Mario de. **Música do Brasil**. Curitaba, São Paulo: Editôra Guaira
Pr   limitado, 1941. 79p. LC A45-888.

Spanish translation:

0989a Andrade, Mario de. **Música del Brasil**. Traducción de Delia Berrabó.
Sp   Buenos Aires: Editorial Schapire, 1944. 128p. (Col. Alba, 17) LC 47-
28413.   ML 232 A725
Chase–325a
Consists of two previously published articles: "Evolução social da música
brasileira," (1930), p. 1-61; "Danças dramáticas iberobrasileiras," (1939), p. 67-
128. Illustrations; no musical examples, index, or bibliography.

Folk Music and Folksong

0990   Alvarenga, Oneyda. **Música popular brasileira**. Rio de Janeiro: Editôra
Pr   Globo, 1950. 330p. LC 51-23360.   ML 3575 B7 A44
Original edition in Spanish:

0990a Alvarenga, Oneyda. **Música popular brasileña**. Traducción de José Lión
Sp   Depetre. México: Fondo de Cultura Económica, 1947. 272p.
Chase–272a   LC A 50-313
Excellent survey covering many aspects of Brazilian folk music–song,
dance, religious music, urban popular music. With 52 plates, (illustrating dances
and instruments), 121 musical examples; and 10-page glossary-format section
describing instruments in paragraph-length entries. Unannotated seven-page
bibliography.

0991   Garcia, Angelica de Rezende. **Nossos avós contavam e cantavam; ensaios
Pr   folclóricos e tradições brasileiras**. Belo Horizonte: Impr. Official, 1949.
191p. LC 50-36580.   M 1689 G3 N6
Popular commentary on song and dance forms of the oral tradition and
their place in popular culture and religious life. With 313 musical examples; 24
illustrations; 22 photographs. No bibliography or index.

0992   Menezes Bastos, Rafael José de. "Las músicas tradicionales del Brasil."
Sp   **Revista musical chilena**, 28 (enero-marzo 1974), 21-77.
ML 5 R238
General survey, descriptive and analytical. Musical examples, maps, three-
page unannotated bibliography.

The next four items are general folklore works with considerable music coverage:

0993   Cascudo, Luis de Camara. **Dicionário do folclore brasileiro.** 2d ed. Rio de
Pr   Janeiro: Instituto Nacional do Livro, 1962. 2v. LC 79-219097.
GR 133 B6 C2773 1962
(1st ed. 1954) Dictionary format with average entry of paragraph length.
Musical examples, illustrations, bibliographic references. Some biographical entries
(e.g., Villa Lobos.)

0994   Araújo, Alceu Maynard. **Folclore nacional.** São Paulo: Edições
Pr   Melhoramentos, 1964. 3v. (2d ed. of v.2, 3, 1967) LC 65-40159 rev.
LC 68-117, LC 68-255.   GR 133 B6 A7
Volume 1: Festas, bailados, mitos e lendas; Volume 2: Danças, recreação,
música. Descriptive study by a sociologist containing no musical analysis, but many
musical examples and song texts. Folk music and dance in the social context. Last
chapter of volume 2 (pp. 369-457) devoted to folk song. Illustrations; name and
topic index.

0995   Almeida, Renato. **Tablado folclórico.** São Paulo: Ricordi Brasileira, 1961.
Pr   175p.   GR 133 B6 A5
Includes song and dance forms; musical examples, illustrations, bibliographic
references.

0996   Lima, Rossini Tavares de. **Abecê do folclore.** 4th ed. São Paulo: Ricordi,
Pr   1968. 294p. LC 72-212459.   GR 133 B6 L46 1968
(1st ed. 1952) Includes "pequeno dicionário musical folclórico," pp. 201-
294: a dictionary-format section with identifications and musical illustrations of
song and dance forms.

Studies of Afro-Brazilian music and its influence:

0997   Alvarenga, Oneyda. "A influência negra na música brasileira." **Boletín**
Pr   **latino-americano de música,** 6 (1946), 357-93.   ML 199 B64
African influence in music and instruments. Analysis of 37 melodies.
Photos of instruments; musical examples; no bibliography.

0998   Herskovits, Melville J.; Waterman, Richard A. "Música de culto afrobahiana."
Sp   **Revista de estudios musicales,** 1 (dic. 1949), 65-127.
ML 5 R203
Descriptive and analytical study of Afro-Bahian cult music. Musical
examples. Descriptive text is by Herskovits; musical transcriptions and analysis
by Waterman.

Afro-Brazilian music is also covered in *0855*, chapter 10. Entry *1005*
deals with African influence in Brazilian popular music.

The next three items are folk dance studies:

0999 Andrade, Mario de. "As danças dramáticas do Brasil." **Boletín latino-**
Pr **americano de música**, 6 (1946), 49-97. ML 199 B64
A part of the author's researches on dramatic folk dances that were subsequently published in three volumes (see following entry.) Photographs; unannotated bibliography of 101 entries.

1000 Andrade, Mario de. **As danças dramáticas do Brasil.** São Paulo: Livraria
Pr Martins, 1959. 3v. (Obras completas, 18) GV 1637 A8
Posthumously published collection of studies describing native "dramatic dances"—music, choreography, instruments. Musical examples, photographs, illustrations; unannotated bibliography of 337 items.

1001 Lima, Rossini Tavares de. **Melodia e ritmo no folclore de São Paulo.** São
Pr Paulo: Ricordi, 1954. 143p. ML 3575 B7 L628
Chase—320a
Study of six dance forms: cururu, fandango, caterete, batuque, samba, jongo. Musical examples, rhythmic analysis. Appendix with notes on instruments and photos.

1002 Lamas, Dulce Martins. "O Centro de Pesquisas Folclóricas da Escola de
Pr/En Música da Universidade Federal do Rio de Janeiro." **Anuario interamericano de investigación musical**, 4 (1968), 161-177. ML 1 T842
Report on the Center for Folklore research, founded by Corrêa de Azevedo in 1943. Describes its five publications, field recording efforts, and commercial record holdings.

See also entries *0975, 0980, 0981, 0982, 0983, 0984, 0988, 0989, 1020.*

Popular Music

1003 Tinhorão, José Ramos. **Música popular, um tema em debate.** Rio de
Pr Janeiro: Editôra Saga, 1966. 165p. LC 66-8000.
ML 2817 B7 T5
Collection of studies and magazine articles originally published 1961-1965. Topics include bossa nova, samba, choro, social and historical commentary. Unannotated bibliography of five items; 16 bibliographic references.

1004 Vasconcelos, Ary. **Panorama da música popular brasileira.** São Paulo:
Pr Livraria Martins, 1964. 2v. (259p. 403p.) LC 65-48523.
ML 232 V35
Volume 1 treats earlier period; biographical information on popular composers. Volume 2 covers the contemporary period, including information on performers. Photos, discography, no indexes.

1005   Tinhorão, José Ramos. **Música popular de índios, negros e mestiços.**
Pr   Petrópolis: Editôra Vozes, 1972. 204p. LC 72-375374.

           ML 3575 B7 T48

Survey of the development of urban popular music in terms of ethnic contributions. Copious documentation and bibliographic references; no index.

1006   Tinhorão, José Ramos. **O samba agora vai–a farsa da música popular**
Pr   **no exterior.** Rio de Janeiro: JCM Ed., 1969. 147p. LC 73-403462.

           ML 2817 B7 T53

Documented historical study of popular music forms, eighteenth to twentieth centuries. No bibliography or index.

1007   Passos, Claribalte. **Música popular brasileira.** Recife: Universidade Federal
Pr   de Pernambuco, 1968. 70p. LC 79-456672.   ML 232 P289

General account of samba and bossa nova development since about 1916. Many names of composers and performers interspersed with some biographical sketches. No musical examples; three-page discography of bossa nova; four photos; no index or bibliography.

1008   Passos, Claribalte. **Vultos e temas da música brasileira; paralelo.** Rio de
Pr   Janeiro: Guanabrara, 1972. 335p. LC 74-227139.

           ML 3575 B7 P4

Aspects of popular music and biographical information on nine composers: Villa Lobos, Henckel Tavares, Chico Buarque de Hollanda, Edu Lobo, Prahnho da Viola, Milton Nascimento, Jorge Ben, Dorival Caymmi, Ary Barroso. List of works, discography, and portraits.

1009   Rangel, Lúcio. **Sambistas & chorões; aspectos e figuras da música popular**
Pr   **brasileira.** São Paulo: P. de Azevedo, 1962. 180p. LC 62-51226.

           ML 232.5 R3

Collection of miscellaneous writings on popular music, including biographical chapters on seven performers. Photos; 45-page basic discography of Brazilian popular music. No bibliography or index.

The next six items are studies of popular genres and dance forms.

The modinha and lundu:

1010   Araújo, Mozart de. **A modinha e o lundu no seculo XVIII: uma pesquisa**
Pr   **histórica e bibliográfica.** São Paulo: Ricordi Brasileira, 1963. 157p.
        NUC 69-112818.

Includes review of previous writings; musical examples. "One of the best historical and bibliographical works on these musical forms" [*Handbook of Latin American Studies*, 32 (1970), p. 470].

1011   Alencar, Edigar de. **A modinha cearense.** Fortaleza, Brasil: Impresa
Pr   Universitaria do Ceará, 1967. 266p. LC 68-32870.

           M 1689 A44 M6

Introductory matter is an 11-page essay on the origin of the modinha, followed by five pages on the modinha in Ceará. Remainder of the book is sort of a composite biographical dictionary and musical anthology—chapters on individual composers, lyricists, and performers with paragraph-length biographical sketches, photos, and extensive musical examples. Includes 16 composers. Unannotated two-page bibliography, index of illustrations, index of song titles.

The samba:

1012   Alves, Henrique L. **Sua excelência o samba**. Palermo, São Paulo: Ed.
Pr   I.L.A. Palma, 1968. 196p. LC 68-116233.   ML 3465 A49
        History and background of the samba with chapters on individual musicians and composers. No name or topic index; 86 bibliographic footnotes; 16 illustrations, index of illustrations.

The bossa nova:

1013   Béhague, Gérard. " 'Bossa' & 'Bossas': Recent Changes in Brazilian
En   Popular Music." **Ethnomusicology**, 17 (May 1973), 209-233.
                                                        ML 1 E77
        A 10-page survey of developments in urban popular music—bossa nova, bossas, followed by four musical examples, unannotated, eight-item bibliography, and selected discography of two pages. Appendix (nine pages) of song texts.

1014   Campos, Augusto de. **Balanço da bossa; antologia crítica da moderna**
Pr   **música popular brasileira**. São Paulo: Editôra Perspectiva, 1968. 195p.
        LC 68-137383.   ML 2817 B7 C34
        Anthology of short articles (average length is 10-20 pages), on bossa nova. Mostly descriptive, no musical examples, one rhythmic notation. Includes transcription of interviews with two performers. No bibliography or index.

1015   Ramalho Neto, A. **Historinha do desafindao: bossa nova**. Rio de Janeiro:
Pr   Casa Editôra Vecchi, 1965. 144p. LC 66-98784.
                                                        ML 2817 B7 R3
        Popular commentary with eight-page discography; numerous photos of musicians; list of performers, ensembles, composers. No index or bibliography.

1016   Tinhorão, José Ramos. **Música popular: teatro & cinema**. Petrópolis:
Pr   Editôra Vozes, 1972. 284p. LC 72-375374.   ML 3575 B7 T5
        Music written for Brazilian film and theatre, mentioning individual composers and their works. Includes chronological list of Brazilian films, 1899-1933, with discussion of their musical elements. No index or bibliography.

        See also coverage of popular music in entries *0975, 0981, 0982, 0983, 0987, 0988, 0990, 1020.*

Opera and Vocal Music

1017   Corrêa de Azevedo, Luiz Heitor. **Relação das óperas de autores brasileiros.**
Pr   Rio de Janeiro: Serviço gráfico do Ministério da Educação e Saude, 1938.
       116p. LC 43-43702.   ML 1717 B8 C6
       Chase—902
       Chronological listing of 97 operas by Brazilian composers with historical
and biographical information.

1018   Chaves Júnior, Edgard de Brito. **Memórias e glórias de um teatro; sessenta**
Pr   **anos de história do Teatro Municipal do Rio de Janeiro.** Rio de Janeiro:
       Companhia Editora Americana, 1971. 683p. LC 72-303094.
                                                        ML 232.8 R5 T43
       Consists of 15-page introductory matter followed by daily chronology,
1909-1970. Separate, chronology-format chapters for performance genre—e.g.,
theatre, operetta, opera, ballet, recitals. Appendix of miscellaneous facts and
photographs. No bibliography or index.

1019   Lange, Francisco Curt. "La ópera y las casas de ópera en Brasil colonial."
Sp   **Boletín interamericano de música**, 44 (nov. 1964), 3-11.
       Documented study with four illustrations. Includes list of 70 works
performed in Vila Rica, Cuyaba, and Rio de Janeiro from 1770 to 1795.

1020   Mariz, Vasco. **A canção brasileira; erudita, folclórica e popular.** 2d ed.
Pr   Rio de Janeiro: Ministerio da Educação e Cultura, Serviço de Documentação,
       1959. 305p. LC 59-52066.   ML 2517 M3
       Chase—361a
       (1st ed. 1948; *Canção de camara no Brasil.*) Study of Brazilian art, folk,
and popular song. Appendices include selected discography, bibliography, list of
selected works by principal composers. Index.

       See also the article on Brazilian art song in entry *0988*.

Church and Religious Music

1021   Braga, Henriqueta Rosa Fernandes. **Música sacra evangélica no Brasil;**
Pr   **contribuição a sua história.** Rio de Janeiro: Livraria Kosmos Editôra,
       1961. 448p. LC 62-66421.   ML 3117 B7
       Historical survey, sixteenth to twentieth century. Biographical section on
composers and writers; a few pictures and musical examples. Unannotated 22-page
bibliography; name and topic index.

       See also the article on sacred music in *0984*.

Music Theory and Musicology

1022   Duprat, Régis. "Metodologia da pesquisa histórica-musical no Brasil."
Pr   **Anais de história,** 4 (1972), 101-108. (Faculdade de Filosofía, Ciências e
Letras de Assis, São Paulo.)   D1 A47
"Useful review of musicological research in Brazilian colonial music since
about 1914" [*Handbook of Latin American Studies,* 36 (1974), p. 486.]

See also the note on musicology in *0976.*

Historical Studies, Chronologies, Contemporary Narratives

1023   Stevenson, Robert. "Some Portuguese Sources for Early Brazilian Music
En   History." **Anuario interamericano de investigación musical,** 4 (1968),
1-43.   ML 1 T842
Information on musical culture in colonial Brazil from Portuguese sources
of that period.

1024   Lange, Francisco Curt. **A organização musical durante o período colonial**
Pr   **brasileiro.** Coimbra, 1966. 106p. (Separate of **International Colloquium**
on Luso-Brazilian Studies, volume 4. DP 501 I5) LC 67-53335.
ML 232.2 L35
Documented historical study, including two-page "basic" bibliography of
the author's writings, published and unpublished. Illustrations, discography of two
entries; no index.

1025   Béhague, Gérard. **The Beginnings of Musical Nationalism in Brazil.** Detroit:
En   Information Coordinators, 1971. 43p. LC 79-174730.
ARBA 72–1079   ML 232 B43
Taken from author' dissertation (Tulane, 1966) Documented study of the
development of a national style, 1870-1920, reflecting folk and popular traditions.
Illustrated primarily by three late-nineteenth century composers: Alexandre Ley,
Brasilio Itibere da Cunha, Alberto Nepomuceno. Some biographical information;
22 musical examples; no bibliography or index.

Regional and Local Histories

1026   Andrade, Ayres de. **Francisco Manuel da Silva e seu tempo, 1808-1865;**
Pr   **una fase do passado musical do Rio de Janeiro à luz de nuovos documentos.**
Rio de Janeiro: Tempo Brasileiro, 1967. 2v., 272, 261p. LC 67-96264.
ML 410 S585 A5
History of musical life in Rio de Janeiro during the life of this composer,
1808-1865. Supplement I is an alphabetical index of musical performances by title
of work. Supplement II is a biographical dictionary with paragraph-format entries.
Many chronologies included in the text. Illustrations, list of Silva's compositions;
no index or bibliography.

1027   Lange, Francisco Curt. "La música en Minas Gerais; un informe preliminar."
Sp   **Boletín latino-americano de música,** 6 (1946), 409-494.

    Chase–354a   ML 199 B64

    Reconstructs history of music in the state of Minas Gerais, from 1710 to
1800. Documented study based on author's discovery of manuscripts. Lange's
research on this topic is extensive, see his bibliography in entry *1024.*

    The musical history of São Paulo is outlined in the next two items:

1028   Rezende, Carlos Penteado de. **Fragmentos para uma história da música**
Pr   **em São Paulo.** São Paulo: Gráf. Municipal, 1954. 30p. (Separate of **IV**
     Centenario da fundação da cidade de São Paulo, São Paulo: Gráf.
     Municipal, 1954. pp. 195-224.)
     Chronology of musical events, 1500-1800.

1029   Rezende, Carlos Penteado de. "Cronologia musical de São Paulo (1800-
Pr   1870)." In Instituto Histórico e Geográfico de São Paulo. **São Paulo em**
     quatro séculos; temas sobre algunos aspectos da história e da geografía
     de São Paulo e assuntos correlatos. São Paulo, 1952. v.2, pp. 233-268.

                  F2631 I6

    Chronology (like the preceding item) for the period 1800-1870; eight
illustrations; unannotated, two-page bibliography.

1030   Salles, Vicente. **Música e músicos do Pará.** Belém: Conselho Estadual de
Pr   Cultura, 1970. 297p.
     Historical survey followed by biographical dictionary of 300 short entries.
Coverage is seventeenth century to present, musical amateurs and professionals.
Illustrations and bibliography.

1031   Brasil, Hebe Machado. **A música na cidade do Salvador (1549-1900)—**
Pr   **complemento da história das artes na cidade do Salvador.** Salvador:
     Prefeitura Municipal do Salvador, 1969. 135p.
     General survey, includes popular and folk music, musical organizations;
bibliography. For a critical review by Jaime Diniz see *Anuario interamericano de
investigación musical*, 7 (1973), 165-171.

    See also entries *1011, 1018, 1039.*

Music Publishing and Music Printing

1032   Salles, Vicente. "Editôras de música no Pará." **Revista brasileira de**
Pr   **cultura,** 4 (avril-junio 1972), 17-35.   NX 533 A1 R48

    Documented study of music publishing in Pará since mid-nineteenth
century. Coverage of publishing and typographical firms, personalities, musical
trends. Copiously illustrated with fine plates of music covers and photographs.
Classified, four-page table of publishers with commentary.

Periodicals and Yearbooks

1033   **Revista brasileira de música**, v.1-10, 1934-1944. Rio de Janeiro: Universidad,
Pr   Instituto Nacional de Música. (irregular)
       Reviews of books by Brazilians, music published in Brazil, new recordings.
A chronicle, including Brazilian musical events.

1034   **Revista brasileira de folclore**, ano 1– . 1961– . Rio de Janeiro: Ministerio
Pr   da Educação e Cultura, Campanha de Defesa do Folclore Brasileiro.
       (irregular) ISSN 0034-7213.   GR 1 R26
       Fine, serious publication with many folk music and ethnomusicological
articles, illustrations, and musical examples. Scope includes other Latin American
countries. Summaries of articles given in English and French; book reviews; bibliography; summary of other folklore journals.

Instruments

1035   Lima, Rossini Tavares de. "Música folclórica e instrumentos musicais do
Pr   Brasil." in **Inter-American Conference on Ethnomusicology**, 1st (*0853*),
       pp. 203-224. also in: **Boletín interamericano de música**, 49 (sept. 1965),
       3-22.
       Description of folk instruments, unannotated bibliography of 17 entries,
five musical examples, photos of instruments and musicians.

       English translation:

1035a Lima, Rossini Tavares de. "Folk Music and Musical Instruments of Brazil."
En   Tr. by Robert R. Krueger. **Student Musicologists at Minnesota**, 4 (1970-
       1971), 219-249.   ML 1 S898
       With translator' discography of four records.

1036   Herskovits, Melville J. "Drums and Drummers in Afro-Brazilian Cult Life."
En   **Musical Quarterly**, 30 (Oct. 1944), 477-492.   ML 1 M725

       Portuguese translation:

1036a Herskovits, Melville J. "Tambores y tamborileiros no culto afrobrasileiro."
Pr   **Boletín latino-americano de música**, 6 (1946), 99-112.
       Drums and their use in Afro-Bahian cult music; photos.

BIOGRAPHICAL SOURCES

1037   **Quem é quem nas artes e nas letras do Brasil; artistas e escritores
Pr   contemporâneos ou falecidos depois de 1945.** Rio de Janeiro: Ministério
       das Relações Exteriores, Departamento Cultural e de Informações, 1966.
       LC 67-71179.   CT 686 Q4
       Music section, pp. 111-180, compiled under direction of Vasco Mariz.
Sections on art and popular music.

1038   Mariz, Vasco. **Dicionário bio-bibliográfico musical (brasileiro e internacional).**
Pr   Rio de Janeiro: Livraria Kosmos, 1948. 246p. LC A 49-2658.
                                                 ML 105 M3
A sort of *Baker's (0175)*. International coverage of composers and
performers with a good percentage of Brazilian and Latin American musicians.
About 2,000 entries, with list of works and bibliographical references. No pictures.

1039   Mariz, Vasco. **Figuras da música brasileira contemporânea.** 2d ed. São
Pr   Paulo: Centrais Impressoras Brasileiras, 1970. LC 77-508466.
        Duckles 74–154 (1st ed.)   ML 390 M273 1970
(1st ed. 1948. Chase–363a) Biographical coverage of 17 composers, 13 of
which are treated in individual chapters of 5 to 10 pages. Gives list of authors'
publications; some documentation in text. No bibliography, index, or photographs.
Elaborate appendix in tabular form is a classified catalog of works with information
on recordings, duration, editions, instrumentation.

1040   Cardoso, Sylvio Tullio. **Dicionário biográfico de música popular.** Rio de
Pr   Janeiro: Empresa Gráfica Ouvidor, 1965. 351p. LC 66-86115.
                                                 ML 105 C38
Biographical dictionary of popular musicians covering Brazilians in part I,
pp. 11-164. Who's who format, paragraph-length entries with titles of songs for
composers, partial discographies for performers. Includes individuals and ensembles;
eight-page photo section; unannotated two-page bibliography.

1041   Diniz, Jaime C. **Músicos pernambucanos do passado.** Recife: Universidade
Pr   Federal de Pernambuco. v.1, 1969, 222p.; v.2, 1971, 219p. LC 76-456674.
                                                 ML 385 D615
Projected three volume work on composers of the colonial period in the
state of Pernambuco. Biographies of 10 composers (five per volume); serious
documented study based on primary sources. Most chapters have an appendix with
chronology, unannotated bibliography of published and manuscript sources,
facsimiles of documents.

See also biographical information in entries *0975, 0976, 0977, 0982,
0983, 0986, 0987, 1004, 1007, 1008, 1011, 1017, 1021, 1025, 1026, 1030.*

GUIDES TO OTHER SOURCES

See also Latin America—General (pp. 103-108).

Selective and Critical Guides

1042   Corrêa de Azevedo, Luiz Heitor. **Bibliografia musical brasileira, 1820-1950.**
Pr   Rio de Janeiro: Ministério da Educação e Saude, Instituto Nacional do
        Livro, 1952. 252p. LC 54-35729. (Coleção B 1: Bibliografia, 9)
        Chase–334a; Duckles 74–750   ML 120 B7 C6

Annotated bibliography of 1,639 entries. Coverage of books on Brazilian music and by Brazilian authors on any musical topic. Includes some articles in Brazilian periodicals. Broad subject arrangement (bibliography, history, esthetics, biography, religion, encyclopedias, etc.); no scores. Illustrations; author index.

1043　Luper, Albert T. "The Musical Thought of Mario de Andrade (1893-
En　1945)." **Anuario interamericano de investigación musical,** 1 (1965), 41-54.　　　　　　　　　　　　　　　　　　　　　ML 1 T842
　　　Review of the life and principal publications of a prolific and significant writer on Brazilian music.

Chase, *A Guide to the Music of Latin America* (*0891*), includes approximately 600 entries for Brazil, pp. 107-157.

Annual and Periodic Lists

Irregular publication, changing format, and changing scope of music coverage characterize the Brazilian national bibliographies.

The oldest of three principal publications:

1044　**Boletim bibliográphico da Biblioteca Nacional,** v.1— . 1918— . new series,
Pr　v.1— . 1951— . Rio de Janeiro: Biblioteca Nacional. (quarterly) LC 21-21648.　　　　　　　　　　　　　　　　　　　　　　Z 907 R585B
　　　Sheehy 76—AA516
　　　Frequency varies (a quarterly originally, then semiannual; quarterly again since 1973). Publication was "interrupted" in the years 1922-1930, 1932-1937, 1939-1944, 1946-1950, and 1968-1972. A classed Dewey arrangement with index. Coverage of scores before 1973 (first installment of volume 16, for 1966, included 11 music books—about one page—and 41 pages of printed music). With volume 18, for 1973, no scores are included (5 music books are listed in the first installment). Prepared by the acquisitions department of the national library on the basis of materials received. Last installment of the year includes list of current periodicals in classified arrangement with title index.

1045　**Bibliografia brasileira,** v.1— . 1938/1939— . Rio de Janeiro, 1941— .
Pr　(irregular) LC 43-7405.　　　　　　　　　　　　　　　　Z 1671 B5
　　　Sheehy 76—AA512
　　　A publication of the Instituto Nacional do Livro. Retrospective coverage for 1938-1955 in irregularly published volumes, 1941-1957. Arrangement is clumsy for locating music books, some titles entered under "música," with other musical subject headings given as cross references; no cross references to musical biographies. Includes song collections and anthologies but no scores. For 1941 there were 17 music entries; 21 for 1955. After nine-year suspension, publication resumed in 1966 (with coverage of 1963) using a classed Dewey arrangement. The 1963 volume contained six music books; that of 1966, 12 music books.

1046 **Bibliografia brasileira mensal**, v.1– . nov. 1967– . Rio de Janeiro: Instituto
Pr Nacional do Livro. (monthly) LC 72-358316. Z 1675 B5
  Sheehy 76–AA515
  Classed Dewey arrangement, with about three music books per issue until
October 1969, when score coverage began. Issue for November 1969 included 68
music items, that of May 1971 contained 84 items. Includes list of publishers
(with addresses) and list of periodicals.

  The next item is useful for the years 1955-1962, not covered by *1045*:

1047 **BBB: Boletim bibliográfico brasileiro**, nov.-dez. 1951– . set.-dez. 1967.
Pr Rio de Janeiro: Estante Publicações, 1953-1967. (bimonthly, irregular)
  LC 58-26371 rev.   Z 1671 B6
  Sheehy 76–AA514
  Commercially produced, a sort of *Publishers Weekly*. Classed Dewey
arrangement with all "700's" items in one author alphabet. Books and song collec-
tions; no scores. Issue of Jan./Feb. 1961 contained two music items; an issue in
1967 contained four.

LISTS OF MUSIC

1048 **Catálogo de obras nacionals; 1° centenario, 1868-1968**. Rio de Janeiro:
Pr Editôra A. Napoleao, 1968. 37p. LC 78-14489.
               ML 120 B7 C42
  Publisher's catalog of about 2,000 works. Classed arrangement (piano,
songs, ensembles, solos) with composer order in each class. Titles of works only,
no date or information; no index.

1049 Lange, Francisco Curt. "Estudios brasileños (Mauricinas)." **Revista de**
Sp **estudios musicales**, 1 (abril 1950), 98-194. ML 5 R203
  (Off-print is LC 58-25317, ML 136 R45 L3)
  Duckles 74–1450; Chase–353a
  Catalog of manuscripts in the Biblioteca Nacional. Three sections: European
composers; Brazilian composers (including those born in Europe); non-score manu-
scripts pertaining to music and musicians. Many photos and facsimiles.

  Stevenson, *Renaissance and Baroque Musical Sources in the Americas*
(*0914*), includes coverage of musical archives in Rio de Janeiro.

  See information on Brazilian compositions in entries *0978, 1008, 1020,
1034, 1044, 1046*. See also the Lists of Music section under Latin America–
General (p. 109).

DISCOGRAPHIES

  The following entries include information on recordings: *0978, 0980,
1002, 1004, 1006, 1007, 1008, 1009, 1013, 1015, 1020, 1035a, 1039, 1040*.

See also the discographies listed under Latin America—General (p. 110).

CHILE

The music bibliography of Chile is distinguished by the long run of the *Revista musical chilena (1068)*, which has established valuable documentation of musical life since 1945 and published serious articles on many aspects of Chilean art and folk music.

THE LANGUAGE OF MUSIC

See under Latin America—General (p. 94).

DIRECT INFORMATION SOURCES

Introductions and General Surveys

The two volumes by Pereira Salas comprise a reliable, comprehensive survey to 1900:

1050   Pereira Salas, Eugenio. **Los orígenes del arte musical en Chile.** Santiago:
Sp   Imprenta Universitaria, 1941. 373p. LC 42-16313.
      Chase—1230, 1296, 1339   ML 232.5 P3 O7
      Historical narrative covering pre-Columbian era to 1850. Includes folk, art, popular, and dance music. Information on composers, list of compositions, 1714-1860 (seven-page list of works arranged by composer giving date and, in some cases, publishing information; also a list of popular music and lullabies). Unannotated 11-page bibliography, 33 pages of illustrations, index of illustrations, subject index, name index.

1051   Pereira Salas, Eugenio. **Historia de la música en Chile, 1850-1900.**
Sp   Santiago: Editorial del Pacífico, 1957. 379p. (Publicaciones de la
      Universidad de Chile) LC 59-18944.   ML 233.4 P4
      Chase—478a
      General narrative covering musical life, opera, ballet, religious music, military music, and music education. Appendix of opera performances; name and title index; index of illustrations.

A general survey with twentieth century coverage:

1052   Claro Valdés, Samuel; Urrutia Blondel, Jorge. **Historia de la música en**
Sp   **Chile.** Santiago: Editorial Orbe, 1973. 192p. (Universidad de Chile,
      Instituto de Investigaciones Musicales.)
      Documented historical narrative, pre-Columbian era to 1971. Topics include Indian music, instruments, religious music. Biographical sketches of 98

composers (74 are twentieth century), including some names of works. A six-page chronology, 1940-1971; appendix with information on music periodicals. Name and topic index; unannotated bibliography of 189 items; 51 photos; no musical examples.

The next three items deal with twentieth century topics:

1053   Salas Viu, Vicente. **La creación musical en Chile 1900-1951**. Santiago:
Sp   Ediciones de la Universidad de Chile, 1952. 477p. LC 53-35962.

    Chase—497a   ML 233 S338

    General survey of musical life 1900-1950 (including compositional trends and musical organizations), followed by lengthy biographical sketches of 40 composers, including lists of works. Unannotated bibliography of two pages, no index.

1054   Escobar, Roberto. **Músicos sin pasado; composición y compositores de**
Sp   **Chile**. Madrid: Editorial Pomaire, 1971. (Ediciones Nueva Universidad)
        267p. LC 72-322868.   ML 3845 E85

    Sociological aspects of twentieth century Chilean music history and musical life. Topics include the lack of a musical nationalism, women composers, and a classification of Chilean composers into categories. Appendix of statistical data. Biographical notes on about 100 Chilean composers; three-page bibliography.

1055   Stevenson, Robert M. "La música chilena en la época de Santa Cruz."
Sp   **Boletín interamericano de música**, 67 (sept. 1968), 3-16.

1055a   Stevenson, Robert M. "Chilean Music in the Santa Cruz Epoch." **Inter-**
En   **American Music Bulletin**, 67 (Sept. 1968), 1-17.

                                            ML 1 I717

    Reviews the achievements of notable twentieth century Chilean musicians.

    See Vinton, *Dictionary of Contemporary Music (0507)*, pp. 138-140 for background summary and survey of current trends, composers, and institutions.

1056   Salas Viu, Vicente. **Músicos modernos de Chile**. Washington: Pan American
Sp   Union, 1944. 29p. (Music series, 11) LC 44-51012 rev.

    Chase—503a   ML 233 S34

    Brief historical survey including information on leading composers. No index; unannotated, two-page bibliography.

Folk Music and Folksong

    In the absence of a comprehensive general work, articles and books on specific topics are included in this section. See also the studies of folk instruments (p. 144).

1057   Barros, Raquel; Dannemann, Manuel. **El romancero chileno.** Santiago:
Sp   Ediciones de la Universidad de Chile, 1970. 119p. LC 70-541339.
ML 3575 C5 B4
Study of the *romance* form; numerous musical examples, 93 bibliographic
references, glossary.

1058   Grebe, María Ester. **The Chilean Verso: a Study in Musical Archaism.**
En   Translated by Bette Jo Hillman. Los Angeles: University of California,
1967. 133p. (Latin American Center. Latin American Studies v.9)
LC 67-65493.   ML 3575 C5 G7
Eighty-page study of a folksong form, a translation of the author's thesis
(University of Chile, 1965). Numerous musical examples, illustrations, six-page
unannotated bibliography; 44-page appendix of *versos*.

1059   Garrido, Pablo. **Biografía de la cueca.** Santiago: Ediciones Ercilla, 1943.
Sp   133p. LC 44-18406.   GV 1639 G37
Descriptive and historical study of a popular dance form. Musical examples,
drawings, song texts. No bibliography or index.

1060   Vega, Carlos. "La forma de la cueca chilena." **Revista musical chilena,** 3
Sp   (mayo-junio 1947), 7-21; (julio-agosto 1947), 15-45.
ML 5 R283
Also published as a separate: Santiago: Universidad de Chile, Instituto de
investigaciones musicales, 1947. (Coleccion de ensayos, 2) 46p. LC 49-
19460.   GV 1796 C82 V4
Chase—421a, 422a
Musical and rhythmical analysis. Second part deals with form and meter
of texts. Musical examples.

1061   Campbell, Ramón. **La herencia musical de Rapanui; etnomusicología de**
Sp   **la Isla de Pascua.** Santiago: Editorial Andrés Bello, 1971. xii, 594p.
LC 73-208788.   ML 360 C29
Comprehensive, scholarly study of Easter Island folk music; forms, instruments, dances. Extremely detailed descriptions and analyses of song types and
individual songs. Numerous photos and musical examples. Index; unannotated
three-page bibliography; 10-page English summary.

1062   Lavín, Carlos. "Criollismo literario y musical"; "Romerías chilenas";
Sp   "La música de los araucanos." **Revista musical chilena,** 21 (enero-marzo
1967), 15-49, 50-56, 57-60.   ML 5 R283
Three documented studies on folk music topics. Musical examples, brief
bibliographies.

Popular Music

1063   Acevedo Hernández, Antonio. **Canciones populares chilenas; recopilación**
Sp   **de cuecas, tonadas, y otras canciones, acompañada de una noticia sobre**
los que han cantado para el público chileno. Santiago: Ediciones Ercilla,
1939. 193p. LC 40-14601.   ML 3575 A23 C2

Text is a 60-page survey of popular song, including information on popular performers. Remainder of book is song texts. No index or bibliography.

See also *1059*: Garrido, *Biografía de la cueca*.

Opera and Vocal Music

1064   Abascal, Brunet, Manuel. **Apuntes para la historia del teatro en Chile:**
Sp   **la zarzuela grande.** Santiago: Imprenta Universitaria, 1941, 1951. 2v.
        LC 43-16824 rev.   ML 1717 A25
        Chase—1268
        Documented historical study of zarzuela performance throughout Chile.
Information on singers and performances; photos. Each volume has name index
and chronology of performances. Volume one covers the period 1628-1871;
unannotated bibliography of 20 items. Volume two has coverage of 1871-1882.

See also *1051*.

Instrumental Music

Two studies of Chilean piano music:

1065   Etzler, Andrea W. **A Survey of Representative Contemporary Solo Piano**
En   **Literature of Chile.** Masters of music dissertation, Indiana University,
        1971. 188p.
        Analysis of major works by 21 Chilean composers, born 1880 to present.
Biographical sketch precedes analysis of the work. Discussion of general trends
and styles.

1066   Grandela, Inés. "La música chilena para piano de la generación joven:
Sp   1925." **Revista musical chilena,** 25 (enero-junio 1971), 35-54.
                                                        ML 5 R283
        Summary of author's musicology thesis, University of Chile. Analytical
survey of piano works by composers born after 1925. Nine musical examples.

Directories

1067   Pan American Union. Music Section. **Chile.** Washington, 1954. (Directorio
En/Sp   musical de la America Latina. Musical Directory of Latin America.) xxiv,
        44p. LC PA 54-51 rev.   ML 21 P2
        Chase—473a
        Information on musical organizations, conservatories, performing ensembles,
libraries, record libraries, music periodicals, music publishers, stores, instrument
makers, radio stations, concert halls, etc. Name index of persons and organizations.

Periodicals and Yearbooks

The outstanding Latin American music journal of longevity:

1068   **Revista musical chilena**, año 1, mayo 1945– . Santiago: Instituto de
Sp   Extension Musical, Universidad de Chile. (quarterly) LC 48-19882.
        ISSN 0035-0192.   ML 5 R283
    Fine, serious publication, with scholarly articles on Chilean folk and art
music, Latin American music, and general music topics. Chronicle of music news
and personalities; concert, book, and music reviews; lists of music, records, and
books received. Issue of enero-junio 1975 (v. 30) includes a history of the journal,
and author, subject indexes to articles, 1967-1974.

Instruments

1069   Henríquez, Alejandro. **Organología del folklore chileno.** Valparaíso:
Sp   Ediciones Universitarias de Valparaíso, 1973. 107p.
                                                                   ML 3575 C5 H4
    A general account, intended as a school text. Discusses origin and type
as well as physical characteristics. Classification chart; 45 illustrations (photos,
drawings). Poor bibliography, no index. Not scholarly or entirely reliable; see
critical review in *Revista musical chilena*, 29 (ab.-sept. 1974).

1070   Lavín, Carlos. "El rabel y los instrumentos chilenos." **Revista musical**
Sp   **chilena**, 10 (enero 1955), 15-28.   ML 5 R283
        Also published as a separate: Santiago: Universidad de Chile, Instituto
        de investigaciones musicales, 1955. (Colección de ensayos, 10)
        Chase–397a, 398a
    Survey of instrument makers in Chile since 1854 (piano, organ, guitar)
followed by section on the *rabel* and *guitarrón*. Unannotated bibliography of 10
items; five musical examples; six photos.

1071   Barros, Raquel; Dannemann, Manuel. "El guitarrón en el Departamento
Sp   de Puente Alto." **Revista musical chilena**, 14 (nov.-dic. 1960), 7-45.
                                                                   ML 5 R283
        Also published as a separate: Santiago: Universidad de Chile, Instituto
        de Investigaciones Musicales, 1961. 41p. (Colección de ensayos, 12)
    Structure and construction of Chilean wide-necked guitar. Includes two-
page glossary of terms; one page of bibliographic references cited.

1072   "Organología vernácula de Chile." **Revista musical chilena**, 28 (oct.-dic.
Sp   1974), 111p.   ML 5 R283
    Special issue consisting of two articles: Grebe, María Ester, "Instrumentos
musicales precolombianos de Chile," pp. 5-55–a scholarly, documented study with
numerous illustrations and five-page unannotated bibliography.

Merino, Luis, "Instrumentos musicales, cultura mapuce, y el *Cautiverio feliz* del maestro de campo Francisco Nuñez de Pineda y Bascunan," pp. 56-95— thoroughly documented study; the text *Cautiverio feliz* is examined for information pertaining to past mapuche musical culture. Unannotated bibliography of four pages.

1073   Isamitt, Carlos. "Un instrumento araucano; la trutruka." **Boletín latino-**
Sp   **americano de música**, 1 (1935), 43-46; "Cuatro instrumentos musicales araucanos." **Boletín latino-americano de música**, 3 (1937), 55-66; "Los instrumentos araucanos." **Boletín latino-americano de música**, 4 (1938), 305-312.   ML 199 B64
       Chase—1322x, 1323, 1324
       Three classic studies of Araucanian Indian instruments. Musical examples and illustrations.

1074   Orrego-Salas, Juan A. "Araucanian Indian Instruments." **Ethnomusicology**,
En   10 (Jan. 1966), 48-57.   ML 1 E77
       Based on the Isamitt articles of the preceding entry. Includes drawings and 11 musical examples; bibliographic references.

BIOGRAPHICAL SOURCES

Entries *1052, 1053, 1054* are the most useful and current sources of biographical information. See also *1055* and *1065*. The one entry in this section is an older work.

1075   Uzcátegui García, Emilio. **Músicos chilenos contemporáneos (datos**
Sp   **biográficos e impresiones sobre sus obras).** Santiago: Imprenta y Encuadernación América, 1919. 236p. LC 43-45016.
       Chase—1266   ML 385 U9
       Biographies of 23 Chilean musicians, composers and performers. Average length is five pages. Photos and musical examples; no bibliography or index.

GUIDES TO OTHER SOURCES

See also the Guides to Other Sources section under Latin America—General (p. 103).

Selective and Critical Guides

Chase, *A Guide to the Music of Latin America (0891)* has approximately 265 entries for Chile, pp. 163-187.

The three items in this section pertain to folk music studies.

1076   Pereira Salas, Eugenio. "Guía bibliográfica para el estudio del folklore
Sp   chileno." **Archivos del folklore chileno**, 4 (1952), 1-112.

                                GR 133 C5 A7

     Also issued as a separate: Santiago: Universidad de Chile, Instituto de
Estudios Musicales, 1952. 112p.

     Contains 248 entries on music, grouped in section 15, "La música
folklórica, tradicional y popular," pp. 76-94. Annotated, classified bibliography
and discography, listing books, articles, records, and music anthologies. Subject
headings include musical topics and forms as well as format of medium (e.g.,
disc, printed music).

1077   Dannemann, Manuel. **Bibliografía del folklore chileno 1952-1965.** Austin:
Sp   University of Texas, Center for Intercultural Studies in Folklore and Oral
       History, 1970. 60p. (Latin American Folklore Series, 2) LC 74-169179

                                Z 5984 C45 D35

     Bibliography of 425 items (mostly articles) in author alphabet with topic
index; entries pertaining to music found under such terms as *cantos, instrumentos*.
Brief descriptive annotations; author index.

1078   Dannemann, Manuel. "Bibliografía folklórica y etnográfica de Carlos
Sp   Lavín A." **Revista musical chilena**, 21 (enero-marzo 1967), 85-88.

                                ML 5 R283

     Unannotated, classified bibliography; 76 published articles, 34 unpublished
articles.

Annual and Periodic Guides

1079   **Servicio bibliográfico chileno. Chilean Bibliographic News Service,**
Sp/En 1940-1971. Santiago: Zamorano y Caperan. (monthly, then quarterly)
       LC 45-27668.   Z 1705 S4
       Winchell 67—AA416 (noted in Sheehy 76—AA543)

     Book dealer's list prepared primarily for foreign clientele. According to
Zimmerman (*0089*), "the only consistent record of Chilean publications for three
decades" (p. 38). Publisher estimated 90 percent coverage of Santiago book
production. Subject arrangement; first specific music heading appeared in 1965,
but previous music titles had been included in folklore and miscellaneous sections.
Covered song books but not scores.

LISTS OF MUSIC

1080   Escobar, Roberto; Yrarrazaval, Renato. **Música compuesta en Chile,**
Sp   **1900-1968.** Santiago: Ediciones de la Biblioteca Nacional, 1969. 257p.
       LC 74-213534.   ML 120 C45 E8

     Classified arrangement by performing medium; gives date, duration,
publication and recording information, library locations in Chile and Indiana
University. Composer index of about 75 names.

1081 Santiago de Chile. Biblioteca Nacional. **Bibliografía musical; composiciones**
Sp   **impresas en Chile y composiciones de autores chilenos publicados en el**
      extranjero. Segunda parte, 1886-1896. Santiago: Establecimiento Poligráfico
      Roma, 1898. 89p.   ML 120 S2 M4
      Chase—1236
      Prepared by Ramón A. Laval; originally appeared in *Anuario de la prensa*
chilena, 1896. (According to Chase, first part was not published.) Lists of music
published in Chile, and by Chileans abroad, 1886-1896.

Compositions, 1714-1860 are listed in *1050*. Folk music and song collections are included in *1076*. See Stevenson, *Renaissance and Baroque Musical Sources
of the Americas (0914)* for holdings of music archives in Santiago.

See also the Lists of Music section under Latin America—General (p. 108).

DISCOGRAPHIES

See *1076*, *1080*. See also the discographies listed under Latin America—
General (p. 110).

COLOMBIA

THE LANGUAGE OF MUSIC

A 100-page glossary of terms pertaining to folk music, folk dance, and
instruments is included in item *1083*. See also item *1086*, and the Language of
Music section under Latin America—General (p. 94).

DIRECT INFORMATION SOURCES

Introductions and General Surveys

Two substantial works of high quality:

1082 Pardo Tovar, Andrés. **La cultura musical en Colombia.** Bogotá: Ediciones
Sp   Lerner, 1966. (Academia Colombiana de Historia, Historia Extensa de
      Colombia, v. 20, Las artes en Colombia, 6) 449p. NUC 69-19116
      Comprehensive, documented historical survey, pre-Hispanic era through
1965. Detailed coverage of performance organizations, music education, musical
institutions. Appendix of 13 pages deals with popular music. Extensive biographical
information, including catalogs of composers works. Handsomely and copiously
illustrated with photographs, plates, and 33 musical examples. Yet another excellent
feature is detailed coverage of Colombian music publications, 1851-1964. Sixty-two
monographs—works of music theory, pedagogy, history, analysis; biographies; folk
music studies—are treated in seven separate bibliography chapters, with full bibliographic information, contents summary, and critical evaluation.

1083   Perdomo Escobar, José Ignacio. **Historia de la música en Colombia.** 3d ed.
Sp   Bogotá: Editorial ABC, 1963. 422p. LC 63-25609
    Chase—542a   ML 234 P47 1963
(1st ed. 1945) General comprehensive survey, including aboriginal music,
pre-Columbian instruments, church music, musicians and composers, musical
organizations, and folk music. Detailed explanations of folk music terms in 100-page
glossary; unannotated 13-page bibliography. Illustrations; photos; name and topic
index. (Expansion of the author's earlier "Esbozo histórico sobre la música
colombiana," in *1084*, pp. 387-570; Chase—1369.)

Collections of Essays, Articles, etc.

1084   **Boletín latino-americano de música** (*0881*), 4 (1938). 861p.
Sp   Volume published in Colombia with 10 articles on Colombian topics,
including folk music, the national orchestra, religious music, and biography of
composer Guillermo Uribe Holguín. Many photographs and musical examples.
(Entries in Chase: 1361, 1369, 1373, 1376, 1378, 1379, 1393, 1401, 1402, 1404,
1405.)

1085   Lima, Emirto de. **Folklore colombiano.** Barranquilla, 1942. 210p. LC
Sp   44-28211.   ML 3575 C7 L5
    Chase—1380, 1387
Collection of 33 essays, mostly on folk music (song and dance forms,
instruments, Indian music) but also includes national composers, national songs,
radio stations, musical institutions. Described by Pardo Tovar in *1082* (p. 388)
as a disordered compilation of uneven writings—folk music articles are based on
direct knowledge, but some other articles lack documentation. Musical examples;
no bibliography or index.

Folk Music and Folksong

The Latin American issue of *Ethnomusicology* (*0852*) includes an article
by George List, "Ethnomusicology in Colombia," pages 70-76. It is a survey of
folk music research, with information on institutions and researchers, two-page
unannotated bibliography updating Chase, and two-page discography of commercial
discs and field recordings.

See also folk music coverage in items *1082* and *1085*.

1086   Davidson, Harry C. **Diccionario folklórico de Colombia; música,**
Sp   **instrumentos y danzas.** Bogotá: Banco de la Republica, Departamento
    de Tall. Graf., 1970. 3v. LC 70-598930.   ML 234 D39
Long and short articles on terms for song and dance forms, instruments.
Name and topic index.

1087   Ocampo López, Javier. **El folclor y su manifestación en las supervivencias**
Sp   **musicales en Colombia.** Tunja: Universidad Pedagógica y Tecnológica de
       Colombia, 1970. 170p. (Ediciones "La Rana y el Aguila.") LC 79-510417.
       ML 3575 C7 O3
       General work, covering European, Indian, and African aspects of Colombian
folk music. Also music and instruments of the Chibcha Indians. Some footnotes, no
musical examples. Drawings, 13-page unannotated bibliography; no index.

1088   Abadía Morales, Guillermo. **La música folklórica colombiana.** Bogotá:
Sp   Universidad Nacional de Colombia, Dirección de Divulgación Cultural,
       1973. 158p. LC 74-207369.   ML 3575 C7 A2
       Survey of folksong and dance forms, native Indian and *mestizo* instruments.
Elaborate classification of song forms. No bibliography or index.

1089   Zamudio, Daniel. "El folklore musical en Colombia." **Revista de las Indias,**
Sp   35 (mayo-junio 1949), suppl. 14, 30p.
       Chase—535a
       Publication of a lecture delivered in 1935 at a music congress in Ibagué.
Analytical study of song and dance forms. Described by Pardo Tovar in *1082*
(pp. 390-391) as a monograph of fundamental importance. Musical examples.

       The remaining five items in this section are studies of particular regions
and peoples:

1090   Pardo Tovar, Andrés; Pinzón Urrea, Jesús. **Rítmica y melódica del folclor**
Sp   **chocoano.** Bogotá: Universidad Nacional de Colombia, 1961. 72p.
       (Monografías del Centro de Estudios Folclóricos y Musicales, 2) LC
       62-51493.   ML 3575 C7 P44
       Analytical study of five song and dance forms. Information on instruments
and appendix dealing with the *bambuco*. Numerous musical examples; no bibliography or index.

1091   Pardo Tovar, Andrés. **Los cantares tradicionales del Baudó.** Bogotá:
Sp   Universidad Nacional de Colombia, 1960. 41p. (Monografías del Centro
       de Estudio Folclóricos y Musicales, 1) LC 62-3229.
                                           ML 3575 C7 P4
       Analysis of instruments, traditional dances, songs; three musical transcrip-
tions, three illustrations, bibliography, and index.

       An English version of this study:

1091a Pardo Tovar, Andrés. "Traditional Songs in Chocó, Colombia." **Inter-**
En   **American Music Bulletin,** no. 46-47 (March-May 1965), 28p. LC 66-
       61257.   ML 1 I717
       Translation of original Spanish text; two-page glossary of musical and
geographical terms (Spanish and Indian); unannotated bibliography of 24 entries;
photo of instruments; maps; eight musical examples.

1092   Bose, Fritz. "Die Musik der Chibcha und ihre heutigen Nachkommen. Ein
Ge   Beitrag zur Musikgeschichte Sü damerikas." **International Archives of
        Ethnography**, 48 no. 2 (1958), 149-198. (Leiden: E. J. Brill)

        GN 1 I6
        History of Chibcha Indian musical culture, before and after Spanish
conquest. Instruments and instrumental music, songs. Extensive unannotated
two-page bibliography; five photos of artifacts; musical examples, pp. 196-198.

1093   Bose, Fritz. "Die Musik der Uitoto." **Zeitschrift für vergleichende
Ge   Musikwissenschaft**, 2 (1934), 1-14, 25-50.   ML 5 Z39
        Chase–1399
        Serious study, covering instruments and music. Description and analysis
of songs; four photos of musicians and instruments; unannotated bibliography of
one and one-half pages.

1094   Pinzón Urrea, Jesús. "La música vernácula del altiplano de Bogotá."
Sp   **Boletín interamericano de música**, 77 (mayo 1970), 15-30.
        Short survey of musical forms and instruments in the central region, the
altiplano or *sabana* of Bogotá. Numerous musical examples; two photos of
instruments.

Popular Music

1095   Restrepo Duque, Hernán. **Lo que cuentan las canciones; cronicón musical.**
Sp   Bogotá: Impreso por Tercer Mundo, 1971. 256p. LC 72-329566.
        ML 3575 C7 R48
        Disc jockey's recounting of popular music in Colombia since late nine-
teenth century. Popular journalistic style. Includes many discographical citations.
Information on popular musicians not easily retrieved due to organizational
format and lack of index. Photos of performers. No bibliography or musical
examples.

1096   Añez, Jorge. **Canciones y recuerdos; conceptos acerca del orígen del
Sp   bambuco y de nuestros instrumentos típicos y sobre la evolución de la
        de la canción colombiana a través de sus más afortunados compositores
        e intérpretes.** Bogotá: Impr. Nacional, 1951. 485p. LC 53-4366.
        ML 234 A5
        Two general chapters on the bambuco and Colombian song, followed
by detailed treatment of the history of concerts, compositions, and performers;
brief biographies; photos, musical examples, song texts. Index of names and
index of songs. No footnotes or bibliography.

1097   Mazuera, M.; Lubín, E. **Orígenes históricos del bambuco, teoría musical
Sp   y cronología de autores y compositores colombianos.** 2d ed. Cali: Imp.
        Departamental, 1972. 238p.
        Two chapters are devoted to the origin and analysis of the *bambuco*. The
rest of the book is a biographical directory of about 50 "músicos vallecaucanos,"
grouped by city. Biographical sketches are one to five pages in length.

Historical Studies, Chronologies, Contemporary Narratives

1098   Stevenson, Robert. **La música colonial en Colombia.** Traducción de Andrés
Sp   Pardo Tovar. Cali, Colombia: Instituto Popular de Cultura de Cali, Depart-
amento de Investigaciones Folklóricas, 1964. 62p. NUC 66-54650.
ML 234 S7
Spanish translation of two articles, item *1098a* and "The Bogotá Musical
Archive," *Journal of the American Musicological Society*, 15 (Fall 1962), 292-315.
(The latter is a catalog of holdings, included in *0914*.) Name index, musical
examples, and bio-bibliography of the author.

1098a   Stevenson, Robert. "Colonial Music in Colombia." **Americas**, 19 (Oct.
En   1962), 121-136.   E 11 A4
Thoroughly documented reconstruction of colonial musical activity.
(Spanish translation also published in *0878a*, 153-171.)

Regional and Local Histories

1099   Stevenson, Robert Murrell. "Bogotá." In **MGG** (*0058*), Supplement A-Dy
Ge   columns 893-898.
Thoroughly documented survey covering music of the precolonial era
Chibcha Indians to events of 1969; one-column bibliography.

Instruments

1100   Pardo Tovar, Andrés; Bermúdez Silba, Jesús. **La guitarrería popular de**
Sp   **Chiquinquirá.** Bogotá, 1963. 58p. (Monografías del Centro de Estudios
Folclóricos, 3) LC 66-80408.   ML 1015 G9 P4
General material on string instruments in Colombia and specific study of
guitar makers in Chiquinquirá. Unannotated three-page bibliography; maps,
drawings, musical examples.

1101   Velásquez M., Rogerio. "Instrumentos musicales del Alto y Bajo Chocó."
Sp   **Revista colombiana de folclor**, 2 (1961), 77-113.
GR 1 R295
Documented article, organized by instrument classification. Appendix of
expressions using musical, dance, and instrumental terms but with nonmusical
meanings. Forty-five bibliographic references; four plates.

BIOGRAPHICAL SOURCES

Items *1082, 1083, 1097* include considerable biographical information.
See also the biographical sources listed under Latin America—General (p. 103).

1102   Zapata Cuéncar, Heriberto. **Compositores colombianos.** Medellín: Editorial
Sp   Carpel, 1962. 280p. LC 63-25612.   ML 390 Z3
       Haphazard collection of about 200 entries, some with portraits and lists of
works. Severely criticized by Pardo Tovar in *1082* (pp. 402-403) for complete lack
of logical, valid organization (arrangement is geographical, by state), for inadequate
information (some entries merely offer name and birthplace), and for depth of
coverage incongruent with a composer's stature and importance. Index of "principal"
biographies.

       Three smaller, similar-style works by the same author offer slightly fuller
coverage of composers already in *1102*, and include additional names:

1103   Zapata, Cuéncar, Heriberto. **Compositores antioqueños.** Medellín: Editorial
Sp   Granamérica, 1973. 130p. LC 74-207371.   ML 106 C64 Z4

1104   Zapata, Cuéncar, Heriberto. **Compositores narinenses.** Medellín: Editorial
Sp   Granamérica, 1973. 41p. LC 74-213535.   ML 106 C64 Z42
       Thirty-six paragraph-length sketches, photos.

1105   Zapata, Cuéncar, Heriberto. **Compositores vallecaucanos.** Medellín:
Sp   Editorial Granamérica, 1968. 96p. LC 72-396423.
                                                     ML 390 Z33
       Fifty-eight sketches, photos.

GUIDES TO OTHER SOURCES

       See also the Guides to Other Sources section under Latin America–General
(pp. 103-108).

Selective and Critical Guides

       The outstanding bibliographical source is *1082*, with coverage of mono-
graphs, 1851-1964. Chase, *A Guide to the Music of Latin America (0891)* includes
85 entries for Colombia, pp. 188-197. See also the note at the beginning of Folk
Music and Folksong (p. 148).

Annual and Periodic Guides

1106   **Anuario bibliográfico colombiano.** v.1– . 1951– . Bogotá: Instituto Caro
Sp   y Cuervo, 1952– . (annual) LC 53-28591 rev.2
       Sheehy 76–AA550   Z 1731 A58
       Classed Dewey arrangement, including books, pamphlets, song collections.
Issue for 1962 included seven music items; that of 1972, two items. List of new
periodical titles.

1107   **Bibliografía colombiana.** v.1– . 1961– . Gainesville, Florida. (semiannual)
Sp   LC 64-4610rev.   Z 1731 B5
       Sheehy 76–AA551
       (Title to 1965, *Fichas para el Anuario bibliográfico colombiano*.) Prepared
by Cuban bibliographer Fermin Peraza and continued after his death by his wife.
Includes books and pamphlets published in Colombia and abroad–the latter written
by Colombians. Author alphabetical arrangement with comprehensive index. Three
music items in 1969 volume, none in 1970.

LISTS OF MUSIC

Holdings of musical archives in Bogotá are listed in *1098* and in *0941*.
Catalogs of composer's works are included in *1082*. See also the Lists of Music
section under Latin America–General (p. 108).

DISCOGRAPHIES

See note at beginning of Folk Music and Folksong (p. 148). See also the
discographies listed under Latin America–General (p. 110).

COSTA RICA

THE LANGUAGE OF MUSIC

See the Language of Music section under Latin America–General (p. 94).

DIRECT INFORMATION SOURCES

Introductions and General Surveys

1108   Araya Rojas, José Rafael. **Vida musical de Costa Rica.** San José: Impr.
Sp   Nacional, 1957. 142p. LC 58-16866.   ML 3572 C6 A7 1957
       Originally an article in *Educación*, 16 (nov.-dic. 1942), 3-79; Chase–1414.
Reprinted with update to 1956. Covers music education, popular music, performance
organizations, religious music, music bibliography, instruments, and national anthem.
Alphabetical list of prominent musicians and composers.

1109   Fonesca, Julio. "Referencias sobre música costarricense." **Revista de**
Sp   **estudios musicales,** 1 (abril 1950), 75-97.   ML 5 R203
       Chase–547a
       Originally an article in *Revista Musical*, 1940-1941; Chase–1415, 1416.
Information on folksong and folk dance forms, instruments, and art music, including
performance ensembles, organizations, and institutions. Thirteen paragraph-length
biographies. Musical examples.

For **MGG** coverage, see *0842*; see also *0848*.

Instruments

1110   Fournier Facio, Gastón. "Descripción de algunos instrumentos musicales
Sp   precolombinos de Costa Rica." **Revista de la Universidad de Costa Rica,**
       30 (julio 1971), 7-75.   AS 65 S3
       "Description of acoustical properties of a certain number of archeological
exemplars. Pieces analyzed include simple and double whistles, various sizes of
ocarinas and percussion instruments. Careful study" [*Handbook of Latin American
Studies*, 34 (1972), p. 578.]

BIOGRAPHICAL SOURCES

See *1108, 1109, 0848*; see also the biographical sources listed under Latin
America–General (p. 103).

GUIDES TO OTHER SOURCES

See also the Guides to Other Sources section under Latin America–General
(pp. 103-108).

Selective and Critical Guides

Chase, *A Guide to the Music of Latin America* (*0891*) includes 29 entries
for Costa Rica, pp. 198-202.

Annual and Periodic Guides

1111   **Anuario bibliográfico costarricense,** v.1– . 1956– . San José, Costa Rica:
Sp   Impr. Nacional, 1958– . (annual) LC 59-52634.
         Sheehy 76–AA555   Z 1453 A65
       Since 1959, a subject arrangement with author index. Volume for 1966
had no headings for music or related topics (e.g., fine arts, folklore); probably
reflects the lack of publication in these areas. Before 1959, separate author and
subject lists, with subject and author index.

LISTS OF MUSIC

See *0849*; see also the Lists of Music section under Latin America–General
(p. 108).

DISCOGRAPHIES

See the discographies listed under Latin America—General (p. 110).

CUBA

THE LANGUAGE OF MUSIC

See the Language of Music section under Latin America—General (p. 94).

DIRECT INFORMATION SOURCES

Introductions and General Surveys

1112 Carpentier, Alejo. **La música en Cuba.** México: Fondo de cultura económica,
Sp   1972. 368p.   ML 207 C8 C3
      Chase—586a
      (1st ed. 1946) Good historical survey of Cuban music and musical culture,
sixteenth century to 1940s. Based on primary sources. Biographical information on
composers; musical examples; six-page unannotated bibliography. No index.

1113 Martín, Edgardo. **Panorama histórico de la música en Cuba.** Habana:
Sp   Universidad de La Habana, 1971. 257p.
      A content summary of this book is found in Stevenson, *A Guide to
Caribbean Music History (0896)*, pp. 41-42. General historical survey.

      The next item draws much information from Carpentier (*1112*) but offers
later coverage of the twentieth century:

1114 Ardévol, José. **Introducción a Cuba: la música.** Habana: Instituto del
Sp   Libro, 1969. 195p. LC 70-286758.   ML 207 C8 A68
      Popular historical survey, sixteenth to twentieth century. Some directory-
type information on musical organizations since 1959 (orchestras, societies,
performers, and schools) but narrative format makes it difficult to extract.
Appendices on music periodicals and education. Musical examples and pictures
are poorly printed. Bibliography; no index.

1115 Sariol, Natalio Galán. "Visión musical de nuestra historia." In **La**
Sp   **enciclopedia de Cuba**, tomo 5, artes, sociedad, filosofía. San Juan:
      Enciclopedia y Clásicos Cubanos, 1974. pp. 307-380.
                                             F 1754 E52
      General historical survey, sixteenth century to 1950. Emphasis on art
music and Cuban composers. Pictures of musicians, composers, and instruments
on nearly every page. Musical examples, including eight nineteenth century
contradanzas. Supplement on percussion instruments (three pages) contains 32
illustrations. Unannotated bibliography at end of volume has 20 music entries.
Name index.

1116   Grenet, Emilio. **Popular Cuban Music; 80 Revised and Corrected Compo-**
En   **sitions Together with an Essay on the Evolution of Music in Cuba.** Habana:
       printing by Carasa and Co., 1939. xlix, 199p. LC A41-2411rev.

  Chase–1487   ML 207 C8 G7

  Published to promote understanding of Cuban music in the United States.
The 41-page introductory essay considers African and Spanish influences, rhythmic
characteristics, genres of music, and dance forms. Over 30 musical examples; also
references to the musical selections.

1117   Ramírez, Serafín. **La Habana artística; apuntes históricas.** Habana: Imp.
Sp   del E. M. de la Capitanía General, 1891. 687p. LC A12-1236.

  Chase–1455, 1470, 1492   ML 207 C8 R2

  History of art music and musical life in nineteenth century Havana.
Includes 200-page biographical dictionary of musicians, also biographical chapters
on Cuban pianists and violinists. Supplement includes opera and concert programs,
musical examples.

Folk Music and Folksong

1118   León, Argeliers. **Música folklórica cubana.** Habana: Ediciones del Dept.
Sp   de Música de la Biblioteca Nacional José Martí, 1964. 148p. LC 65-78030.

              ML 3565 C8 L5

  Spanish and African influences, dance forms, and instrumental music.
Musical examples and drawings of instruments. "A semi-popular, politically-slanted
introduction to the subject which fails to make a distinction between 'folk' and
'popular' or 'composed' music" [*Handbook of Latin American Studies*, 28 (1966),
p. 343].

1119   Ortiz Fernández, Fernando. **La africanía de la música folklórica de Cuba.**
Sp   2d ed. Habana: Editora Universitaria, 1965. 489p. LC 67-56054.

  Chase–559a   ML 3565 O69 1965

  (1st ed. 1950) Part I of a monumental, seven-volume study of Afro-Cuban
music (see also *1120, 1127*). Songs and dances of Black Africa analyzed in detail,
with 83 illustrations (mostly musical examples). Unannotated 10-page bibliography;
no index.

1120   Ortiz Fernández, Fernando. **Los bailes y el teatro de los negros en el**
Sp   **folklore de Cuba.** Habana: Ministerio de Educación, Dirección de Cultura,
       1951. xvi, 466p. LC 51-6608.   ML 3565 O693
       Chase–560a

  Continuation of preceding item. Dance and pantomime music, also the
theatrical quality of Afro-Cuban songs and ballads. Thoroughly documented study,
including social aspects of the music; 27 illustrations and musical examples.

   Information on Afro-Cuban music (based on Ortiz) is included in item
0855.

Popular Music

1121   **Signos**, 2 (nov. 1969). Habana: Consejo Nacional de Cultura, Biblioteca
Sp   José Martí.   NX 7 S56
       Special issue devoted to popular dance forms. Illustrations, musical
examples.

Opera and Vocal Music

1122   Tolón, Edwin Teurbe; Gonzáles, Jorge A. **Óperas cubanas y sus autores.**
Sp   Habana: 1943. 472p. LC 43-21186.   ML 1714 T6
       Chase–1461x
       Cited by Carpentier (*1112*) as a well-documented study. Covers 12
composers of Cuban opera. Portraits, no bibliography or index.

1123   Tolón, Edwin Teurbe; González, Jorege A. **Historia del teatro en la**
Sp   **Habana.** Santa Clara, Cuba: Direccion de Publicaciones, Universidad
       Central de las Villas, 1961. 170p. LC 65-57087.
                                              PN 2402 H3 T6
       Documented general historical narrative with coverage to 1850. Seven out
of the 10 chapters are devoted to opera. Unannotated four-page bibliography. No
index, illustrations, or musical examples.

Church and Religious Music

1124   Macía de Casteleiro, María. **La música religiosa en Cuba.** Habana: Ucar
Sp   García, 1956. 137p. LC 57-21653.   ML 2914 M3
       History of Cuban church music in the nineteenth and twentieth centuries.
Biographical information for organists, choirmasters, and composers (including
titles of sacred compositions). Coverage of sixteenth to eighteenth centuries via a
summary of Carpentier (*1112*), pp. 30-59.

1125   Hernández Balaguer, Pablo. "La capilla de música de la Catedral de
Sp   Santiago de Cuba." **Revista musical chilena**, 18 (oct.-dic. 1964), 14-16.
                                              ML 5 R283
       Documented scholarly study, based on primary sources (which are quoted
extensively in the text). Illustrations and musical examples.

Periodicals and Yearbooks

1126   **Revista de Música.** año 1-2, 1960-1961. Habana: Biblioteca Nacional José
Sp   Martí, Departamento de Música. (quarterly) LC 65-68182.
                                              ML 5 R208
       Fine serious publication with articles on Cuban and general music topics
with brief news summary. (Brief life-span of two volumes.)

Instruments

1127   Ortiz Fernández, Fernando. **Los instrumentos de la música afrocubano.**
Sp   Habana: Dirección de Cultura del Ministerio de Educación, 1952-1955.
5v. LC 53-35955.   ML 480 O72
Chase—561a
Continuation of *1120*. A thorough study, describing physical and social
aspects of more than 2,500 types of instruments. Illustrated with photos and
drawings. Index to all figures at the end of volume 5. Bibliography; no general
index.

1128   Courlander, Harold. "Musical Instruments of Cuba." **Musical Quarterly,**
En   28 (Apr. 1942), 227-240.   ML 1 M725
Brief descriptive survey of Afro-Cuban instruments based on author's field
visits. Includes 18 photographs, three drawings.

BIOGRAPHICAL SOURCES

See items *1117, 1122, 1124*.

GUIDES TO OTHER SOURCES

See also the Guides to Other Sources listed under Latin America—General
(pp. 103-108).

Selective and Critical Guides

Stevenson, *A Guide to Caribbean Music History* (*0896*) lists 36 index
entries for Cuba. Chase, *A Guide to the Music of Latin America*(*0891*) contains
approximately 160 entries, pp. 203-217.

Annual and Periodic Lists

The current national bibliography:

1129   **Bibliografía cubana,** v.1, 1959/62— . Habana: Biblióteca Nacional José
Sp   Martí. (annual) LC 71-378138.   Z 1511 B5
Sheehy 76—AA566
Classed Dewey subject arrangement, with comprehensive index. Music
section includes scores and books, often with contents note. Volume for 1965
contained seven music items, volume for 1970 contained one.

The pre-revolutionary national bibliography:

1130 **Anuario bibliográfico cubano**, v.1-30, 1937-1965. Habana; Gainesville.
Sp (annual) LC 38-8616.   Z 1511 A61
     Sheehy 76—AA564
(Volumes 25-30, 1961-1966, issued in Gainesville and Coral Gables,
Florida.) Title and arrangement vary. Until 1955, author arrangement with subject
index; then a classed arrangement. Title became *Bibliografía cubana* in 1953. Both
formats include music books and scores; 1956 volume contained about 15 scores
and 20 books.

The continued bibliographic efforts of Fermin Peraza, editor of the
preceding item, produced the following publication for the years 1966-1968:

1131 **Revolutionary Cuba: a Bibliographical Guide**, 1966-1968. Coral Gables,
En Florida: University of Miami Press, 1967-1970. (annual) LC 68-21369.
     Sheehy 76—AA567   Z 1511 A653
Materials about and published in Cuba since the Castro regime. Author
arrangement, with subject-title-author index. Six music items for 1966; two for
1967; three for 1968. Scores and books.

LISTS OF MUSIC

1132 Hernandez Balaguer, Pablo. **Catálogo de música de los archivos de la
Sp Catedral de Santiago de Cuba y del Museo Bacardí.** Habana: Biblioteca
Nacional José Martí, 1961. 59p. LC 68-130407.
     Duckles 74—1469   ML 136 S35 C35
Catalog of works by Cuban composers in the archives of the Cathedral
and museum of Santiago. General classified arrangement: vocal religious, vocal
secular, instrumental, piano, chamber music, etc. Within classes, alphabetical by
composer. A 20-page introduction of historical background and biographical
information on composers.

See also *1129, 1130, 1131* and Lists of Music section under Latin
America—General (p. 108).

DISCOGRAPHIES

See the discographies listed under Latin America—General (p. 110).

DOMINICAN REPUBLIC

THE LANGUAGE OF MUSIC

See the Language of Music section under Latin America—General (p. 94).

DIRECT INFORMATION SOURCES

Introductions and General Surveys

1133 Coopersmith, Jacob Maurice. **Music and Musicians of the Dominican**
En/Sp **Republic.** Washington: Division of Music and Visual Arts, Dept. of
Cultural Affairs, Pan American Union, 1949. 146p. LC 50-60386.
Chase—620a   ML 207 D6 C62
Historical survey of folk and art music, including song and dance forms,
instruments, composers. Index, discography, bibliography. Photos, map, musical
examples.

1134 García, Juan Françisco. **Panorama de la música dominicana.** Ciudad
Sp Trujillo: Secretaría de Estado de Educación y Bellas Artes, 1947. 46p.
LC 55-16168.   ML 207 D6 G3
Chase—621a
General historical survey including many paragraph-length biographies
of musicians. No index or illustrations; unannotated bibliography of six entries.

1135 Valldeperes, Manuel. "La música en la República Dominicana." **Boletín**
Sp **interamericano de música,** 77 (mayo 1970), 31-44.
Brief historical survey, with emphasis on late nineteenth century and
twentieth century composers. Mentions music education, folk music. Unannotated
bibliography of eight items.

1136 Hernández, Julio Alberto. **Música tradicional dominicana.** Santo Domingo:
Sp Julio D. Postigo, 1969. 202p. (Colección artistas dominicanos, 1)
NUC 71-93909
Survey of folk and popular forms. Text is 89 pages (including musical
examples and song texts) followed by a 100-page anthology of musical compositions.
Unannotated bibliography of one page; no index.

See also *1141.*

Collections of Essays, Articles, etc.

1137 Rodríguez Demorizi, Emilio. **Música y baile en Santo Domingo.** Santo
Sp Domingo: Librería Hispaniola, 1971. 227p. LC 74-215423.
ML 207 D6 R6
Collection of newspaper articles since 1945. Topics include instruments,
folk and popular dances, personalities of art and popular music, *merengue*,
orchestras. Index, no bibliography.

1138 Nolasco, Flerida De. **La música en Santo Domingo y otros ensayos.** Ciudad
Sp Trujillo: Impresora Dominicana, 1956. 163p.   ML 220 N65 M8 1956
Chase—1540

(1st ed. 1939) Includes approximately 100 pages of general material on folk music and musical history. Musical examples, two-page unannotated bibliography, no index.

Folk Music and Folksong

1139   Lizardo, Fradique. **La canción folklórica en Santo Domingo.** San Cristóbal:
Sp   Imp. Benemérita, 1958. 83p. (Publ. de la Sociedad Folklorica Dominicana, 1)
        "A short introduction, including material on classification of folk songs and on instruments and their geographic distribution, is followed by some 20 examples, first of song texts, then of music" [*Handbook of Latin American Studies*, 21 (1961), p. 381].

1140   Lizardo, Fradique. **Danzas y bailes folklóricos dominicanos.** Santo
Sp   Domingo: Taller, 1974. 329p.   GV 1635 L78
        Comprehensive survey of folk dance forms, including historical background and choreography. Glossary of instrument names; photos, drawings, diagrams; musical examples. Comprehensive seven-page unannotated bibliography; no index.

1141   Marchena, Enrique de. **Del areito de Anacona al poema folklórico; Brindis**
Sp   **de Salas en Santo Domingo.** Ciudad Trujillo: Editora Montalvo, 1942.
        95p. LC 45-14157.   ML 3565 M19
        Chase–1538
        General survey of folk music and miscellaneous musical history. Musical examples, illustrations, two-page unannotated bibliography; no index.

1142   Arzeno, Julio. **Del folk-lore musical dominicano.** Santo Domingo: Imp.
Sp   "La Cuna de America," Roques Roman Hnos., 1927. 135p. LC 29-3055.
        Chase–1537   ML 3565 A8 F7
        Survey of folk music–song and dance forms. Musical examples; one-page bibliography of the author's publications; no index.

See also *1133, 1136, 0862.*

Popular Music

See items *1136, 1137.*

BIOGRAPHICAL SOURCES

1143   Domínguez, Franklin. "Biografía de los compositores dominicanos."
Sp   **Revista de educación,** 29 (enero-abril 1959), 38-85. (Santo Domingo:
        Secretaría de Estado de Educación y Bellas Artes.)
        Biographical information on 10 composers.

See also *1133, 1134, 1135,* and the biographical sources listed under Latin America—General (p. 103).

GUIDES TO OTHER SOURCES

See also the Guides to Other Sources section under Latin America—General (pp. 103-108).

Selective and Critical Guides

Chase, *A Guide to the Music of Latin America* (*0891*) includes 22 entries for the Dominican Republic, pp. 220-225. Stevenson, *A Guide to Caribbean Music History* (*0896*) lists five index entries for the Dominican Republic.

General Lists and Library Catalogs

See *0897.*

Annual and Periodic Guides

See *0904, 0907.*

LISTS OF MUSIC

See the Lists of Music section under Latin America—General (p. 108).

DISCOGRAPHIES

See the discographies listed under Latin America—General (p. 110).

ECUADOR

THE LANGUAGE OF MUSIC

See entry *1147*; see also the Language of Music section under Latin America—General (p. 94)

DIRECT INFORMATION SOURCES

Introductions and General Surveys

1144   Moreno Andrade, Segundo Luis. "La música en el Ecuador." In Gonzalo
Sp   Orellana, J., **El Ecuador en cien años de independencia.** Quito: Imprenta
de la Escuela de Artes y Oficios, 1930. pp. 187-276.

     Chase–1556   F 3708 O38

General survey of folk and art music in broad chronological arrangement.
Information on religious music and music education. Brief, paragraph-length biographical sketches of musicians (including lists of works) in a regional (and non-
alphabetical) arrangement.

Moreno's major musicological work is a lengthy, three-volume expansion
of the previous item; only volume one has been published so far:

1145   Moreno Andrade, Segundo Luis. **Historia de la música en el Ecuador.**
Sp   Quito: Editorial Casa de la Cultura Ecuatoriana, 1972. v.1, 225p. LC
73-328088.   ML 235 M67

Coverage of folk, Indian, and pre-Hispanic music, organized by regions.
Photos, musical examples, pictures (including instruments and their ranges), some
footnotes. No bibliography or index. According to the review by Charles Sigmund,
"Moreno's study is a unique and valuable contribution because he was the only
professionally trained musician who had observed indigenous ceremony so extensively.
He worked before the invention of the modern portable tape recorder at a time when
Indian ceremony was practiced more freely and with less western influence than it is
today. It would be impossible for a modern scholar to duplicate his studies" [*Anuario
de investigación musical*, 8 (1972), 171].

Volumes II and III are described by Sigmund in *1158*. Volume II treats the
impact of Western music on the traditional Ecuadorian music, and includes 50
musical examples. Volume III covers musical institutions, art music, church music,
and music education. Organization is geographical. Lists of musicians and their
contributions.

Collections of Essays, Articles, etc.

1146   Alexander, Francisco. **Música y músicos: ensayos en miniatura.** Quito:
Sp   Editorial Casa de la Cultura Ecuatoriana, 1970. 284p. LC 73-867807.
         ML 60 A425 M9

Collection of newspaper articles that have appeared since 1935. Broad
subject arrangement, with Ecuadorian topics in sections 5 ("Musica y músicos
ecuatorianos") and 6 ("Conciertos y recitales en Quito"), pp. 211-284. Name index.

See also *1157*.

Folk Music and Folksong

Ecuador is included in Raoul and Marguerite d'Harcourt's studies of Andean
folk music; see entries *0866, 0873, 0874*. See also *1145*.

1147   Carvalho Neto, Paulo de. **Diccionario del folklore ecuatoriano.** Quito:
Sp   Editorial Casa de la Cultura Ecuatoriana, 1964. 488p. LC 65-51658.
                                                      GR 133 E3 C293
       Comprehensive dictionary of folklore terms, including musical forms,
songs, dances, and instruments. Alphabetical arrangement with numerous indexes
and extensive prefatory matter explaining the study and use of the book. Illustrations; unannotated 10-page bibliography.

1148   Moreno Andrade, Segundo Luis. **Música y danzas autóctonas del Ecuador.**
Sp/En **Indigenous Music and Dances of Ecuador.** English version by Jorge Luis
       Pérez, final chapter by C. W. Ireson. Quito: Editorial "Fray Jodoco
       Ricke," 1949. xii, 158p. LC 51-7063rev.   ML 235 M7
       Spanish and English versions in parallel columns. Deals with Indian cere-
monial music, dances. Lengthy treatment of instruments, including illustrations
with ranges. Musical examples; photos; no index or bibliography.

       The next four items are studies of particular regions and peoples:

1149   Instituto Ecuatoriano de Folklore. **Folklore de Lican y Sicalpa.** Quito:
Sp   Casa de la Cultura Ecuatoriana, 1962. 67p. NUC 65-57. (Publicaciones
       especiales, 1) Director de la investigación: Paulo de Carvalho Neto.
       Includes description of dances, instruments, and musical style. Illustrations;
three musical examples.

1150   List, George. "Music in the Culture of the Jíbaro Indians of the Ecuadorian
En   **Montaña.**" In **Inter-American Conference on Ethnomusicology. 1st.** (*0853*),
       pp. 131-151.

       Reprinted as an article:

       List, George. "Music in the Culture of the Jíbaro Indians of the Ecuadorian
       Montaña." **Inter-American Music Bulletin,** no. 40-41 (March-May 1964),
       1-17.   ML 1 I717
       Documented article with 18 illustrations: musical examples, photos, map,
drawing.

1151   Ramón y Rivera, Luis Felipe. "Música afroecuatoriana." **Folklore americano,**
Sp   15-16 (1967-1968), 70-86.   GR 1 F327
       Based on a 22-day field visit. Description and analysis of Afroecuatorian
music of the Pacific coast; information on the marimba; photos; eight musical
examples.

1152   Whitten, Norman E., Jr.; Fuentes, C. Aurelio. "*¡Baile marimba!* Negro Folk
En   Music in Northwest Ecuador." **Journal of the Folklore Institute,** 3 (Aug.
       1966), 168-191.   GR 1 I5
       Description of the *marimba*–dancing, instruments, song texts. No photos
or bibliography.

Historical Studies, Chronologies, Contemporary Narratives

Studies of Inca musical culture are entered under Latin America—General; see items *0873, 0874, 0875.*

1153   Moreno Andrade, Segundo Luis. **La música de los Incas; rectificación a la**
Sp   **obra intitulada La musique des Incas et ses survivances por Raúl y**
       Margarita d'Harcourt. Quito: Editorial Casa de la Cultura Ecuatoriana,
       1957. 179p. LC 57-46790rev.   ML 3575 P4 H32
       An attack on *0874*, in defense of Ecuadorian music. Deals with musical
systems and offers 50 corrected versions of musical examples from the d'Harcourt
study. According to Charles Sigmund in *1158*, "Many of Moreno's arguments are
faulty and he often fails to provide sufficient evidence to make his views more
convincing than those of the d'Harcourts . . . the substance involved in the argument
is often too petty to warrant the considerable effort of publishing a book" (p. 92).
Musical examples; no index or bibliography.

1154   Stevenson, Robert. "Music in Quito, Four Centuries." **Hispanic American**
En   **Historical Review**, 43 (May 1963), 247-266.   F 1401 H5
       (For Spanish version, see *0878a*, pp. 172-194) Thoroughly documented,
detailed reconstruction of church music activity in Quito, 1534-1911.

Instruments

1155   Casa de la Cultura Ecuatoriana. **Museo de instrumentos musicales de la**
Sp   **Casa de la Cultura Ecuatoriana.** Quito, 1961. 71p. LC 67-39570.
                                                       ML 462 Q58 C4
       Classified catalog of the museum's instrument collection, with 22 photo-
graphs. (Also reproduces "opinions of visitors to the museum.")

1156   Zeller, Richard. **Instrumentos y música en la cultura guangala.** Guayaquil,
Sp   Ecuador: Cromos y Segura, 1971. 86p. LC 72-320781.
                                                       ML 3547 Z44
       Catalog of 40 instruments with precise description and commentary;
photos. Unannotated two-page bibliography, no index. (An archeological study.)

       See also information on the *marimba* in items *1151, 1152.*

BIOGRAPHICAL SOURCES

1157   Astudillo Ortega, José María. **Dedos y labios apolíneos.** Cuenca: Casa de la
Sp   Cultura Ecuatoriana, Nucleo del Azuay, 1956. 125p. LC 57-36620.
                                                       ML 235 A8
       Collection of 40 short essays, of which about 30 are biographical sketches.
Average length is two to three pages. Musicians and composers, in vague, topical
arrangement. Table of contents, but no bibliography or index.

See also *1144*.

GUIDES TO OTHER SOURCES

See also the Guides to Other Sources listed under Latin America—General (pp. 103-108).

Selective and Critical Guides

1158　Sigmund, Charles. "Segundo Luis Moreno (1882-1972): Ecuador's Pioneer
En　　Musicologist." **Anuario de investigación musical**, 8 (1972), 71-104.

ML 1 T842

Extracted from the author's Ph.D. dissertation (University of Minnesota, 1971) Biographical summary with descriptive and critical information on Moreno's publications. Photos, musical examples, and bibliography of Moreno's published and unpublished writings—19 unannotated entries.

Chase, *A Guide to the Music of Latin America (0891)* includes 32 entries for Ecuador, pp. 226-230.

LISTS OF MUSIC

See the Lists of Music section under Latin America—General (p. 108).

DISCOGRAPHIES

See the Language of Music Section under Latin America—General (p. 94).

EL SALVADOR

THE LANGUAGE OF MUSIC

See the Language of Music section under Latin American—General (p. 94).

DIRECT INFORMATION SOURCES

Introductions and General Surveys

1159　González Sol, Rafael. **Datos históricos sobre el arte de la música en El
Sp　　Salvador.** San Salvador: Imprenta Mercurio, 1940. 74p. LC 43-48148.

Chase—1585　　　　　　　　　　　　　　　ML 220 Sl G6

Also reprinted as an article:

González Sol, Rafael. "Datos histórica sobre el arte de la música en El Salvador." **Anales del museo nacional "David Guzmán,"** 1 (oct.-dic. 1950), 42-68.   F 1481 S35

Chase—635a

Historical survey with information on orchestras, military bands, musical publications, music schools, composers, native instruments, performers, and musical activity.

See also *0848*.

Folk Music and Folksong

1160 Sp   Baratta, María de. "Ensayo sobre música indígena de El Salvador." **Revista de estudios musicales**, 1 (abril 1950), 61-74.   ML 5 R203

Chase—631a

Information on Indian song and dance forms; musical examples.

1161 Sp   Baratta, María de. **Cuzcatlán típico; ensayo sobre etnofonía de El Salvador, folklore, folkwisa y folkway.** San Salvador: Ministerio de Cultura, 1951-1952. 2v. (740p.) LC 52-64779rev.

Chase—629a   GR 118 S1 B3

Coverage of folk music and dance, instruments, pre-Hispanic musical culture and dance. Oversize-format volumes with many photos and illustrations (some in color); musical examples and song texts. Unannotated two-page bibliography; detailed table of contents; no index.

BIOGRAPHICAL SOURCES

See *0848*; see also the biographical sources listed under Latin America— General (p. 103).

GUIDES TO OTHER SOURCES

See also the Guides to Other Sources section under Latin America—General (pp. 103-108).

Selective and Critical Guides

Chase, *A Guide to the Music of Latin America* (*0891*) includes 22 entries for El Salvador, pp. 231-234.

LISTS OF MUSIC

See *0848*; see also the Lists of Music section under Latin America—General (p. 108).

DISCOGRAPHIES

See the discographies listed under Latin America—General (p. 110).

GUATEMALA

THE LANGUAGE OF MUSIC

See Latin America—General (p. 94).

DIRECT INFORMATION SOURCES

Introductions and General Surveys

1162　Vásquez A., Rafael. **Historia de la música en Guatemala.** Guatemala: Tip.
Sp　　Nacional, 1950. 346p. LC 54-41331.　　ML 220 G9 V3
　　　Comprehensive historical survey covering art, folk, and popular music.
Includes opera, musical organizations, and biographical information. Topical
arrangement. No documentation in text; no bibliography or index.

1163　Díaz, Victor Miguel. "La Música." In **Las bellas artes en Guatemala.**
Sp　　Guatemala: Tipografía nacional, 1934. p. 518-595.

　　　　Chase—1593　　　　　　　　　　N 6576 D5
　　　Fairly comprehensive survey covering musical history, instruments, fiesta
music, folk and popular song and dance, conservatories, concert life, and musical
activities. Paragraph-length biographies of musicians, colonial era to the twentieth
century. Drawings and photos.

1164　Castellanos, J. Humberto. "Breve historia de la música en Guatemala."
Sp　　**Boletín de Museos y Bibliotecas,** segunda epoca, 3 (oct. 1943), 112-121,
　　　(enero 1944), 147-154; 4 (abril 1944), 20-28, (julio 1944), 66-74, (oct.
　　　1944), 97-94. Guatemala City: Biblioteca Nacional.

　　　　Chase—639a　　　　　　　　　　Z887 G91 B
　　　Historical survey, pre-colonial era to the twentieth century, including
information on Indian music, church music, musical theatre, and folk music. Last
installment is an unfinished, illustrated biographical dictionary of composers with
coverage through the letter A.

　　　See also Sider, "The Art Music of Central America—Its Development
and Present State" (*0848*).

Folk Music and Folksong

1165   Chenoweth, Vida. **The Marimbas of Guatemala**. Lexington: University of
En   Kentucky Press, 1964. x, 108p. LC 63-12386   ML 1040 C5
        Study of the instrument and its music. Many drawings and musical examples;
unannotated bibliography of three pages; index.

1166   Paret-Limardo de Vela, Lise. **Folklore musical de Guatemala**. Guatemala:
Sp   Tipografía Nacional, 1962. 54p. LC 62-51966   ML 3572 G9 P4
        Text of 19 pages is a brief survey, with photos, followed by musical
examples. No bibliography.

1167   Castillo, Jesús. **La música Maya-Quiché (región guatemalteca)**.
Sp   Quetzaltenango: Tip. E. Cifuentes, 1941. 88p. LC 43-43227
        Chase—1630   ML 3547 C3
        Attempts reconstruction of ancient Indian musical culture, including
instruments, scales, and bird songs. Illustrations, photos, and musical examples.
No bibliography or index.

Historical Studies, Chronologies, Contemporary Narratives

1168   Sáenz Poggio, José. **Historia de la música guatemalteca desde la monarquía**
Sp   **española, hasta fines del año de 1877**. Guatemala: Imprenta de la Aurora,
        1878. 80p.   ML 220 S2
        Historical survey including chapters on opera, military music, and music
education. Three pages on native Indian music. No table of contents, index, bibliography, or musical examples (omissions to be pardoned in 1878, no doubt).

1169   Stevenson, Robert M. "European music in sixteenth-century Guatemala."
En   **Musical Quarterly**, 50 (July, 1964), 341-52.   ML 1 M725
        Thoroughly documented reconstruction of church music activity in
sixteenth century Guatemala. Musical examples.

Regional and Local Histories

1170   Stevenson, Robert M. "Guatemala Stadt." **MGG** (*0058*), supplement
Ge   Fus-Hy, columns 551-555.
        Comprehensive historical survey, including Indian instruments, the colonial
era, and the twentieth century. Unannotated bibliography of one-third of a column.

Instruments

See Chenoweth, *The Marimbas of Guatemala* (*1165*).

1171 Armas Lara, Marcial. **Orígen de la marimba, su desenvolvimiento y otros**
Sp **instrumentos músicos.** Guatemala: Tipografía Nacional, 1970. 116p. LC 72-
303374 ML 1040 A62
Survey of marimba and brief treatment of other instruments. A descriptive
study, with many photos and an index of the illustrations. No documentation in
text; no index or bibliography.

See also Hammond, "Classic Maya Music" (*0878*).

BIOGRAPHICAL SOURCES

See *1162, 1163, 1164, 0848*, and the biographical sources listed under
Latin America—General (p.103).

GUIDES TO OTHER SOURCES

See also the Guides to Other Sources section under Latin America—General
(pp. 103-108).

Selective and Critical Guides

Chase, *A Guide to the Music of Latin America* (*0891*) includes 63 entries
for Guatemala, pp. 235-241.

LISTS OF MUSIC

1172 "Catálogo de las composiciones musicales de autores guatemaltecos que
Sp se conservan en el archivo musical del museo." **Revista del Museo Nacional
de Guatemala; Seccion de Historia y Bellas Artes**, época 3, (mayo/junio
1945), 60-64, (julio, agosto y sept. 1945), 118-127, (dic. 1946), 60-68.
Chase—641a, 642a N910 G8 A5
Lists of works by composer, in alphabetical order.

See also *0848*, and the Lists of Music section under Latin America—General
(p. 108).

DISCOGRAPHIES

See the discographies listed under Latin America—General (p. 110).

GUYANA

1173   Brathwaite, Percy A. **Musical Traditions: Aspects of Racial Elements with**
En   **Influence on a Guianese Community.** Georgetown: C. A. Welshman, 1962.
        55p. LC 66-666.   ML 3575 B75 B7
        Subtitled "A Short Treatise on the Original Basis of Music, the Rituals and
Cultural Trends in the Approach to Guianese Folk-lore." Information on song and
dance forms of Guyana, dealing with contributions and influences of the country's
six ethnic peoples. A loose compilation of brief articles on various aspects of musical
culture (song, dance, instruments). Many drawings, some photos, poor quality paper.

        Stevenson, *A Guide to Caribbean Music History* (*0896*) includes five index
entries for Guyana. Chase, *A Guide to the Music of Latin America* (*0891*) includes
four entries for Guyana (entered as "British Guiana"), p. 158.

HAITI

THE LANGUAGE OF MUSIC

        Entries *1175* and *1176* include glossaries of Creole terms, with some names
of musical forms and instruments. For French terms, see entries *0005, 0006* in
Volume 1.

DIRECT INFORMATION SOURCES

Introductions and General Surveys

1174   Dumervé, Constantin. **Histoire de la musique en Haïti.** Port-au-Prince:
Fr   Imprimerie des Antilles, 1968. 319p. LC 68-124220.
                                                                 ML 207 H3 D84
        Popular historical survey of folk and art music, followed by 54 biographical
sketches of composers—with pictures and some lists of works. No bibliography or
index.

Folk Music and Folksong

1175   Courlander, Harold. **The Drum and the Hoe; Life and Lore of the Haitian**
En   **People.** Berkeley: University of California Press, 1960. xv, 371p. LC 60-
        8760.   GR 121 H3 C65 1960
        Chase—651a
        Extensive coverage of folk music in eight chapters dealing with folksong,
dance, and musical instruments. Photos, 186 musical transcriptions, glossary of
Creole terms (including names of songs and instruments). Annotated discography
of nine entries; unannotated three-page bibliography; index.

1176   Courlander, Harold. **Haiti Singing.** Chapel Hill: The University of North
En   Carolina Press, 1939. xii, 273p. Reprint—New York: Cooper Square
         Publishers, 1973. (Library of Latin American History and Culture)
         LC 72-95270. ISBN 0-8154-0461-1.   ML 3565 H3 C7 1973
         Chase—1647
         (1st ed. 1939) Comprehensive study of Haitian folk music—songs, dances,
music of the *Vodoun* and other rituals. Anthology of 126 musical transcriptions;
photos, drawings, musical examples; glossary of common Creole terms. Unannotated
one-page bibliography; index.

1177   Paul, Emmanuel Casseus. **Notes sur le folklore d'Haiti, proverbs et chansons.**
Fr   Port-au-Prince: Imp. Telhomme, 1946. 80p. LC 47-16942.
         Chase—654a   PM 7854 H3 P35
         Includes approximately 30 pages of description of folksong forms. Musical
examples; texts. No bibliography, index, or table of contents.

         The *Encyclopédia des musiques sacrées (0510)*, v.1, includes an article by
Laura Boulton, "Le culte *Vaudou*," pp. 105-110. The article contains photos, illustrations, musical examples, and a short bibliography and discography.

         See also *0862*.

Instruments

1178   Courlander, Harold. "Musical Instruments of Haiti." **Musical Quarterly**, 27
En   (June 1941), 371-383.   ML 1 M725
         Chase—1649
         Study describing drums and percussion instruments; illustrations.

BIOGRAPHICAL SOURCES

         See *1174*.

GUIDES TO OTHER SOURCES

         See also the Guides to Other Sources section under Latin America—General
(pp. 103-108).

Selective and Critical Guides

         Stevenson, *A Guide to Caribbean Music History (0896)* lists 14 index entries
for Haiti. Chase, *A Guide to the Music of Latin America (0891)* includes 25 entries
for Haiti, pp. 242-244.

General Lists and Library Catalogs

See *0897, 0901.*

Annual and Periodic Lists

See *0904, 0907.*

LISTS OF MUSIC

See *1174*; see also the Lists of Music section under Latin America–General (p. 108).

DISCOGRAPHIES

See *1175*, the note following entry *1177*, and the discographies listed under Latin America–General (p. 110).

HONDURAS

THE LANGUAGE OF MUSIC

See Latin America–General (p. 94).

DIRECT INFORMATION SOURCES

Introductions and General Surveys

1179 Adalid y Gamero, Manuel de. "La música en Honduras." **Revista del archivo**
Sp   **y biblioteca nacional**, 17, (nov. 1938), 299-301, (enero 1939), 500-501,
      (feb. 1939), 594-596.   F 1501 R45
      Chase–1662
      Brief survey of Indian and art music.

1180 Coello Ramos, Rafael. "La cultura musical del pueblo hondureño." **Boletín**
Sp   **latino-americano de música**, 4 (1938), 91-94.   ML 199 B64
      Chase–1663
      Laments lack of musical culture, especially a conservatory. Characterizes
Honduras' music as *marimbas* and government bands. Some information on music
education.

See also *0848, 0840, 0842.*

Folk Music and Folksong

1181 Manzanares, Rafael. "La etnomusicología hondureña." **Folklore**
Sp **americano,** 11-12 (1963-1964), 68-91.   GR 1 F327
General comments on folk music followed by information on the instrument *caramba*. Text is six pages; rest is photos, drawings, musical examples. Briefer
version published in *0853*.

Instruments

1182 Manzanares, Rafael. "Instrumentos musicales tradicionales de Honduras."
Sp **Boletín interamericano de música,** 69-70 (enero-marzo 1969), 6-11.
Five-page survey of musical instruments, with three photos, one drawing,
and one musical example. Also published in *0854*.

BIOGRAPHICAL SOURCES

1183 Manzanares, Rafael. "Músicos de Honduras." **Boletín interamericano de**
Sp **música,** 81 (julio-oct. 1971), 26-28.
Half-page biographies of five prominent musicians. Photos.

See also *0848*.

GUIDES TO OTHER SOURCES

See also the Guides to Other Sources section under Latin America—General
(pp. 103-108).

Selective and Critical Guides

Chase, *A Guide to the Music of Latin America (0891)*, includes 13 entries
for Honduras, pp. 245-246.

LISTS OF MUSIC

See *0848*; see also the Lists of Music section under Latin America—General
(p. 108).

DISCOGRAPHIES

See the discographies listed under Latin America—General (p. 110).

JAMAICA

DIRECT INFORMATION SOURCES

Introductions and General Surveys

1184   Baxter, Ivy. **The Arts of an Island: the Development of the Culture and**
En   **of the Folk and Creative Arts in Jamaica, 1494-1962 (Independence).**
       Metuchen, N.J.: Scarecrow, 1970. xv, 407p. LC 71-14849. ISBN 0-
       8108-0303-8.   NX 527 B38
       Includes eight chapters with information on folk music, history of art
music (seventeenth to twentieth centuries), and dance. General bibliography;
index.

Folk Music and Folksong

1185   Lewin, Olive. "Jamaica's Folk Music." **Yearbook of the International**
En   **Folk Music Council**, 3 (1971), 15-22.   ML 1 I719
       Brief general survey with musical examples.

1186   Roberts, Helen H. "A Study of Folk Song Variants Based on Field Work
En   in Jamaica," **Journal of American Folk-Lore**, 38 (April-June 1925),
       149-216.   GR 1 J8
         Chase—1680
       Includes 95 musical transcriptions.

1187   Roberts, Helen H. "Possible Survivals of African Song in Jamaica." **Musical**
En   **Quarterly**, 12 (July 1926), 340-358.   ML 1 I725
         Chase—1678
       African influence in Jamaican folk music; musical examples.

1188   Roberts, Helen H. "Some Drums and Drum Rhythms of Jamaica." **Natural**
En   **History**, 24 (March-April 1924), 241-251.   QH 1 N13
         Chase—1679
       Includes musical examples.

1189   Jekyll, Walter. **Jamaican Song and Story.** London: David Nutt, 1907.
En   288p. (Publication of the Folk-Lore Society, 55) LC 7-23639.
         Chase—1676
       Anthology of songs and stories with a 10-page appendix discussing African
and English influences in Jamaican music. Musical transcriptions.

       See also *0862.*

GUIDES TO OTHER SOURCES

       See also the Guides to Other Sources listed under Latin America—General
(pp. 103-108).

Selective and Critical Guides

1190   Jamaica Library Service. **Jamaica: a Select Bibliography, 1900-1963.**
En   Kingston: Jamaica Independence Festival Committee, 1963. 115p.
       LC 70-235435.   Z 1541 J35
       Includes 14 music entries: books, articles, lecture, printed music. Locations
indicated, Name index.

       Stevenson, *A Guide to Caribbean Music History (0896)*, lists 19 index
entries for Jamaica. Chase, *A Guide to the Music of Latin America (0891)*, lists
nine entries for Jamaica, p. 247.

General Lists and Library Catalogs

      See *0897, 0901*.

Annual and Periodic Guides

1191   **Jamaican National Bibliography**, v.1– . 1968– ; new series, v.1 1975– .
En   Kingston: Institute of Jamaica, West India Reference Library, 1969– ,
       new series, 1976– . (annual) LC 72-3929.   Z 1549 I5
         Sheehy 76–AA747
       Continues *Jamaican Accessions* (1965-67). A cumulative volume for
1964-70 was published in 1973. Coverage of Jamaican publications and other
materials about Jamaica: books, pamphlets, articles, microfilms, classified list
of periodicals and newspapers. Music covered in "arts" section—includes books,
articles, printed music, song collections, even songs published in periodicals. New
series began in 1975 (numbered volume 1) using a classed Dewey arrangement,
with author-title index and list of publishers. Detailed bibliographic information.
Two music entries (song collections) in this volume. Publication to be continued
as a quarterly with annual cumulation.

      See also *0904, 0907*.

LISTS OF MUSIC

      See *1190, 1191*; see also the Lists of Music section under Latin America—
General (p. 108).

DISCOGRAPHIES

      See the discographies listed under Latin America—General (p. 110).

MEXICO

THE LANGUAGE OF MUSIC

See Volume I (especially entries *0040-0043*) for dictionaries of Spanish terms. Specifically Mexican terms (song and dance forms, instruments) may be found in the Mexican "OED":

Santamaria, Francisco J. *Diccionario de Mejicanismos*. México: Editorial Porrua, 1959.

Terms are defined and illustrated with a series of quotations.

For Indian musical terms:

1192　Stanford, Thomas. "A Linguistic Analysis of Music and Dance Terms from
En　　Three Sixteenth-Century Dictionaries of Mexican Indian Languages."
　　　Anuario interamericano de investigación musical, 2 (1966), 101-159.
　　　　　　　　　　　　　　　　　　　　　　　　　　　ML 1 T842
　　　A 15-page study of terms from sixteenth century dictionaries of the
Mixteco, Nahuatl, and Tarasco Indians, followed by vocabularies for each language.
Terms are arranged under general subject headings (*canto, danza, instrumentos*)
with Spanish definitions.

See also *0839*.

DIRECT INFORMATION SOURCES

Introductions and General Surveys

For *MGG* coverage, see *0842* and *1220*.

1193　Stevenson, Robert Murrell. **Music in Mexico, a Historical Survey**. New York:
En　　Crowell, 1952. 300p. LC 52-10379.　　　　ML 210 S8
　　　Chase—862a
　　　Excellent, documented study of comprehensive scope—all periods (pre-
Conquest to twentieth century) and all musical topics (folk, art, popular, and
religious music; instruments; opera; composers). Musical examples and extensive
11-page unannotated bibliography. Index.

Other historical surveys:

1194　Saldívar, Gabriel. **Historia de la música en Mexico (épocas pre-cortesiana**
Sp　　**y colonial)**. México: Secretaría de Educación Pública, Impreso en los
　　　talleres de la Editorial "Cultura," 1934. 324p. LC 36-5142.
　　　Chase—1723　　　　　　　　　　　　ML 210 S16 H5
　　　Good general historical survey covering Indian music, European art music
in Mexico (sixteenth to early nineteenth century) and folk music. Musical examples,
illustrations, nine-page classed, unannotated bibliography; no index.

1195   Galindo, Miguel. **Nociones de historia de la música mejicana.** Colima: Tip.
Sp   de "El Dragón," 1933. 636p. LC 35-24803.   ML 210 G3 N6
       Chase—1702
       Comprehensive historical survey, pre-Cortesian era to mid-nineteenth
century. Includes folk, art, popular and religious music. Photos, illustrations,
musical examples. Unannotated seven-page bibliography; index.

1196   Mayer-Serra, Otto. **Panorama de la música mexicana desde la independencia
Sp   hasta la actualidad.** México: El Colegio de México, 1941. 196p. LC 42-
       21498.   ML 210 M19 P2
       Chase—1706
       Documented general survey, nineteenth century through development of
musical nationalism. Coverage of popular, folk, and art music (religious, opera,
instrumental). Unannotated, seven-page classified bibliography; name index; index
of musical examples and plates.

1197   Baqueiro Fóster, Gerónimo. **La música en el período independiente.**
Sp   México: Secretaría de Educación Pública, Instituto Nacional de Bellas
       Artes, Dept. de Música, 1964. 607p. (Historia de la música en México,
       3) NUC 67-87311   ML 210 B22
       (Series number is ML 210 M49)
       General survey of art music in eighteenth and nineteenth centuries. Topics
covered include opera and musical theatre, music education, orchestra development,
concert activity, beginnings of musical nationalism. Illustrations, musical examples.
Unannotated two-page bibliography; index.

1198   Orta Velázquez, Guillermo. **Breve historia de la música en México.** México:
Sp   Librería de M. Porrúa, 1971. 495p. LC 72-598928.
                                        ML 210 O77
       Popular, journalistic-style historical narrative covering native Indian music,
colonial and modern eras. Many photographs, illustrations, musical examples. No
bibliography, footnotes or index.

       Two brief surveys:

1199   **México; cincuenta años de revolución.** México: Fondo de Cultura Económica,
Sp   1963. pp. 439-520.   F1234 M592
       Part 4, "La Cultura," includes two music chapters. Baqueiro Fóster,
Gerónimo. "La música," pp. 439-477—historical survey of art music (orchestras,
opera, education, concerts). Mendoza, Vicente T. "La música tradicional," pp.
481-520—survey of folk music (origins, forms) with musical examples and texts.

1200   Mayer-Serra, Otto. **El estado presente de la música en México.** (English
Sp/En translation by Frank Jellinek) Washington, D.C.: Pan American Union
       Music Division, 1946. 47p. LC 47-28452.   ML 210 M19 P2
       Chase—814a
       Text is 24 pages, given once in each language. Covers art and folk music,
with biographical information on composers Carlos Chávez, Manual Ponce, and
Silvestre Revueltas.

1201   Campos, Rubén M. **El folklore y la música mexicana; investigación acerca**
Sp   **de la cultura musical en México (1525-1925).** Publicaciones de la Secretaría
      de Educación Pública, México: Talleres gráficos de la nación, 1928. 351p.
      LC 28-24547.   ML 3570 C33
      Chase—2043
      Development of folk music and Mexican musical idiom. Concludes with
survey of musical life and culture in the mid-1920s (musicians, composers, orchestras,
conservatories). Many illustrations—photos of musicians, drawings, musical examples.
Appendix of 100 songs. No bibliography. Index of musical examples and illustrations,
no subject index.

      A brief survey of contemporary musical developments (composers, institu-
tions, trends) is included in Vinton, *Dictionary of Contemporary Music* (*0507*),
pp. 479-482.

Folk Music and Folksong

      For an historical survey, see the preceding entry, *1201*.

1202   Mendoza, Vicente T. **Panorama de la música tradicional de México.** México:
Sp   Impr. Universitaria, 1956. 257p. LC 57-2103.   ML 3570 M35
      Chase—726a
      Detailed analytical study of traditional song and dance music (folk,
popular). Text is 110 pages and includes musical examples and 15 bibliographies
(15-20 entries each, unannotated) on specific topics. Appendix includes 231
musical illustrations, their texts, and 49 illustrations.

1203   Mendoza, Vicente T. **La canción mexicana; ensayo de clasificación y**
Sp   **antología.** México: Instituto de Investigaciones Estéticas, Universidad
      Nacional Autónoma de México, 1961. 671p. LC 62-4632.
                                                 ML 3572 M5 M5
      Introductory essay of 124 pages discusses categories and classification
of Mexican folk song, including Indian, Spanish, native Mexican, and popular
songs. Anthology of 314 songs; 11 illustrations; index of songs.

1204   Mendoza, Vicente T. **El romance español y el corrido mexicano; estudio**
Sp   **comparativo.** México: Ediciones de la Universidad Nacional Autónoma,
      1939. xviii, 833p. LC 40-13710.   ML 3570 M36 R5
      Chase—2023
      Text of 230 pages studies the origin and development of the Mexican ballad
(*corrido*) from the Spanish *romance*; 23 illustrations (photos, drawings, musical
examples) and 600-page anthology of *corridos* and *romances*. Index, no bibliography.

1205   Stanford, E. Thomas. "The Mexican **Son." International Folk Music**
En   **Council Yearbook,** 4 (1972), 66-86.   ML 1 I719
      Study of a particular song and dance form; instruments, musical analysis,
texts. Musical examples, 14 bibliographic footnotes.

1206   México (City). Instituto Nacional de Bellas Artes. Departamento de Música.
Sp   **Investigación folklórica en México.** Introd. y notas: Baltasar Samper.
Expediciones de investigación: Francisco Domínguez, Luis Sandi y Roberto
Téllez Giron. México: INBA, Departamento de Música, Sección de
Investigaciones Musicales, 1962, 1964. 2v. (651p., 384p.) LC 63-24080.
                                       ML 3570 M43 I6
Based on extended field research in 1931, 1937, and 1939. Maps, photos,
extended musical examples, transcriptions. Material on dances, instruments, fiestas,
song texts. Bibliography; many indexes–names, topics, instruments, illustrations.

Stevenson, *Music in Aztec and Inca Territory (0875)*, is a scholarly and
authoritative source for coverage of Indian music.

The remaining entries in this section deal with Indian music. Their emphasis
is reconstruction of the pre-Conquest musical culture:

1207   Martí, Samuel. **Canto, danza y música precortesianos.** México: Fondo de
Sp   Cultura Económica, 1961. 379p. LC 62-30284.
                                       F 1219 M38
Historical, documented narrative with much material (text, illustrations)
taken from the first edition of *1227*. Musical examples, 180 pictures, eight-page
unannotated bibliography. Name and topic index. For a critical review by Robert
Stevenson, see *Ethnomusicology* 6 (Sept. 1962), 230-232.

1208   Castellanos, Pablo. **Horizontes de la música precortesiana.** México: Fondo
Sp   de Cultura Económica, 1970. 153p. LC 71-543654.
                                       ML 210.2 C35
Popular narrative survey of instruments, forms, and musical systems.
Unannotated bibliography of 50 entries; four-page glossary of Maya and Nahuatl
terms; 23-item discography. Illustrations and index of illustrations.

1209   Boilés, Charles. "The Pipe and Tabor in Mesoamerica." **Anuario**
En   **interamericano de investigación musical,** 2 (1966), 43-74.
                                       ML 1 T842
Documented study of Indian flute and drum music. Mechanical aspects
of the instruments; detailed musical analysis. Photos, drawing, musical examples.

Popular Music

1210   Campos, Rubén M. **El folklore musical de las ciudades; investigación acerca**
Sp   **de la música mexicana para bailar y cantar.** Mexico: Secretaría de Educación
       Pública, 1930. 467p. LC 41-6447rev.   ML 3530 C3
       Chase–1917
Survey of song and dance music of the nineteenth and early twentieth
centuries. Many photographs of musicians. Index of illustrations; 85 musical texts
(dances in piano arrangement). No index or bibliography.

1211   Geijerstam, Claes Af. **Popular Music in Mexico.** Albuquerque: University
En   of New Mexico Press, 1976. LC 75-17373. ISBN 0-8263-0414-1.

                     ML 3570 G44

Prepared from author's doctoral dissertation (Uppsala University).
Deals with traditional forms and urban popular music. Of questionable authority—
based on secondary sources and 12 informants. Bibliography, index.

See also coverage of this topic in *1193, 1195, 1196, 1201, 1203.*

Opera and Vocal Music

1212   Olavarria y Ferrari, Enrique de. **Reseña histórica del teatro en México,**
Sp   **1538-1911.** 3d ed. . . . puesta al día de 1911 a 1961. México: Editorial
Porrua, 1961. 5v. (xxx, 3,680p.) LC 78-223202.

                     PN 2311 O43

Comprehensive, five-volume work with much coverage of opera and musical
theatre. Photos, index of illustrations. Volume 5 has chronology of performances,
1911-1961. Separate, comprehensive 290-page index volume, with indexes of names,
organizations, theatres, publications, geographic names. (The index, a sixth volume,
has LC card number 75-391772.)

1213   Cardon, Hugh Frederick. **A Survey of Twentieth-century Mexican Art Song.**
En   Ph.D. dissertation, University of Oregon, 1970. 106p. **Dissertation Abstracts**
31A (1971), 5444. Microfilm ed., Ann Arbor: University Microfilms,
71-10703.

Organized by composer with brief biographical information and description
of works in art song medium. Composers are in chronological arrangement within
style classifications. Includes early twentieth century composers and modern avant
garde. List of compositions for each composer, in alphabetical order, with name of
poet, range, publisher, date. Musical examples; unannotated five-page bibliography.

Church and Religious Music

1214   Estrada, Jesús. **Música y músicos de la época virreinal.** México: Secretaría
Sp   de Educación Pública, 1973. 165p. LC 74-228332.

                     ML 210 E8

Survey of colonial-era church music activities, based on Cathedral archives.

1215   Stevenson, Robert. "Mexico City Cathedral Music: 1600-1750." **The**
En   **Americas,** 21 (Oct. 1964), 111-135.   E 11 A4

Spanish version:

1215a   Stevenson, Robert. "La música en la catedral de México: 1600-1750."
Sp   **Revista musical chilena,** 19 (abril-junio 1964), 11-31.

                     ML 5 R238

Detailed, thoroughly documented reconstruction of colonial-era musical
activity of the Mexico City cathedral.

Historical Studies, Chronologies, Contemporary Narratives

Studies of pre-Conquest Indian music have been entered under Folk Music and Folksong (p. 179). See entries *1207-1209*. See also Stevenson, *Music in Aztec and Inca Territory* (*0875*).

1216   Stevenson, Robert. "Mexican Colonial Music Manuscripts Abroad." **Notes,**
En   29 (Dec. 1972), 203-214.   ML 27 U5 M695
       Description of items in the Newberry Library, Chicago, with biographical
information on composers, especially Juan de Lienas, Fabian Ximeno, and Manuel
de Zumaya.

1217   Pulido, Esperanza. **La mujer mexicana en la música (hasta la tercera**
Sp   **decada del siglo XX).** México: Ediciones de la Revista Bellas Artes, 1958.
       126p. LC 60-17129.   ML 210 P8
       Documented study with bibliographic footnotes. A historical survey, pre-
Conquest to the 1930s, covering the participation of women in folk and art music.
Nineteenth and twentieth century women treated in brief biographical sketch format.
No name or topic index; 16 pages of photos and illustrations.

1218   Godoy, Susan. **Mexican Music from 1920-1953.** Ph.D. dissertation, Radcliffe
En   College, 1961. 3v. (Call number Rad. T/G589 in the Harvard University
       Archives, Pusey Library, Harvard University.)
       Text (first volume) is chronologically organized survey of stylistic evolution;
based partially on personal interviews with several Mexican composers. Classified
bibliography (bibliographies, lists of music, books and articles) but no index. List
of compositions consulted. Volumes 2 and 3 are musical examples.

1219   Malmström, Dan. **Introduction to Twentieth Century Mexican Music.**
En   Uppsala: Akad. avh. Uppsala Univ., 1974. 167p. LC 74-175179.   ISBN
       91-7222-050-3.   ML 210.5 M25
       Includes discography (pp. 153-156) and bibliography (pp. 157-161).

Regional and Local Histories

1220   Stevenson, Robert. "Mexiko Stadt." **MGG** (*0058*), supplement.
Ge   Authoritative, documented article of four columns.

1221   Romero, Jesús C. **La música en Zacatecas y los músicos zacatecanos.**
Sp   México: Univ. Nacional Autónoma de México, 1963. 202p. LC 63-48400.
                                                                   ML 210.8 Z11 R6
       A 90-page collection of brief biographical sketches (one to three pages
each, with lists of works) followed by a 75-page chronology of musical events,
1700-1920, in paragraph format. Notes on music education and religious music;
no coverage of folk music. Bibliography of the author's publications; no index.

1222 Ruiz Carvalho de Baqueiro, Eloisa. **Tradiciones, folklore, música y músicos**
Sp   **de Campeche.** Campeche: Publicaciones del Gobierno del Estado de
      Campeche, 1970. 141p. LC 71-542133.   ML 3570 R859
      Popular survey covering folk, art, and popular music. Photos and musical
examples; unannotated three-page bibliography.

Directories

1223 Pan American Union. Music Section. **México.** Washington, 1956. xi, 69p.
Sp   (Directorio musical de la América Latina. Musical Directory of Latin
      America) LC PA 57-124.
      Listing of musical institutions, including conservatories, orchestras,
publishers, periodicals, concert halls, and radio stations. Some listings of personnel.

Periodicals and Yearbooks

1224 **Revista musical mexicana.** v.1-6, 1941-1946. México. (monthly)
Sp   Articles on Mexican musicians and general music topics. Musical news—
concerts, personalities, performing organizations, conferences, necrology.

·1225 **Nuestra música.** año 1-7, 1946-1952. México. LC 51-26729.
Sp   ML 5 N85
      Edited by Adolfo Salazar, Jesús Bal y Gay, and Rodolfo Halffter. Fine,
serious publication; documented articles on Mexican and general music topics.
Musical examples and drawings.

1226 **Heterofonía: revista musical bimestral.** v.1– . 1968– . México. (bimonthly)
Sp   LC 64-10. ISSN 0018-1137.
      Brief serious articles on Mexican and general music topics; musical news;
book reviews. English abstracts of articles. Indexed in *The Music Index* (*0289*).

Instruments

1227 Martí, Samuel. **Instrumentos musicales precortesianos.** 2d ed. México:
Sp   Instituto Nacional de Antropología e Historia, 1968. 378p. LC 79-403059.
                                                      ML 482 M3 1968
      (1st ed. 1955) Description of Indian instruments, some with scale and
range. Photos, some color; musical examples; no documentation in text. Name
and topic index; three-page unannotated bibliography.

      See also *1209* and *0873*.

BIOGRAPHICAL SOURCES

1229　Grial, Hugo de. **Músicos mexicanos. Con un apéndice sobre el orígen e**
Sp　**historia de las más famosas canciones revolucionarias y populares de**
México. México: Editorial Diana, 1965. 275p. LC 66-38410.
ML 385 G85
About 250, popular-style biographical sketches of eighteenth, nineteenth, and twentieth century musicians. No lists of works or pictures. No bibliography or index.

1230　Alvarez Coral, Juan. **Compositores mexicanos.** México: Editores Asociados.
Sp　S. de R. L., 1971. 195p. LC 72-219346.　ML 390 A46
Twenty-five biographies (one to three pages in length) of deceased nineteenth and twentieth century composers of art and popular music. Portraits, musical examples; unannotated seven-page bibliography.

1231　Moncada García, Francisco. **Pequeñas biografías de grandes músicos**
Sp　**mexicanos.** México: Ediciones Framong, 1966. 291p. LC 67-40661.
ML 385 M6
Sixty biographical sketches (three to eight pages)–popular style, with pictures. Mentions some titles, but no lists of works. Name index; unannotated bibliography of 24 items.

See also biographical information in entries *1200, 1201, 1213, 1216, 1217, 1221.*

GUIDES TO OTHER SOURCES

See also the Guides to Other Sources section under Latin America–General (pp. 103-108).

Selective and Critical Guides

1232　Huerta, Jorge A. **A Bibliography of Chicano and Mexican Dance, Drama,**
En　**and Music.** Oxnard, Calif.: Colegio Quetzalcoatl, 1972. 59p. LC 72-176491.
ML 120 M5 H8
Separate music section arranged under headings "Mexican, Pre-Columbian, Aztlan." Books, journals; records included for "Mexican" section also.

1233　Moedana Navarro, Gabriel. "Biobibliografía del profesor Vicente T.
Sp　Mendoza." in **25 Estudios de Folklore: homenaje a Vicente T. Mendoza**
y Virginia Rodríguez Rivera. México: Universidad Nacional Autónoma
de México, Instituto de Investigaciones Estéticas, 1971. pp. 9-55.
GR 70 V4
Unannotated bibliography of 355 entries in chronological order; includes reviews.

Chase, *A Guide to the Music of Latin America (0891)* includes approximately 600 entries for Mexico, pp. 248-316.

Annual and Periodic Lists

The following bibliographic publications all follow a classed Dewey subject arrangement, with music in class 78 or under the heading *Bellas Artes*.

The source for current bibliography:

1234 **Bibliografía mexicana**, 1– . enero-feb. 1967– . México: Biblioteca Nacional.
Sp   (bimonthly)   Z1411 B53
     Sheehy 76–AA783
Includes music books and scores, two to three per bimonthly installment for 1970. Author, title, subject index.

Early attempt at publication of a national bibliography:

1235 **Anuario bibliográfico mexicano.** 1931-1933 and 1940-41/42. México:
Sp   Secretaria de Relaciones Exteriores, 1932-1934, 1942-1944. LC 32-
     13182rev.   Z 1411 A62
     Sheehy 76–AA769
Includes music books and scores. Volume for 1941 had seven entries, that for 1942 had 11.

After a 25-year interval, publication of an annual bibliographic record was resumed:

1236 **Anuario bibliográfico**, v.1– . 1958– . México: Biblioteca Nacional, 1967– .
Sp   (annual) LC 72-452004.   Z 1411 M5
     Sheehy 76–AA785
Copies examined had no scores. Volume for 1961 had 11 music books; that of 1962 (published in 1974) had nine. Title and author index.

LISTS OF MUSIC

Stevenson, *Renaissance and Baroque Musical Sources in the Americas (0914)*, includes descriptions of the contents of many Mexican musical archives (cathedrals, libraries, private collections).

1237 Spiess, Lincoln; Stanford, Thomas. **An Introduction to Certain Mexican**
En   **Musical Archives.** Detroit: Information Coordinators, 1969. 90p. LC 73-
     12866.   ML 136 M49 S7
Preliminary report from scholars preparing a full catalog of several music archives. Summary of the contents (colonial music and some nineteenth-century works), list of composers, and supplement with transcriptions and illustrations.

See also information on compositions in entries *1213, 1216, 1218, 1221,*
1234, 1235, and the Lists of Music section under Latin America—General (p. 108).

DISCOGRAPHIES

1238 Stanford, Thomas. **Catálogo de grabaciones del laboratorio de sonido del**
Sp **Museo Nacional de Antropología.** México: Instituto Nacional de Antropología
e Historia, 1968. 471p. LC 68-109009. ML 155.32 S73
Classified catalog of record holdings of the Instituto; arranged by language
and subject. "The lack of table of contents, indexes, divisions into chapters or
geographical origin of the materials, and systematic cross-references make use of
the catalogue quite difficult" [*Handbook of Latin American Studies,* 32 (1970),
p. 480].

1239 Mexico (City). Instituto Nacional de Bellas Artes. Departamento de Música.
Sp **Música folklórica mexicana; inventorio de discos grabados por la sección**
de investigaciones musicales del I.N.B.A. México, 1952. 78p.
Folk music recordings, listed by title of song, with information on
instruments, place, and date of recording; 924 entries.

See also information on recordings in entries *1208, 1219, 1232,* and the
Discographies section under Latin America—General (p. 110).

NETHERLANDS ANTILLES

1240 Boskaljon, Rudolf Frederik Willem. **Honderd jaar muziekleven op Curaçao.**
Du Assen, Netherlands: VanGorcum, 1958. 188p. LC 59-29971.
ML 207 C87 B7
Chronology, 1850-1955, of musical activity and events. Paragraph summary
of pre-1850 musical activity. No bibliography or index; no illustrations or musical
examples. For a four-page English summary, see *0896,* p. 7.

Stevenson, *A Guide to Caribbean Music History* (*0896*) lists eight
index entries for Curaçao.

NICARAGUA

THE LANGUAGE OF MUSIC

See the Language of Music section under Latin America—General (p. 94).

DIRECT INFORMATION SOURCES

Introductions and General Surveys

1241 Delgadillo, Luis A. "La música indígena y colonial en Nicaragua." **Revista**
Sp   **de estudios musicales**, 1 (abril 1950), 43-60.   ML 5 R203
      Chase—877a
      Brief survey of folk music (song and dance forms, instruments) and history
of musical life in capital city Managua. Musical examples.

   See also *0848*.

Folk Music and Folksong

1242 Mejía Sánchez, Ernesto. **Romances y corridos nicaragüenses**. México:
Sp   Imprenta Universitaria, 1946. 123p. LC 47-22918.
                                                          PQ 7516 M4
      Anthology of song texts with 26-page survey on the song forms and their
historical background.

BIOGRAPHICAL SOURCES

1243 Vega Miranda, Gilberto. **Breviario del recuerdo; antología de músicos**
Sp   **nicaragüenses**. Managua, Nicaragua: Secretaría de Educación Pública,
      1945. 212p. LC 48-17864.   ML 220 V43
      Chase—883a, 887a
      Contains 44 two- to three-page biographies of Nicaraguan musicians (not
arranged in any alphabetical or chronological order). Photos, some musical examples;
appendix of Nicaraguan popular songs. No bibliography or index.

   See also *0848* and the biographical sources listed under Latin America—
General (p. 103).

GUIDES TO OTHER SOURCES

   See also the Guides to Other Sources section under Latin America—General
(pp. 103-108).

Selective and Critical Guides

   Chase, *A Guide to the Music of Latin America* (*0891*), lists 29 entries for
Nicaragua, pp. 317-319.

LISTS OF MUSIC

See *0848*; see also the Lists of Music section under Latin America—General (p. 108).

DISCOGRAPHIES

See the Discographies section under Latin America—General (p. 110).

PANAMA

THE LANGUAGE OF MUSIC

See the Language of Music section under Latin America—General (p. 94).

DIRECT INFORMATION SOURCES

Introduction and General Surveys

See *0848*.

Folk Music and Folksong

1244   Garay, Narciso. **Tradiciones y cantares de Panamá. Ensayo folklórico.**
Sp   Bruxelles: Presses de l'expansion, 1930. 203p. LC 32-7559.
     Chase—2285   ML 3572 G2
     First-person narrative recounting first-hand observations of folk musical
culture. Numerous musical examples, photos; no bibliography or index.

1245   Zárate, Manuel F. **Tambor y socavón; un estudio comprensivo de dos temas
Sp   del folklore panameño, y de sus implicaciones históricas y culturales.**
Panamá: Ediciones del Ministerio de Educación, Dirección Nacional de
Cultura, 1968. 408p. LC 73-380629.   ML 3572 Z37
     Survey of folk music; song and dance forms, instruments. Photos, song
texts: two-page, unannotated bibliography; no index.

1246   Schaeffer, Myron. "El tamborito." **Boletín del instituto de investigaciones
Sp   folklóricas,** 1 (julio 1944), 1-29. (Panamá: Universidad Interamericana.)
     Chase—894a
     Study of a particular dance form, with texts and musical examples.

1247   Schaeffer, Myron. "La mejorana, canción típica panameña." **Boletín del**
Sp   **instituto de investigaciones folklóricas,** 1 (nov. 1944), 1-50. (Panama,
        Universidad Interamericana.)
        Chase—895a
        Detailed study of a specific song form; musical examples.
        English version: "The Mejorana: a typical song of Panama." *Canadian*
Music Journal, 4 (Spring 1960), 4-22.

1248   Densmore, Frances. **Music of the Tule Indians of Panama.** Washington:
En   Smithsonian Institution, 1926. (Smithsonian miscellaneous collections,
        vol. 77 no. 11) 39p. LC 26-26378.   ML 220 P2 D5
                                     also F 1565.3 M9 D3
        Based on author's study of eight Tule Indians visiting in Washington, D.C.
Covers vocal and instrumental music, songs, and instruments. Five photos, musical
examples; no bibliography or index.

        See also Espinosa, Luis Carlos; Pinzón Urrea, Jesús. "La heterofonía en la
música de los indios cunas del Darién," in *0853*, pp. 119-129.

Directories

1249   Pan American Union. Music Section. **Panamá.** Washington, 1956. 18p.
Sp/En   (Directorio musical de la América Latina. Musical directory of Latin
        America.) LC PA 56-125.   ML 21 P24
        Directory of musical institutions, organizations, performance ensembles,
theatres, faculty members, schools, and radio stations. Index.

Instruments

1250   Zárate, Manuel F. "Tambores de Panamá." **Folklore americano,** 11-12
Sp   (1963-1964), 5-21.   GR 1 F327
        Illustrated study of Panamanian drums.

BIOGRAPHICAL SOURCES

        See *0848*; see also the biographical sources listed under Latin America—
General (p. 103).

GUIDES TO OTHER SOURCES

        See also the Guides to Other Sources under Latin America—General
(pp. 103-108).

Selective and Critical Guides

Chase, *A Guide to the Music of Latin America* (*0891*) includes 15 entries for Panama, pp. 320-321.

LISTS OF MUSIC

See *0848*; see also the Lists of Music section under Latin America—General (p. 108).

DISCOGRAPHIES

See the Discographies section under Latin America—General (p. 110).

PARAGUAY

THE LANGUAGE OF MUSIC

See the Language of Music section under Latin America—General (p. 94).

DIRECT INFORMATION SOURCES

Introductions and General Surveys

1251 Boettner, Juan Max. **Música y músicos del Paraguay.** Asunción: Edición
Sp   de Autores Paraguayos Asociados, 1956. 294p. LC 57-44877.

   Chase—900a   ML 239 P3 B6

General historical survey including Indian and folk music, dance, instruments. Chapters on "guitars and guitarrists," "harps and harpists," etc., with paragraph-length biographical sketches. Also a 28-page biographical dictionary with brief identifications. Musical examples, drawings, photos. Unannotated bibliography of 294 entries; no index. Certainly the "all-purpose" reference source for Paraguayan music.

Collections of Essays, Articles, etc.

1252 Cardozo Ocampo, Maurício. **Mis bodas de oro con el folklore paraguayo**
Sp   **(memorias de un Pychäi).** Asunción, 1972. 316p. LC 72-364840.

                                      ML 239 P3 C4

Mostly a collection of song texts, with discographical information cited for many. Also some miscellaneous short essays (about two pages long) on various musical topics; native musical idiom, the Paraguayan harp, performing groups, and biographies of musicians. Many photos; no musical examples, no index, no bibliography.

Folk Music and Folksong

Two books by Alberto Dalmidio Baccay pertain to Paraguay and north-eastern Argentina. They are listed in the chapter on Latin America. See entry *0864*, *Música regional y metodo*; and entry *0865*, *Vitalidad expresiva de la música guaraní*.

BIOGRAPHICAL SOURCES

1253 **Biografía de nuestros artistas.** (n.p.), 1959. 49p. LC 64-37691.
Sp   ML 385 B62
   Contains two- to five-page biographies of nine Paraguayan musicians. Photos, no bibliography, index, or table of contents.

   Entries *1251*, *1252* deserve mention as biographical sources as well.

GUIDES TO OTHER SOURCES

   Chase, *A Guide to the Music of Latin America* (*0891*) lists 22 entries for Paraguay, pp. 322-325.
   See also the Guides to Other Sources section under Latin America–General (pp. 103-108).

LISTS OF MUSIC

   See the Lists of Music section under Latin America–General (p. 108).

DISCOGRAPHIES

   See *1252*; see also the discographies listed under Latin America–General (p. 110).

PERU

THE LANGUAGE OF MUSIC

   See the Language of Music section under Latin America–General (p. 94).

DIRECT INFORMATION SOURCES

Introductions and General Surveys

1254 Raygada, Carlos. "Guía musical del Perú." **Fénix, Revista de la Biblioteca**
Sp   **Nacional,** 12 (1956-1957), 3-77, 13 (1963), 1-82, 14 (1964), 3-95.
                                                                    Z 761 F35

Fine comprehensive reference work, mostly biographical coverage of performers, scholars, educators, and composers (with list of works) but also organizations, institutions, periodicals, and historical topics (e.g., *capella*, *conciertos*, *capilla virreinal*). Alphabetical arrangement—an encyclopedia format. Entries vary in length from brief paragraph to several pages. Part 1: A—Camperós, José de. Part 2: Campo, Toribio—Many, Juanita. Part 3: Marañon español—Vega.

1255   Raygada, Carlos. "Panorama musical del Perú." **Boletín latino-americano**
Sp   **de música**, 2 (1936) 169-214.   ML 199 B64
       Chase—2317
       Documented article with information on Peruvian music history, song and dance forms, Indian music, musical institutions and activities.

Collections of Essays, Articles, etc.

1256   Stevenson, Robert Murrell. **The Music of Peru: Aboriginal and Viceroyal**
En   **Epochs.** Washington: Pan American Union, 1960. xii, 331p. LC 60-62370.
       Chase—962a   ML 236 S8
       Collection of thoroughly documented, detailed historical studies covering ancient Peruvian instruments, Inca music instruction, colonial church music, early opera, early Peruvian folk music and music in colonial Bolivia ("high Peru"—see annotation for *0971*). Unannotated bibliography of 17 pages; 100-page musical supplement and musical examples; index.

Folk Music and Folksong

Peruvian folk music has been studied by Raoul and Marguerite d'Harcourt; see entries *0873*, *0874*. See also Stevenson, "Early Peruvian Folk Music," in entry *1256*, and studies of pre-colonial Indian music and instruments under Historical Studies . . . (p. 193) and Instruments (p. 194).

1257   Holzmann, Rodolfo. **De la trifonía a la heptafonía en la música tradicional**
Sp   **peruana.** Lima: Federación Universitária de San Marcos, 1968. 51p.
       LC 71-200927.   ML 3575 P4 H64
       Reprinted from *San Marcos; revista de cultura general, segunda época*, 8 (marzo-mayo 1968), 5-51. AS 88 SE. Subtitled "una evaluación analítica de 21 melodías del folklore musical del Perú." Analytical study with 59 musical examples and six unannotated bibliographic references.

1258   Romero, Emilia. **El romancero tradicional en el Perú.** México: Colegio de
Sp   México, 1952. 136p. LC 52-68287.   PQ 8380 R6
       Historical survey of the *romance* form. Numerous musical examples; bibliographic footnotes; index.

1259   Romero, Fernando. "De la 'samba' de África a la 'marinera' del Perú."
Sp   **Estudios afrocubanos**, 4 (1940), 82-120.   F 1789 N3 E8
        Chase—2379
        Traces evolution of *zamacueca* to twentieth century *marinera*, popular
Peruvian dance form.

Opera and Vocal Music

1260   Stevenson, Robert Murrell. **Foundations of New World Opera, with a**
En   **Transcription of the Earliest Extant American Opera, 1701**. Lima:
        Ediciones CULTURA, 1973. 300p.   ML 1717 S83
        Historical study of early Peruvian opera, including a study and transcription
of Tomás de Torrejón y Velasco's opera *La púrpura de la rosa*.

1261   Claro, Samuel. "Música dramática en el Cuzco durante el siglo XVIII y
Sp   catálogo de manuscritos de música del seminario de San Antonio Abad
        (Cuzco, Perú) **Yearbook for Inter-American Musical Research**, 5 (1969),
        1-48.   ML 1 T842
        Scholarly, documented 23-page study of colonial-era musical theatre in
Cuzco followed by 16-page classed catalog of music manuscripts in the Cuzco
seminary of San Antonio Abad. Musical examples.

See also the opera chapter in *1256*. See *1270*.

Church and Religious Music

1262   Sás Orchassal, Andrés. **La música en la Catedral de Lima durante el**
Sp   **Virreinato**. Lima: Universidad Nacional Mayor de San Marcos; Instituto
        Nacional de Cultura, 1971-1972. 3v. (280p. 232p. 460p.) LC 74-226756.
                                                          ML 3017 P47 S27
        Posthumous publication of a monumental historical work. Detailed study
of music and musicians of the Lima Cathedral in the colonial era. Volume one is in
narrative format with appendix of three-page unannotated bibliography and
chronology, 1565-1813. Second and third volumes are a biographical dictionary;
name index in each volume.

        A short summary of this material is found in *0878a*: Sás' article "La vida
musical en la Catedral de Lima durante la colonia," pp. 8-53.

See also *1256*.

Historical Studies, Chronologies, Contemporary Narratives

        Studies of Inca musical culture have been entered under Latin America.
See entries *0873, 0874*, and *0875*. Studies of ancient Peruvian instruments are
entered under Instruments (p. 194). Stevenson's *The Music of Peru; Aboriginal*

and Viceroyal Epochs (*1256*) covers ancient and colonial topics. Colonial-era opera and church music are treated under those headings (see p. 193).

1263   Castro Franco, Julio. **Música y arqueología.** Lima: Editorial Eterna, 1961.
Sp   44p. NUC 69-68358.   ML 3575 P4 C36
        Pre-Incaic and Inca music. Based on archeological discoveries—mostly instruments, also pictorial works. Ten-page section of photographs: instruments, artifacts. A summary of the author's longer work by this title (not yet published).

1264   Castro, José. "Sistema pentafónico en la música indígena precolonial del
Sp   Perú." **Boletín latino-americano de música,** 4 (1938), 835-850.
        Chase—2393   ML 199 B64
        Scholarly article with documentation and musical examples. Chase notes that the article was written in 1908.

Regional and Local Histories

1265   Stevenson, Robert Murrell. "Cuzco." **MGG** (*0058*), Supplement A-Dy,
Ge   columns 1673-1678.
        Comprehensive historical survey, 1043 to the present. Unannotated bibliography of one-half column.

1266   Stevenson, Robert Murrell. "Lima." **MGG** (*0058*), Supplement Hy-Lö,
Ge   columns 1138-1139.
        Authoritative historical survey, 1535 to the present. Unannotated bibliography of one-fourth column.

        See also *1261, 1262*.

Instruments

        See Stevenson, "Ancient Peruvian Instruments," in *1256*.

1267   Jiménez Borja, Arturo. "Instrumentos musicales peruanos." **Revista del**
Sp   **museo nacional,** 19-20 (1950-1951), 37-190.   F 3401 L56
        Chase—920a

        Also published as a separate:

        Lima. Museo de la Cultura Peruana. Colección Arturo Jiménez Borja. **Instrumentos musicales del Perú.** Lima, 1951. LC A52-10651.
                                                            ML 486 P4 L5
        Text of about 40 pages is scholarly article, followed by 100 pages of photos and drawings. Organization is by instrument classification (e.g., *cordófono, aerófono*, etc.). No index or bibliography. Includes modern and ancient instruments.

1268   Mead, Charles Williams. "The Musical Instruments of the Inca."
En   **Anthropological Papers of the American Museum of Natural History**, 15
        pt. 3 (1924), 313-347.   GN 2 A27
        Chase—2446
        Organized according to instrument classification (percussion, wind
instruments, etc.). Many plates, drawings, and musical examples.

1269   Sás Orchassal, Andrés. "Ensayo sobre la música nazca." **Boletín latino-**
Sp   **americano de música**, 4 (1938), 221-234.
        Chase—2422
        Scholarly study with musical examples and photos of instruments.

See also information on instruments in *1263, 0873, 0874*, and *0875*.

Miscellaneous

1270   Prieto, Juan Sixto. "El Perú en la música escénica." **Fénix, Revista de la**
Sp   **Biblioteca Nacional**, 9 (1953), 278-351.   Z 761 F35
        Chronological listing of operas, ballets, and other dramatic musical works
with Peruvian subject matter, 1658-1927. Bibliographic information and performance
history; mostly European composers and productions. Appendix of other vocal and
instrumental works. Many illustrations. Title, composer, and librettist indexes;
bibliography of 90 sources consulted.

BIOGRAPHICAL SOURCES

1271   Barbacci, Rodolfo. "Apuntes para un diccionario biográfico musical
Sp   peruano." **Fenix, Revista de la Biblioteca Nacional**, 6 (1949), 414-510.
        Chase—942a   Z 761 F35
        Biographical dictionary; most entries are of paragraph length, although
some are longer and quote texts of documents and programs. Includes Peruvian
musicians (giving lists of works) and visiting artists (coverage of Peruvian activities
only). Includes information from some primary sources subsequently destroyed
by a fire in the National Library.

See also *1254, 1262*.

GUIDES TO OTHER SOURCES

        See also the Guides to Other Sources under Latin America—General
(pp. 103-108).

Selective and Critical Guides

        Chase, *A Guide to the Music of Latin America (0891)*, includes 230 entries
for Peru, pp. 326-345.

Annual and Periodic Guides

1272   **Anuario bibliográfico peruano**, v.1– . 1943– . Lima: Biblioteca Nacional,
Sp   1945– . (irregular) LC 45-21745.   Z 1851 A5
         Sheehy 76–AA825
         Frequency varies; triennial since 1955. Classed arrangement, including
music scores, articles, books. Lists Peruvian imprints and foreign imprints (on
Peruvian topics) in separate sections. Periodical section also. Volume for 1964-1966
listed 52 music items, including concert programs, article reprints, scores, school
texts, pamphlets.

LISTS OF MUSIC

   Stevenson, *Renaissance and Baroque Musical Sources in the Americas*
(*0914*), includes description of musical archives in Cuzco and Lima.

   See also *1261* and the Lists of Music section under Latin America–General
(p. 108).

DISCOGRAPHIES

See the Discographies section under Latin America–General (p. 110).

PUERTO RICO

THE LANGUAGE OF MUSIC

See the Language of Music section under Latin America–General (p. 94).

DIRECT INFORMATION SOURCES

Introductions and General Surveys

1273   Muñoz Santaella, María Luis. **La música en Puerto Rico; panorama**
Sp   **histórico-cultural.** Sharon, Conn.: Troutman Press, 1966. 167p.
         LC 67-546.   ML 207 P8 M8
         General survey, covering Spanish and American influences, music of the
nineteenth and twentieth centuries, religious music, opera, folk music. Brief
biographical sketches of composers and musicians; lists of opera casts. Based on
author's Ed.D. dissertation (Teachers College, Columbia University, 1958).
Musical examples; five-page unannotated bibliography; no index.

1274   Bloch, Peter. **La-le-lo-lai; Puerto Rican Music and Its Performers.** New York:
En   Plus Ultra Educational Publishers, 1973. 197p. LC 73-157051.
                                                                        ML 207 P8 B6
        Brief popular style survey covering folk, popular, and art music. Chapters
on popular musicians. Name index; unannotated three-page bibliography listing
some records. Photos.

1275   Callejo Ferrer, Fernando. **Música y músicos puertorriqueños.** Reimpresión–
Sp   San Juan: Editorial Coqui, 1971. 283p.
        Chase–2479
        (original ed., 1915: *Música y músicos portorrigueños.* 316p.). Consists
of a 40-page historical survey (1660 to 1914); 40-page treatment of folk and
popular forms; and 200-page biographical dictionary in classified arrangement
(e.g., instrumentalists, singers, composers, etc.). Index.

        The next two items are brief surveys in general works on Puerto Rico:

1276   Ribes Tovar, Federico. **Enciclopedia puertorriqueña ilustrada. The Puerto**
Sp/En **Rican Heritage Encyclopedia.** San Juan: Plus Ultra Educational Publishers,
        1970. 3v.   F 1958 R5
        Some musical information in each volume. Volume one has biographies of
three musicians, pp. 168-182. Volume 2, biographical information on Puerto Rican
musicians in New York City, pp. 199-220. Volume 3 includes section "Music and
Folklore of Puerto Rico," pages 207-229: survey of song and dance forms, instruments
and paragraph biographies of eight Puerto Rican composers; four illustrations. Parallel
English and Spanish texts. No music bibliography.

1277   Babín, María Teresa. "El folklore y las bellas artes." In **La Cultura de Puerto**
Sp   **Rico.** San Juan: Instituto de Cultura Puertorriqueña, 1970. pp. 77-126.
                                                                        F 1960 B28
        Includes a short survey of folk music, dance forms, eminent composers and
performers, musical history, and musical life.

Folk Music and Folksong

1278 ·   López Cruz, Francisco. **La música folklorica de Puerto Rico.** Sharon, Conn.:
Sp   Troutman Press, 1967. xi, 202p. LC 68-949.   ML 3565 P8 L7
        Attractive, popular-style book that is essentially an anthology of song and
dance genres with informative and descriptive background information on individual
forms. Includes secular and religious music. Extensive musical examples; 51 bibliographic references; index of song titles.

1279   Puerto Rico. University. Social Science Research Center. **Estudio etnográfico**
Sp   **de la cultura popular de Puerto Rico; Morovis: vista parcial del folklore de**
        Puerto Rico. Pedro C. Escabi, editor. San Juan, 1970. xiv, 380p. NUC
        73-75607.
        Folk music forms and instruments, pp. 294-358. Musical examples,
phonodisc.

1280   López Cruz, Francisco. **El aguinaldo en Puerto Rico (su evolución).** San
Sp   Juan: Instituto de Cultura Puertorriqueña, 1972. 46p. LC 72-374590.
                                                        ML 3565 P8 L65
       Brief analysis and history of a particular folk song form. Musical examples
and 25 bibliographic citations.

1281   McCoy, James A. **The Bomba and Aguinaldo of Puerto Rico as They Have**
En   **Evolved from Indigenous, African, and European Cultures.** Ph.D. disserta-
       tion, Florida State University, 1968. 185p. **Dissertation Abstracts**
       29/07-A, p. 2294. Ann Arbor: University Microfilms, order number
       69-00590.
       Studies the development of two folk music genres; musical examples.

       See also *0862.*

Opera and Vocal Music

1282   Pasarell, Emilio. **Orígenes y desarrollo de la afición teatral en Puerto Rico.**
Sp   2d ed. San Juan: Departamento de Instrucción Pública, 1969. 535p.
                                                        PN 2431 P3 1969
       (Original ed., in 2 volumes, 1951, 1967) Narrative chronology including
opera, operetta, zarzuela, concerts, and religious festivals. Many illustrations and
photos; appendix with list of works performed in alphabetical and chronological
order. Unannotated five-page bibliography; no index.

Church and Religious Music

1283   Muñoz Santaella, María Luisa. "La música religiosa en Puerto Rico."
Sp   **Educación,** 13 (nov. 1963), 25-38. (Hato Rey, Puerto Rico)
                                                        L45 E4525
       Documented historical study with musical examples.

Historical Studies, Chronologies, Contemporary Narratives

1284   Martínez, María Cadilla de. "La histórica danza de Puerto Rico en el siglo
Sp   xvi y sus posteriores evoluciones." **Revista musical chilena** 6, (otoño 1959),
       43-77.   ML 5 R238
       Chase—974a
       Historical study: scholarly, documented article with musical examples; no
bibliography.

BIOGRAPHICAL SOURCES

       See *1273, 1274, 1275, 1276.*

GUIDES TO OTHER SOURCES

See also the Guides to Other Sources under Latin America–General (pp. 103-108).

Selective and Critical Guides

1285   Thompson, Annie Figueroa. **An Annotated Bibliography of Writings**
En   **About Music in Puerto Rico.** Ann Arbor: Music Library Association, 1975.
       34p. (MLA Index and Bibliography Series, 12) LC 74-30256. ISBN 0-
       914954-02-4. ISSN 0094-6478.   ML 120 P8 T5
       Coverage from 1844 to 1972. Author sequence with topic index. Brief
(one to three sentences) annotations. Includes monographs, articles, dissertations,
master's theses.

   Stevenson, *A Guide to Caribbean Music History (0896)*, lists 17 index
entries for Puerto Rico.

   Chase, *A Guide to the Music of Latin America (0891)*, has approximately
21 entries for Puerto Rico, pp. 346-347.

Annual and Periodic Lists

See *0904, 0907.*

LISTS OF MUSIC

See the Lists of Music section under Latin America–General (p. 108).

DISCOGRAPHIES

See entry *1274*; see also the Discographies section under Latin America–
General (p. 110).

SURINAM

1286   Herskovits, Melvile J.; Herskovits, Frances S. **Suriname Folklore.** New
En   York: Columbia University Press, 1936. 766p. (Columbia University
       Contribution to Anthropology, volume 27). LC 37-15342.
                                                      E51 C7
       Chase–1550
       Transcriptions and musicological analysis by M. Kolinski. Part three of the
book is devoted to music. Analysis of urban and rural songs, musical instruments.
Text is 40 pages, followed by 200-page anthology of musical transcriptions.
Unannotated, six-page bibliography.

1287 Kiban, Robert Janki. **Muziek, zang, en dans van de Karaiben in Suriname.**
Du Paramaribo: Stichting Etnologische Kring Suriname, 1966. 26p. LC 67-
79339. ML 207 S9 K5
"Brief study of music, song and dance among the Caribs of Surinam, based
on first-hand observation. Usefulness is considerably curtailed by the absence of
musical notations" [*Handbook of Latin American Studies*, 30 (1968), p. 362].

1288 Arya, Usharbudh. **Ritual Songs and Folksongs of the Hindus of Surinam.**
En Leiden: E. J. Brill, 1968. 178p. LC 76-383436.
ML 207 S9 A8
Introduction is 37-page, serious, documented study of Indian Hindu songs,
musical instruments, and their social context. Balance of work is anthology of 100
song texts and translations. Unannotated, classified bibliography of four pages.
Index.

1289 Panhuys, L.-C. van. "Les chansons et la musique de la Guyane néerlandaise."
Fr **Journal de la Société des Américanistes de Paris,** new series, 9 (1912),
27-39. E51 S68
Chase—1550x
Brief survey with six musical examples.

Stevenson, *A Guide to Caribbean Music History (0896)*, includes 24 index
entries for Surinam.

Chase, *A Guide to the Music of Latin America (0891)*, lists nine entries
for Surinam (entered as "Dutch Guiana"), p. 225.

TRINIDAD AND TOBAGO

DIRECT INFORMATION SOURCES

1290 Elder, Jacob D. **Evolution of the Traditional Calypso of Trinidad:**
En **A Socio-historical Analysis of Song-change.** Ph.D. dissertation, University
of Pennsylvania, 1966. 410p. **Dissertation Abstracts,** 27/10-A, (April
1967), p. 3382. Ann Arbor: University Microfilms, order number
67-3066.
Analysis and description of changes in traditional Negro song-form, the
calypso. Studies form and texts; social context.

1291 Elder, Jacob D. **From Congo Drum to Steelbands; a Socio-historical**
En **Account of the Emergence and Evolution of the Trinidad Steel Orchestra.**
St. Augustine, Trinidad: University of the West Indies, 1969. 47p.
ML 207 T759 E4
Originally published in 1968 under the title *Social Development of the
Traditional Calypso of Trinidad and Tobago (from Congo Drum to Steel Band).*
(Original edition: LC 79-20093).

1292   Espinet, Charles S.; Pitts, Harry. **Land of the Calypso, Origin and Develop-**
En   **ment of Trinidad's Folk Song.** Port-of-Spain, Trinidad: Guardian
       Commercial Printery, 1944. 74p. LC 44-12715.

Chase–1078a   ML 3565 E8
Description and history of the calypso. Photos, no index or bibliography.

1293   Waterman, Richard Alan. **African Patterns in Trinidad Negro Music.** Ph.D.
En   dissertation, Northwestern University, 1943. 261p.
       Analysis of 45 songs, studying retention of African musical styles and
patterns. Review of the literature; 47 musical transcriptions.

See also *0862*.

GUIDES TO OTHER SOURCES

Stevenson, *A Guide to Caribbean Music History* (*0896*), lists 16 index
entries for Trinidad.

Chase, *A Guide to the Music of Latin America* (*0891*), includes five entries
for Trinidad under "West Indies," pp. 384-385.

For general bibliographic coverage of the Caribbean, see *0897, 0901, 0904,
0907.*

DISCOGRAPHIES

See the Discographies section under Latin America–General (p. 110).

URUGUAY

THE LANGUAGE OF MUSIC

See the Language of Music section under Latin America–General (p. 94).

DIRECT INFORMATION SOURCES

Introductions and General Surveys

1294   Ayestarán, Lauro. **La música en el Uruguay.** Montevideo: Servicio Oficial
Sp   de Difusión Radio Eléctrica, 1953. 817p. LC 54-22274.

Chase–990a, 1001a   ML 237 A9
The outstanding work on music in Uruguay—a comprehensive, thoroughly
documented history with coverage to 1860. Detailed treatment of folk and art
music; topics include primitive music, Indian music, Negro music, opera (with
performance chronologies), religious music, popular "salon" music, national songs,

military music, education, music businesses and publishing. Biographical information on 31 composers with lists of their works. Bibliography listing nine of the author's previous publications. A large, handsome volume with numerous illustrations, plates, and musical examples. Name index and index of illustrations.

1295 Salgado, Susana. **Breve historia de la música culta en el Uruguay.** Montevideo:
Sp AEMUS, Biblioteca de Poder Legislativo, 1971. 350p. LC 73-306221.
ML 237 S25
Historical survey of art music, with emphasis on the post-1860 period not covered in the preceding work. Topical organization; subjects include religious, theatrical, chamber, symphonic, and salon music; composers. Classified catalog of works for 18 composers; name index.

See also *1301*.

Folk Music and Folksong

1296 Ayestarán, Lauro. **El folklore musical uruguayo.** 2d ed. Montevideo: Arca,
Sp 1972. 182p.   ML 3575 U78 A9 1972
(1st ed. 1967) Collection of short studies (5-10 pages), mostly on individual song and dance forms. Also covers Afro-Uruguayan music and instruments. Musical examples; no index or bibliography.

1297 Mendoza de Arce, Daniel. **Sociología del folklore musical uruguayo.**
Sp Montevideo: Editorial Goes, 1972. 269p. LC 72-373810.
ML 3575 U78 M45
Sociological interpretation of Uruguayan folk music. Unannotated, nine-page bibliography; no index.

1298 Viglietti, Cédar. **Folklore musical del Uruguay.** Montevideo: Ediciones
Sp del Nuevo Mundo, 1968. 127p. NUC 70-19695.
(1st ed. 1947, *Folklore en el Uruguay, la guitarra del gaucho, sus danzas y canciones.* ML 237 V5; LC 48-22467) Survey of folksong and dance forms, including historical and descriptive information. Five-page musical supplement, one-page unannotated bibliography listing only authors (no titles or bibliographic information); no index.

Historical Studies, Chronologies, Contemporary Narratives

1299 Ayestarán, Lauro. **Crónica de una temporada musical en el Montevideo**
Sp **de 1830.** Montevideo: Ediciones Ceibo, 1943. 108p. LC A44-5200.
Chase—998a   ML 237.8 M6 A9
Comprehensive reconstruction of musical activity in 1830 Montevideo— including opera, ballet, musical theatre, musical personalities. Musical examples; illustrations; unannotated five-page bibliography.

Regional and Local Histories

See the preceding item, *1299*.

Instruments

1300   Ayesterán, Lauro. "El tamboril Afro-uruguayo." **Boletín interamericano**
Sp   **de música**, 68 (nov. 1968), 3-14.
        (reprinted from *Music in the Americas, 0854*) Study of the tamboril and
its music. Drawings, musical examples.

BIOGRAPHICAL SOURCES

1301   Lagarmilla, Roberto. **Músicos uruguayos.** Montevideo: Edit. Medina, 1970.
Sp   91p. (Colección cien temas básicos, 5) NUC 72-105849.
                                                    ML 385 L3 M9
        Diminutive, pocket-sized volume, but nonetheless a useful and
well-organized reference work. Biographies of 40 Uruguayan composers in
chronological arrangement, length ranges from one paragraph to three pages.
Mentions names of works. Name index. Additional features are a 10-page
chronology of Uruguayan music history, 1802-1970; 28-page overview of
Uruguayan music and music history; five-page survey of women in Uruguayan
music; and unannotated bibliography of 28 items.

1302   **Ciento cincuenta años de música uruguaya.** Montevideo: Mosca Hermanos,
Sp   1975. (Ediciones del sesquicentenario)
        Program of a concert series printed with 21-page biographical dictionary of
paragraph-length sketches (in chronological arrangement) of 47 Uruguayan composers,
1825-1975.

        See also *1294*.

GUIDES TO OTHER SOURCES

        See also the Guides to Other Sources section under Latin America—General
(pp. 103-108).

Selective and Critical Guides

1303   Ayestarán, Lauro. "Bibliografía musical uruguaya." **Revista de la Biblioteca**
Sp   **Nacional, Montevideo**, 1 (1966), 13-82.   Z 907 M72
        "A useful, although incomplete annotated bibliography of 505 references
to books, monographs and music periodicals from Uruguay. The first part is divided
into four main sections: a) works printed in Uruguay exclusively dedicated to music,

b) works printed in Uruguay which contain music scores or important music references, c) music librettos printed in Uruguay, d) works printed abroad with detailed information on Uruguayan music and musicians. Of particular importance is the section on Uruguayan music periodicals since this information is not available in any other source" [*Handbook of Latin American Studies*, 32 (1970), p. 481].

1304   Ayestarán, Lauro. **Fuentes para el estudio de la música colonial uruguaya.**
Sp   Montevideo: Impresora uruguaya, 1947. 57p. LC A48-2146.

     Chase–1000a   ML 120 U7 A9

     Separate from the *Revista de la facultad de humanidades y ciencias*, 1 (April 1947), 315-358. (Montevideo, Universidad de la República.) Bibliography of colonial documents containing references to music. Classified by topic (folk music, opera, military music, religious music, etc.), chronological order within topics. Documents date from 1573 to 1839; 147 entries, all with brief content summary.

1305   "Bibliografía de Lauro Ayestarán." **Revista histórica, segunda época**, 39
Sp   (Dic. 1968), 525-589. (Montevideo, Museo Histórico Nacional)

                                            G 989.1006 M765 R
     "Brief biography accompanies the extensive bibliography of this noted Uruguayan folklorist and musicologist (1913-1966)" [annotation by J. R. Scobie, *Handbook of Latin American Studies*, 32 (1970), p. 481].

     Chase, *A Guide to the Music of Latin America (0891)* has approximately 53 entries for Uruguay, pp. 359-365.

Annual and Periodic Guides

1306   **Anuario bibliográfico uruguayo**, 1946-49, new series, 1968– . Montevideo,
Sp   Biblioteca Nacional, 1947-51, 1969– . (annual) LC 48-14586.

     Sheehy 76–AA932   Z 1881 A5
     Classed arrangement. Since 1968, uses Library of Congress classification (e.g., music publications entered under "M", "ML" and "MT"). Entries give an LC classification number. Volume for 1968 had 13 music entries; that of 1973, two music entries. Contains a classed list of periodicals; author index.

LISTS OF MUSIC

     See *1294, 1295*. See Stevenson, *Renaissance and Baroque Musical Sources of the Americas (0914)* for holdings of music archives in Montevideo.

     See also the Lists of Music section under Latin America–General (p. 108).

DISCOGRAPHIES

     See the discographies listed under Latin America–General (p. 110).

VENEZUELA

THE LANGUAGE OF MUSIC

See the Language of Music section under Latin America—General (p. 94).

DIRECT INFORMATION SOURCES

Introductions and General Surveys

1307　Calcaño, José Antonio. **Contribución al estudio de la música en Venezuela.**
Sp　　Caracas: Editorial "Élite", 1939. 127p.　　ML 239 C2 C6
　　　　Chase—2611
　　　　Documented historical survey, including native Indian music and instruments,
folk music and folk instruments. Musical examples; no bibliography or index.

Regional and local histories are entered here in the absence of other
comprehensive surveys:

1308　Calcaño, José Antonio. **La ciudad y su música; crónica musical de Caracas.**
Sp　　Caracas: Conservatorio Teresa Carreño, 1958. 518p. LC 59-40736.
　　　　Chase—1064a　　　　　　　ML 238.8 C3 C3
　　　　Comprehensive historical survey of musical activity in Caracas, colonial
era through the twentieth century. Includes biographical information, concert life,
church music, musical organizations. Many illustrations; appendix of historical
sources; name index; unannotated nine-page bibliography.

1309　Calcaño, José Antonio. **400 años de música caraqueña.** Caracas: Círculo
Sp　　Musical, 1967. 98p. LC 67-98172.　　　　ML 238.8 C3 C34
　　　　Handsome, large-format, lavishly illustrated coffee-table volume with a
general historical survey of Caracas musical life, 1567-1967. Biographical information, appendix of historic documents.

1310　Silva Uzcátegui, Rafael Domingo. "Música y músicos del Estado Lara";
Sp　　"Cultura musical." In **Enciclopedia Larense, tomo II.** Caracas: Gobierno
　　　　del Estado Lara, 1941. pp. 397-481.　　　F 2331 L3 S5
　　　　Regional music history with much information on performance organizations and musicians. Also deals with folk music—song and dance forms. Photographs;
no bibliography or index.

Folk Music and Folksong

Thanks to the scholarship of Luis Felipe Ramón y Rivera and Isabel Aretz,
Venezuela has a rich literature of folk music studies. The first item is a general but
comprehensive work:

1311   Ramón y Rivera, Luis Felipe. **La música folklórica de Venezuela.** Caracas:
Sp   Monte Acila Editores, 1969. 240p. LC 73-217695.
                                            ML 3575 V3 R289
       Survey of Venezuelan folk music. Chapters organized by social function or
subject matter (e.g., children's songs, work songs, songs from religious celebrations,
dances, popular and entertainment music). Includes 107 musical examples, numerous
photos, a two-page list of song and dance names. No index or bibliography.

       Three brief surveys:

1312   Aretz, Isabel. "El folklore musical de Venezuela." **Revista musical chilena,**
Sp   22 (abril-dic. 1968), 53-82.   ML 5 R283
       Good general survey, including information on instruments, song and dance
forms. Unannotated one-page bibliography; illustrations.

1313   Ramón y Rivera, Luis Felipe. **Música indígena, folklórica y popular de**
Sp   **Venezuela.** Buenos Aires: Ricordi Americana, 1967. 66p. LC 70-235747.
                                            ML 3575 V3 R293
       Introductory survey of folk, popular, and native forms. Musical examples;
no bibliography or index.

1314   Cardona, Miguel; Ramón y Rivera, Luis Felipe, *et al.* **Panorama del folklore**
Sp   **venezolano.** Caracas: Universidad Central de Venezuela, 1959. 223p.
       (Biblioteca de cultura universitaria, 3)
       Includes a 35-page chapter on folk music by Ramón y Rivera, and a 30-page
dance chapter by Isabel Aretz. Emphasis on the social context. Charts, photos, five-
page unannotated bibliography; no index.

       The remaining entries are studies of forms or ethnic groups:

1315   Ramón y Rivera, Luis Felipe. **La canción venezolana.** Maracaibo:
Sp   Universidad del Zulia, 1972. 235p. LC 72-221779.
                                            ML 3575 V3 R26
       History, classification and analysis of Venezuelan song types. Numerous
musical examples; one-page unannotated bibliography.

1316   Aretz, Isabel. **El tamunangue.** Barquisimeto, Venez.: Universidad Centro-
Sp   Occidental, 1970. 169p. LC 73-293077.   GV 1796 T2 A7
       Detailed study of a particular music and dance form. Photos, drawings,
musical examples. Unannotated two-page bibliography; detailed table of contents;
index of all illustrative matter but no topic index.

1317   Ramón y Rivera, Luis Felipe. **El joropo, baile nacional de Venezuela.**
Sp   Caracas: Ministerio de Educación, Dirección de Cultura y Bellas Artes,
       1953. 131p. LC 53-3284.   GV 1796 J7 R3
       Text is 92 pages, followed by 31 pages of music. Detailed study including
history, musical analysis, and instruments. Photos, musical examples. Unannotated
one-page bibliography; no index.

1318   Ramón y Rivera, Luis Felipe. **La música afrovenezolana.** Caracas:
Sp   Universidad Central de Venezuela, Imprenta Universitaria, 1971. 174p.
        LC 72-346052.   ML 3575 V3 R287
        Comprehensive survey including dances and fiestas, melody, rhythm,
instruments. Based on field research. Musical examples, photos, bibliography,
index, and discography.

1319   Ramón y Rivera, Luis Felipe; Aretz, Isabel. **Folklore tachirense.** Caracas:
Sp   Biblioteca de autores tachirenses, 1961-1963. 2v. LC 63-48174. (778p.,
        641p.)   GR 133 V4 R3
        Pages 15-146 of volume 1 deal with song and dance forms, instruments.
Numerous musical examples.

1320   Barral, Basilo M. de. **Los indios guaraunos y su cancionero: historia,**
Sp   **religión y alma lírica.** Madrid: Consejo Superior de Investigaciones
        Científicas, Departamento de Misionología Española, 1964. 594p.
        LC 75-226273.   ML 3575 A2 B38
        Serious and comprehensive study of the Guarauno Indians' musical
culture. Numerous musical examples and illustrations. Name index; no bibliography.

1321   Baltasar de Matallana, *padre*. **La música indígena. Taurepán, tribu de la**
Sp   **gran sabana.** Caracas: Editorial Venezuela, 1939. 36p. LC 40-32391.
                                               ML 3575 B34 M8
        Chase—2642
        A speech given August 6, 1938. Survey of folksong and dance forms.
Photos, musical facsimiles. No bibliography or index. Published also as an article
(without photos and musical examples): "La música indígena Taurepán." *Boletín
latino-americano de música*, 4 (1938), 649-664.   ML 199 B64

        Numerous other fine studies have appeared in the *Boletín del Instituto de
Folklore*. See entry *1326*.

Popular Music

        See coverage in *1311* and *1313*.

Opera and Vocal Music

1322   Churión, Juan José. **El teatro en Caracas.** Caracas: Tip. Vargas, 1924. 230p.
Sp   LC 38-13499.   PN 2552 C3 C5
        Chase—2614
        Includes section "La lírica y la ópera," pages 159-198—a brief history of
opera in Venezuela to 1881. No bibliography or index.

Historical Studies, Chronologies, Contemporary Narratives

1323   La Plaza, Ramón de. **Ensayos sobre el arte en Venezuela.** Caracas: Impr.
Sp   al vapor de "La Opinión nacional," 1883. 262p. LC 9-22439.
    Chase—2615   N 6730 L2
    Includes "La música," pages 88-171; historical information on art music
and musicians. No bibliography or index; a 56-page musical supplement.

1324   Plaza, Juan Bautista. **Música colonial venezolana.** Caracas: Ministerio de
Sp   Educación, 1958. 34p. LC 60-17131.   ML 238 P6
    Brief summary of colonial art music; information on composers and their
works.

1325   Plaza, Juan Bautista. "Music in Caracas during the Colonial Period."
En   **Musical Quarterly,** 29 (April 1943), 198-213.   ML 1 M725
    Chase—2621
    Musical activity in Caracas, 1770-1811. Information on composers; two
musical facsimiles.

Regional and Local Histories

See entries *1308, 1309, 1310, 1322.*

Periodicals and Yearbooks

1326   **Boletín del Instituto de Folklore,** v.1— . Sept. 1953— . Caracas: Ministerio
Sp   de Educación, Dirección de Cultura y Bellas Artes, Instituto de Folklore.
ISSN-0505-1398.   GR 133 V4 V45a
Important folk music studies have appeared in this publication, including:

> Aretz, Isabel. "El polo; historia, música, poesía." Vol. 3 (dic. 1959),
> 227-273.

> Aretz, Isabel. "El maremare como expresión musical y coreográfica."
> Vol. 3 (jul. 1958), 45-104.

Articles are illustrated with photos and musical examples. Book reviews
are another feature.

Instruments

1327   Aretz, Isabel. **Instrumentos musicales de Venezuela.** Cumaná, Ven.:
Sp   Universidad de Oriente, 1967. 317p. LC 77-200923.
                  ML 486 V45 A7
    Scholarly, comprehensive work, organized according to instrument classifica-
tion (e.g., cordófonos, aerófonos, etc.). Includes 78 musical examples, photos and
illustrations, 10-page glossary of instrument names; eight-page unannotated bibliography. Index of music examples and illustrations.

BIOGRAPHICAL SOURCES

1328   Venezuela. Dirección de Educación Primaria y Normal. **Músicos**
Sp   **venezolanos.** Caracas, 1962. 15p. LC 65-66188.
                                                    ML 238 V43 F6 no. 1
       Aimed at school children; two-page sketches of five composers born in
the eighteenth century. Mentions some works. Unannotated bibliography of four
entries.

       See also *1308.*

GUIDES TO OTHER SOURCES

       See also the Guides to Other Sources section under Latin America–General
(pp. 103-108).

Selective and Critical Guides

1329   Aretz, Isabel. "La etnomusicología en Venezuela: primera bibliografía
Sp   general." **Boletín interamericano de música**, 55 (sept. 1966), 3-9; no. 56
       (nov. 1966), 3-34.
       Comprehensive reference work. First part is introduction and bibliographic
essay; part two is a classified, unannotated bibliography of 610 entries, covering
books, articles, recordings, and printed music.

1330   Mambretti, Mabel. "Aportes para una bibliografía general del folklore, la
Sp   etnomúsica y afines de Venezuela: años 1968-1970." **Revista venezolana
       de folklore, segunda época,** 3 (sept. 1970), 129-148.
       "Approximately 120 unannotated items listing books, pamphlets, articles
in journals, and newspaper articles about Venezuelan folklore and related subjects"
[*Handbook of Latin American Studies*, 34 (1972), p. 109].

       Chase, *A Guide to the Music of Latin America (0891)*, has approximately
139 entries for Venezuela, pp. 366-383.

Annual and Periodic Guides

1331   **Bibliografía venezolana**, año 1– . enero-marzo 1970– . Caracas: Centro
Sp   Bibliográfico Venezolano. (quarterly 1970; 1971– semi-annual)
       LC 77-615481.   Z 1911 B5
         Sheehy 76–AA937
       Classed Dewey arrangement, covering books, pamphlets, and foreign
imprints by Venezuelans or on Venezuelan topics. Music is included under "Bellas
artes," with all 700's in one alphabet by author. Includes scores. The issue for
oct./dic. 1970 included five music items; that of julio/dic. 1973 listed eight music
entries. Also a list of new periodical titles, in title order (not classed).

The next item provides retrospective coverage:

1332   **Anuario bibliográfico venezolano.** 1942-1954. Caracas: Tip. Americana,
Sp   1944-1960. (irregular) LC 44-9260.   Z 1911 A7
      Sheehy 76–936
      Alphabetical main entry arrangement (usually an author) with author,
title, subject index. Volume for 1942 had 20 music entries, including non-Venezuelan
imprints on Venezuelan topics. Song collections and periodical articles listed, but not
scores. The volume for 1949-1954 leads to six items via the index term "música";
but there are other music books, such as biographies.

LISTS OF MUSIC

      See *1329*. See also the Lists of Music section under Latin America–General
(p. 108).

DISCOGRAPHIES

      See *1329*. See also the discographies listed under Latin America–General
(p. 110).

APPENDIX:

Revisions for Volume I

This section revises and amplifies the entries in Volume I, numbers 0001 through 0503.

0009   Vannes. *Add:* Reprint—New York: Da Capo Press, 1970. (Da Capo Press Music Reprint Series).

0010   Wotton. *Add*: Reprint—St. Clair Shores, Mich.: Scholarly Press, 1972.

0017   Wentworth. *Note*: For musical terms, superseded by Gold, *0506*.

0037   **Entsiklopedicheskii** . . . *Add*: Duckles 74—20.

0040   Bobillier. *Change*: Duckles 74—278 *to*: Duckles 74—279.

0052   Janovka. *Add*: Reprint—Hilversum: Frits A. M. Knuf, 1973.

0053   Brossard. *Add*: Reprint—Hilversum: Frits A. M. Knuf, 1965.

0056   Grassineau. *Add*: Reprint—New York: Broude, 1967.

0063   Riemann. *Add*: Ergänzungsbände. I: A-K, 1972; II: L-Z, 1975. *Add* to Shedlock translation: Reprint—St. Clair Shores, Mich.: Scholarly Press, 1972.

0065   Thompson. *Note*: 10th ed., edited by Bruce Bohle. New York: Dodd, Mead, 1974.

0069   **Enciclopedia** . . . *Change*: Duckles 74—16 *to* Duckles 74—45. [Note erroneous reference in Duckles index.]

0070   **Encyclopaedia Britannica.** *Note*: 15th ed., as **New Encyclopaedia Britannica in 30 Volumes**, 1974. A completely revised format, comprising an outline of knowledge in one volume, ten volumes of short articles, and nineteen volumes of long articles. No separate index volume. Review: *ARBA* 75—77. Musical content appears to be accurate, more up-to-date than the later printings of the fourteenth edition (e.g., the Leonard Bernstein article gives recent information [cf. comments at *0070* in our Volume I], yet the Boulez article still cites no works later than 1966), but unbalanced. No music editor is identified; among the authors are Bruno Nettl, Nicolas Slonimsky, William Malm, and Ralph T. Daniel. Malm's essay on East Asian music is a particularly useful survey. Biographical articles are a strength; American musicians are especially well treated. But the overriding flaw in the fifteenth edition, lack of an index, severely limits the value of this set for information needs in music.

0072   **Encyclopédie** . . . *Change*: Féderov *to* Fédorov.

0076   LaBorde. *Add*: Reprint–Graz: Akademische Druck- u. Verlagsanstalt.

0077   **Larousse** . . . *Add*: Italian edition–**Dizionario musicale Larousse**. A cura di Delfino Nava. Milano: Edizioni Paoline, 1961. 3v.

0079   Mendel. *Add*: Reprint of 2d ed. (1880-83)–Hildesheim: Georg Olms.

0082   **Musikens** . . . *Note*: 2d ed., vols. 2 and 3, 1961.

0091   Abbiati. *Note*: 2d ed., 1967– .

0096   Burney. *Add*: Reprint–Graz: Akademische Druck- u. Verlagsanstalt, in preparation.

0098   Hawkins. *Add*: Reprint of 1875 ed.–Graz: Akademische Druck- u. Verlaganstalt, 1969. 2v.

0101   **New Oxford** . . . Another volume has appeared: (vol. 10):
        Cooper, Martin. **The Modern Age, 1890-1960**. 1974. 764p.
        ML 160 N44 v. 10

0103   Prentice-Hall . . . Another volume has appeared:
        Brown, Howard Mayer. **Music in the Renaissance**. 1976.
        ML 172 B86
        Note also: 2d eds. of Seay (1975) and Hitchcock (1974).

p. 32   Two RidiM publications have been issued. They are cited in the Update as number *0508* and *0509*.

0121   Koch. *Add*: Duckles 74–1560.

0137   Benton. *Note*: Part 3, 1972, covering Spain, France, Italy and Portugal.

0141   Lincoln. *Note*: 5th ed., 1974.

0143   **Music Yearbook**. *Note*: change of title and publisher in latest edition *to*: **British Music Yearbook: a Survey and Directory with Statistics and Reference Articles for 1975**. Ed. Arthur Jacobs. New York: Bowker, 1975. 801p. ISBN 0-85935-024-X.
        ARBA 76–998.

0144   **Musical America** . . . This ought to have been shown as an open entry (1972– .); it is an annual continuation.

0149   **Who's Who** ... *Note*: 7th ed., 1975. New title and publisher: **International Who:s Who in Music and Musicians' Directory** (Cambridge, Eng.: Melrose Press, 1975), 1,348p. LC 73-91185. ISBN 0-900332-31.

    ARBA 76–1004   ML 106 G7 W44

Some 12,000 entries, worldwide scope. Appendices for orchestras, music organizations, competitions and awards, festivals, concert halls and opera houses, conservatories. List of "masters of the King's/Queen's music." All coverage is international, as opposed to the British nature of earlier editions.

0159   Herkowitz. *Note*: 2d ed. 1975. ARBA 76–983.

0170   Bull. *Add*: Volume II, 1974. 567p. ARBA 75–1152.
Supplements the base volume with new information on some 4,000 persons, and gives references on 4,000 new names.

0182   **Compositores** ... *Note*: Latest volume seen is 18 (1972).

0187   Eitner. *Add*: Reprint–Graz: Akademische Druck- u. Verlagsanstalt, 1959-60.

0191   Fétis. *Add*: Reprint of 2d ed.–Brussels: Éditions Culture et Civilisation, 1972.

0203   **Sohlmans** ... *Note*: 2d ed., 1975– . Vol. I, A-Ampo.

0206   Besterman. *Note*: Various subject sections also published separately, including **Music and Drama; a Bibliography of Bibliographies** (Totowa, N.J.: Rowman and Littlefield, 1971. xii, 365p.)
About 1,700 entries, taken from the Besterman 4th ed. ML 113 B43

0210   Pruett. *Note*: 3d ed., compiled by Linda Solow, 1974. 40p.

0216   Duckles. *Add*: ARBA 75–1123.

0223   Reese. *Change*: Duckles 74–534 *to*: Duckles 74–782.

0254   Paris. *Add*: Reprint–Hildesheim: Georg Olms, 1971.

0260   **Répertoire** ... *Add*: **Cumulative Index I-V, 1967-71** [1975]

0269   **Subject** ... *Note*: The current list of publications formerly given in **Publishers Weekly** now appears separately as the **Weekly Record.** v.1– . Sept. 1974– . Z1219 W4

0271
0273   **Bibliographie de la France** and **Biblio** merged in 1972 to form a new publication: **Bibliographie de la France–Biblio.** The annual cumulation also took a new title: **Les livres de l'année–Biblio**; and the monthly

cumulation became **Livres du mois–Biblio**. Books are listed in classified order. Music scores are found in supplements. See Winchell 76–AA613.

0288   **Bibliographia** ... *Note*: In May 1976, volumes for 1968-72 had appeared, with volumes for 1973-74 announced to be in preparation.

0300   **Social** ... *Note*: In 1974 this work was divided into **Humanities Index** and **Social Sciences Index**. Each covers about 260 periodicals. Articles are indexed by author and subject, and book reviews are listed by author in a separate section.

0302   **Subject** ... *Note*: "Class lists in parts" for several subject fields were issued in certain years: 1915-19 and 1920-22. Music was class list "H." A convenient cumulative index for British journals of this period appears in the Update at number *0520*.

0315   Marconi. *Note*: Has been published, 1975. Lists items covered since 1802 by Poole's (*0298*), the Wilson services (*0297, 0299, 0300, 0301*, etc.), the major British and Canadian indexes. Indicates which index treated each journal, and for what years. Thirty journal titles begin with "music" or "musical." LC 76-12242. ISBN 0-87650-005-x.

0335   **Comprehensive** ... *Note*: A five-volume supplement, 1973, has appeared.

0429   Brussels. *Note*: a further volume, covering the 18th century, was issued in 1974 (viii, 519p.).

0442   Internationales ... *Note*: another **Nachtrag**, 1969/70. 44p.

0444   Barlow. *Note*: Rev. ed., 1975. ISBN 0-517-52446-5, LC 75-15687. Minor changes only.

0458   Cooper. *Note*: This was published, 1975.

0480   **Katalog** ... *Note*: Cover and title-page title for recent issues is: **Bielefelder Katalog; Katalog der Schallplatten klassischer Musik** (for the classical catalog; title varies for the spoken and jazz/pop catalogs). In 1974, separate reprints of catalogs in several areas were issued: classical, dance/pop, spoken, jazz, and cassettes.

0485   Maleady. *Note*: Annual publication has continued, with volumes covering 1973 and 1974. Cf. ARBA 75–1154.

0489   Armitage. *Note*: Annual publication has continued, with volumes covering 1973 and 1974. Cf. ARBA 75–1169.

0491   Moon. *Note*: 3d ed.[?] : **A Bibliography of Jazz Discographies Published since 1960**. (1972). 32p. ML 128 J3 M6

0496   Rust. *Note*: The third volume cited seems not to have been published.

0501   Murrells. *Note*: 2d ed. [not so identified on title page] with new title:
       The Book of Golden Discs (London: Barrie and Jenkins, 1974), 503p.
       Indexes through 1970, with some data into 1972.

0502   New York ... *Note*: 3d ed., 1972.

GUIDE TO USE
OF THE AUTHOR-TITLE INDEX

As stated in the Introduction, both the Author-Title Index and the Subject Index are cumulative, covering Volumes I and II of *Information on Music*. All authors of works cited (including co-authors and institutional authors) and all works (including variant titles, translations, series) are presented in this section, interfiled in one alphabet. The filing mode is word by word (*New York Times Index* before Newberry Library). Initial articles, in any language, are ignored in filing. Proper names are grouped before other entries (Price, Steven D., before *Price Guide to Collectors' Records*). Dates or numerals appearing as the initial element of a title are filed as if spelled out in the language of the work (e.g., *150 anos de musica no Brasil* . . . filed as if spelled *Cento e cinqüenta anos de musica no Brasil*).

Names beginning with the prefix Mc are arranged as if written Mac (McWhirter before Madeira). Simple proper names come before compound names: Hernández, Julio, before Hernández Balaguer, Pablo. In Spanish names, the prefix *de* is considered to be part of the following substantive; thus, de Jong (dejong) follows Degrada.

Initials file as letters, ahead of words, but acronyms (clusters of initials treated as words) are filed as though they were words: ASCAP after Artis. *Catalog* and *catalogue* are not interfiled; the spelling of the word is retained and filing follows the spelling.

Letters bearing the umlaut are treated as though followed by *e*; *ä* filed like *ae*, *ö* like *oe*, etc.

AUTHOR-TITLE INDEX

The * after a number indicates that the Update section of this volume carries supplementary information regarding the title.

Aarhus, Denmark. Statsbiblioteket. *Fagkataloger* . . . , *0370*
Abadía Morales, Guillerma. *La música folklórica colombiana, 1088*
Abascal Brunet, Manuel. *Apuntes para la historia del teatro en Chile: la zarzuela grande, 1064*
Abbiati, Franco. *Storia della musica, 0091*
Abecê do folclore (Lima), *0996*
Aber, Adolf. *Handbuch der Musikliteratur* . . . , *0099, 0211*
Abert, Hermann J. *Illustriertes Musik-Lexikon, 0174*
Abkurzungen in der Musik Terminologie; eine Übersicht (Schaal), *0046*
Abraham, Gerald. *Encyclopaedia Britannica, 0070; New Oxford History of Music, 0101*
Abrahams, Roger D. *Anglo-American Folksong Style, 0635*
Accademia Filarmonica, Bologna. *Catalogo della collezione d'autografi* . . . , *0116*
Accademie e biblioteche d'Italia, 0398
Acevedo Hernández, Antonio. *Canciones populares chilenas; recopilación de cuecas, tonadas, y otras canciones, acompañada de una noticia sobre los que han cantado para el público chileno, 1063*
Acquarone, Francisco. *História da música brasileira, 0983*
Acta Bibliothecae Universitatis Varsoviensis, *0237*
Acta musicologica, 0284, 0317, 0341
Adalid y Gamero, Manuel de. "La música en Honduras," *1179*
Adams, John Stowell. *Adams' New Musical Dictionary* . . . , *0001*
Adams' New Musical Dictionary . . . (Adams), *0001*
Adkins, Cecil. *Doctoral Dissertations in Musicology, 0337;* "Index to Acta musicologica," *0317;* "Musicological Works in Progress," *0341*
Adler, Guido. *Handbuch der Musikgeschichte* . . . , *0092*
Adlung, Jakob. *Anleitung zur musikalsichen Gelahrtheit* . . . , *0212*
Ägypten (Hickmann), *0119*
Aeolian Company, New York. *Duo-Art Piano Music; a Classified Catalog of Interpretations of the World's Best Music Recorded by More Than Two Hundred and Fifty Pianists for the Duo-Art Reproducing Piano, 0475*
"Aerófonos prehispánicos andinos" (Fortún), *0972*

"African Music in British and French America" (Epstein), *0861*
African Patterns in Trinidad Negro Music (Waterman), *1293*
La africanía de la música folklórica de Cuba (Ortiz), *1119*
"The Afro-American Legacy (to 1800)" (Stevenson), *0860*
Age of Humanism (Abraham), *0101*
El aguinaldo en Puerto Rico (su evolución) (López Cruz), *1280*
Aires nacionales de Bolivia (Vargas), *0968*
Akademie der Wissenschaften und der Literatur. *Abhandlungen der Geistes und Sozialwissenschaftlichen Klasse, 0047*
Albina, Diāna. *Mūzikas terminu vārdīnca, 0031*
Albrecht, Otto. *Census of Autograph Music Manuscripts of European Composers in American Libraries, 0397; Mary Flagler Cary Music Collection, 0415*
Album Musical (Kinsky), *0120*
Aldrich, Richard. *Concert Life in New York, 1902-1923, 0735*
Alencar, Edigar de. *A modinha cearense, 1011*
Alexander, Francisco. *Música y músicos; ensayos en miniatura, 1146*
Alexander, Franz. *Kleine Musikgeschichte in Jahresübersichten, 0105; Zitatenschatz der Musik* . . . , *0156*
Algemene muziekencyclopedie, 0060
Allen A. Brown Music Collection (Boston Public Library), *0228, 0373*
Allen, Walter C. *Studies in Jazz Discography I. 0489*
Allgemeine Litteratur der Musik: oder Anleitung zur Kenntniss musikalischer Bücher (Forkel), *0217*
Allgemeines Bücher-Lexikon, oder vollständiges alphabetisches Verzeichnis aller von 1700 bis zu ende 1892 erschienenen Bücher (Heinsius), *0274*
Allorto, Riccardo. *La Rassegna musicale, indice generale . . . 1928-52, 0324*
Almanach Hachette, vol. I, p. 46
Almanack (Whitaker), *0154*
Almeida, Renato. *Danses africaines* . . . , *0859; História da música brasileira, 0975; Tablado folclórico, 0995*
Alt-Amerika, Musik der Indianer in präkolumbischer Zeit (Martí; Besseler; Bachmann), *0119, 0872*

The Black Perspective in Music, 0777a
Black Song: The Forge and the Flame . . .
(Lovell), *0777*
Blancheton. See *Inventaire critique du Fonds Blancheton, 0436*
Blesh, Rudi. *They All Played Ragtime: The True Story of an American Music, 0763*
Bloch, Peter. *La-le-lo-lai; Puerto Rican Music and Its Performers, 1274*
Blom, Eric. *Dictionary of Music and Musicians, 0059; General Index to Modern Musical Literature in the English Language* . . . , *0306; Music and Letters: Index to Volume I-XL, 0321*
The Blue Book of Broadway Musicals (Burton), *0799*
The Blue Book of Hollywood Musicals (Burton), *0800*
The Blue Book of Tin Pan Alley . . . (Burton), *0801*
Bluegrass (Artis), *0645*
Bluegrass Music News, 0649
Bluegrass Unlimited, 0650
Blues and Gospel Records, 1902-1942 (Godrich; Dixon), *0836*
Blues People; Negro Music in White America (Jones), *0772*
The Bluesmen. The Story and the Music of the Men Who Made the Blues (Charters), *0674*
Blum, Fred. *Music Monographs in Series* . . . , *0356*
Blume, Friedrich. *Die evangelische Kirchenmusik, 0095; Die Musik in Geschichte und Gegenwart* . . . , *0058; Répertoire internationale des sources musicales, 0419*
BMI Canada, Ltd. *Yes, There is Canadian Music, 0598*
Board of Music Trade of the United States of America. *Complete Catalogue of Sheet Music and Musical Works* . . . 1870, *0825*
Bobillier, Marie. "Bibliographie der bibliographies musicales," *0208; Diccionario de la música* . . . , *0040*
Böhm, László. *Zenei műszótár* . . . , *0029*
Boethius, vol. I, p. 12
Boettner, Juan Max. *Música y músicos del Paraguay, 1251*
"Bogotá" (Stevenson), *1099*
Bohn, Emil. *Bibliographie der Musik-Druckwerke bis 1700, welche in der Stadtbibliothek, der Bibliothek des Academischen Instituts für Kirchenmusik und der Königlichen und Universitäts Bibliothek zu Breslau Aufbewahrt werden* . . . , *0422; Die musikalischen Handschriften des XVI. und XVII. Jahrhunderts in der Stadtbibliothek zu Breslau* . . . , *0400*

Boilés, Charles. "The Pipe and Tabor in Mesoamerica," *1209*
Boletim bibliográfico brasileiro; revista dos editôres, 1047
Boletim bibliográphico da Biblioteca Nacional (Rio de Janeiro), *1044*
Boletín del Instituto de Folklore, 1326
Boletín interamericano de música, 0882
Boletín latino-americano de música, 0881
Boletín latino-americano de música. (Special issue on Brazil), *0984*
Boletín latino-americano de música. (Special issue on Colombia), *1084*
Bollettino delle pubblicazione italiane ricevute per diritto di stampa, 1866-1957, 0276
Bologna. Liceo Musicale. Biblioteca. *Catalogo della biblioteca, 0372*
The Bomba and Aguinaldo of Puerto Rico as They Have Evolved from Indigenous, African, and European Cultures (McCoy), *1281*
Bonaccorsi, Alfredo. *Nuovo dizionario musicale Curci, 0177*
Bonner Beiträge zur Anglistik, 0026
Bonner Katalog . . . (Deutscher Musikverlger-Verband), *0441*
Book of World-Famous Music, Classical, Popular and Folk (Fuld), *0163*
Book Review Digest, 0352
Book Review Index, 0353
Books in Print, 0269
Books in the Hirsch Library, with Supplementary List of Music (British Museum), *0230*
Bosch, Mariano. *Historia del teatro en Buenos Aires, desde el virreinato hasta el estreno de "Juan Moreira," 0944*
Bose, Fritz. "Die Musik der Chibcha und ihre heutigen Nachkommen," *1092*; "Die Musik der Uitoto," *1093*
Boskaljon, Rudolf Frederik Willem. *Honderd jaar muziekleven op Curaçao, 1240*
" 'Bossa' & 'Bossas': Recent Changes in Brazilian Popular Music" (Béhague), *1013*
Boston Public Library. *Catalogue of the Allen A. Brown Collection of Music* . . . , *0373; Dictionary Catalog of the Music Collection, 0228*
Botsiber, Hugo. *Geschichte der Ouvertüre und der freien Orchesterformen, 0099*
Bozzarelli, Oscar. *Ochenta años de tango platenese, 0938*
Bradley, Ian L. *A Selected Bibliography of Musical Canadiana, 0584*
Braga, Henriqueta Rosa Fernandes. *Música sacra evangélica no Brazil: contribuição a sua história, 1021*

I. S. A. M. Monographs. *0786, 0794*
IAML (International Association of Music
    Libraries). P. 34; *0165*
Iampol'skii, I. M. *Entsiklopedicheskii*
    muzykal'nyi slovar', *0037*
Iconographie musicale (Lesure), *0125*
The Iconography of Music: An Annotated
    Bibliography (Crane), *0113*
Illustreret musikleksikon (Panum; Behrend),
    0021
Illustriertes Musik-Lexikon (Abert),
    0174
Imported Records and Tapes (Peters), *0479*
Index général (1917-66) (Revue de
    musicologie), *0326*
The Index of American Popular Music
    (Burton), *0802*
"Index of Articles on Canadian Musicians
    Found in Periodicals and Other
    Sources" (National Library of Canada),
    0594
"Index of Pictures of Canadian Musicians
    Found in Periodicals" (National Library
    of Canada), *0595*
An Index to Acta musicologica (Adkins;
    Dickinson), *0317*
Index to American Doctoral Dissertations,
    1955/56– , *0334*
"An Index to Biographical Information on
    Rock Musicians" (Fischer), *0782*
Index to Biographies of Contemporary
    Composers (Bull), *0170*
Index to Book Reviews in the Humanities,
    0354
Index to Latin American Periodical Litera-
    ture, 1929-1960 (Pan American Union),
    0308
An Index to Musical Festschriften and
    Similar Publications (Gerboth), *0361*
"Index to Musical Necrology," *0197*
Index to Papers Read before the Members . . .
    1874-1944 (Royal Musical Associa-
    tion), *0323*
"Index to Record Reviews . . . " (Myers),
    0484
An Index to Selected Anthologies of Music
    (Loyan), *0395*
Index to the Times (The Times. L0ndon),
    0295
Index to Top-Hit Tunes, 1900-1950
    (Chipman), *0805*
Indexed Periodicals (Marconi), *0315**
Indexing of German and English Music
    Periodicals before 1949 (Foy), *0314*
Indiana. University. Archives of Traditional
    Music. *Catalog of Phonorecordings of*
    Music and Oral Data, 0531
Indiana University Humanities Series,
    0024

Indiana. University. School of Music. Latin-
    American Music Center. *Latin American*
    Music Available at Indiana University, 0908;
    Music from Latin America Available at
    Indiana University: Scores, Tapes, and
    Records, 0908
Indice generale . . . 1928-52 (Allorto), *0324*
Indice general de publicaciones periodicas
    latino-americanas. Humanidades y
    ciencias sociales, 0309
Indici de la Rassegna musicale (annate
    XXIII-XXXII, 1953-62) e dei Quaderni
    della Rassegna musicale (N. 1, 2, 3,
    1964-65) (Degrada), *0325*
Indici dei volumi I a XX (1894-1913)
    (Parigi), *0327*
Indici dei volumi XXI a XXXV (1914-28)
    (Salvatori; Concina), *0328*
Indici della Rivista musicale italiana, 1929-
    55 (Degrada), *0329*
Indigenous Music and Dances of Equador
    (Moreno Andrade; Pérez), *1148*
Los indios guaraunos y su cancionero:
    historia, religión y alma lírica (Barral),
    1320
"A influência negra na música brasileira"
    (Alvarenga), *0997*
Information Please Almanac, vol. I, p. 46
Institute for Studies in American Music.
    Monographs. *0786, 0794*
Institute for Studies in American Music.
    Newsletter, 0760
Instituto Ecuatoriano de Folklore. *Folklore*
    de Lican y Sicalpa, 1149
Instrumental Music Printed before 1600; A
    Bibliography (Brown), *0427*
Instrumentenkunde (Heinitz), *0095*
"Un instrumento araucano; la trutruka,"
    1073
"Los instrumentos araucanos" (Isamitt),
    1073
Los instrumentos de la música afrocubano
    (Ortiz Fernández), *1127*
Los instrumentos musicales aborígenes y
    criollos de la Argentina (Vega), *0955*
"Instrumentos musicales, cultura
    mapuche . . . (Merino), *1072*
Instrumentos musicales de Venezuela
    (Aretz), *1327*
"Instrumentos musicales del Alto y Bajo
    Chocó" (Velásquez), *1101*
Instrumentos musicales del Perú (Lima. Museo
    de la Cultura Peruana), *1267*
"Instrumentos musicales peruanos"
    (Jiménez), *1267*
"Instrumentos musicales precolombianos
    de Chile" (Grebe), *1072*
Instrumentos musicales precortesianos
    (Martí), *1227*

México: cincuento años de revolución
(Baqueiro Fóster; Mendoza), *1199*
Mexico (City). Instituto Nacional de Bellas
Artes. Departamento de Música. *Investigación folklórica en México, 1206*
Mexico (City). Instituto Nacional de Bellas
Artes. Departamento de Música. *Música folklorica mexicana . . . , 1239*
"Mexico City Cathedral Music: 1600-
1750" (Stevenson), *1215*
"Mexiko Stadt" (Stevenson), *1220*
Meyer, André. *Collection musicale André Meyer, 0127*
Meyer, Kathi. *Katalog der Musikbibliothek Paul Hirsch, 0231*
Meyers enzyklopädisches Lexikon in 25 Bänden, Vol. I, p. 26
Meysel, Anton, *0258*
"Michaud," Vol. I, p. 60
Michel, Francois. *Encyclopédie de la musique, 0072*
Microfilm Abstracts, 0331
Middle East and North Africa, Vol. I, p. 60
Mies, Paul. *Musik im Umkreis der Kulturgeschichte, Ein Tabellenwerk aus der Geschichte der Musik, Literatur, bildenden Künste, Philosophie und Politik Europas, 0110*
Milan. Conservatorio di Musica "Giuseppe Verdi." Biblioteca. *Catalogo della biblioteca, Letteratura musicale e opere teoriche, Parte prima: manoscritti e stampe fino al 1899, 0232*
Miller, Allan. *Historical Atlas of Music: A Comprehensive Study of the World's Music, Past and Present, 0160*
Mis bodas de oro con el folklore paraguayo . . . (Cardozo Ocampo), *1252*
The Miscellaneous Manuscripts, 0425
Missouri Music (Krohn), *0731b*
Mitjana, Rafael. *Catalogue critique et descriptif des imprimés de musique des XVIe et XVIIe siècles . . .* (Uppsala), *0438*
"Mittelamerika" (Pahlen; Mendoza), *0842*
Mize, J. T. H. *International Who Is Who in Music, 0138*
Modern Music Makers; Contemporary American Composers (Goss), *0785*
Die moderne Musik seit der Romantik (Mersmann), *0095*
A modinha cearense (Alencar), *1011*
A modinha e o lundu no século XVIII: uma pesquisa histórica e bibliografica (Araújo), *1010*
Moedana Navarro, Gabriel. "Biobibliografía del professor Vicente T. Mendoza," *1233*
Mokrý, Ladislav, *0198*
Monatshefte für Musikgeschichte, 17. Jhg, Beilage, 0278

Moncada García, Francisco. *Pequeñas biografías de grandes músicos mexicanos, 1231*
Moniteur des dates, Vol. I, p. 60
Moogk, Edward B. *Roll Back the Years: History of Canadian Recorded Sound and Its Legacy, 0554*
Moon, P. *Bibliography of Jazz Discographies, 0491*
Moore, John Weeks. *Complete Encyclopedia of Music, 0080*
More Chapters of Opera . . . (Krehbiel), *0692e*
Moreno Andrade, Segundo Luis. *Historia de la música en el Ecuador, 1145; La música de los Incas . . . , 1153;* "La música en el Ecuador," *1144; Música y danzas autóctonas del Ecuador. Indigenous Music and Dances of Ecuador, 1148*
Morgenstern, Sam. *Dictionary of Musical Themes . . . , 0444; Dictionary of Opera and Song Themes, 0445; Dictionary of Vocal Themes, 0445*
Morse, David. *Motown and the Arrival of Black Music, 0685*
Moser, Hans Joachim. *Musik Lexikon, 0062, 0111, 0212*
Moses, Julian Morton. *Collectors' Guide to American Recordings, 0473; Price Guide to Collectors' Records, 0474*
Motown and the Arrival of Black Music (Morse), *0685*
Mount Allison University. Library. *Catalogue of Canadian Folk Music in the Mary Mellish Archibald Library and Other Special Collections, 0589a*
Moyand Lopez, Rafael. *La cultura musical cordobesa, 0951*
Mueller, John Henry. *The American Symphony Orchestra; a Social History of Musical Taste, 0765a*
La mujer mexicana en la música (hasta la tercera década del siglo xx) (Pulido), *1217*
Muleskinner News, 0651
Multi Media Reviews Index, 0528
Munich. Bayerische Staatsbibliothek, *0413*
Munksgaards musik leksikon (Praem), *0020*
Muñoz Santaella, María Luisa. *La música en Puerto Rico; panorama histórico-cultural, 1273;* "La música religiosa en Puerto Rico," *1283*
Murrells, Joseph. *Daily Mail Book of Golden Discs, 0501**
Museo de instrumentos musicales de la Casa de la Cultura Ecuatoriana (Casa de la Cultura Ecuatoriana), *1155*
Museo storico musicale di "S. Pietro a Majella" (Naples. R. Conservatorio di Musica), *0129*

Museum of New Mexico. Research Records [series], *0631*
Music (Bryant), *0213*
Music A to Z (Sacher), *0085*
Music and Books About Music in Roorbach's Bibliotheca Americana, 1820-61 (Dempsey), *0265*
Music and Dance in California and the West, 0725
Music and Dance in Latin American Urban Contexts: A Selective Bibliography (Davis), *0895*
Music and Dance in New York State (Spaeth), *0738*
Music and Dance in Pennsylvania, New Jersey and Delaware (Spaeth), *0728*
Music and Dance in Texas, Oklahoma, and the Southwest (Whitlock), *0745*
Music and Dance in the Central States (Saunders), *0726*
Music and Dance in the New England States (Spaeth), *0732*
Music and Dance in the Southeastern States (Spaeth), *0744*
Music and Dance of the Tewa Pueblos (Kurath; Garcia), *0631*
Music and Letters, 0321
Music and Letters: Index to Volumes I-XL (Blom; Westrap), *0321*
Music and Musicians in Early America (Lowens), *0716*
Music and Musicians of Maine (Edwards), *0731a*
Music and Musicians of Pennsylvania (Rohrer), *0738b*
Music and Musicians of the Dominican Republic (Coopersmith), *1133*
Music and Some Highly Musical People (Trotter), *0776*
Music Article Guide, 0290
Music Cultures of the Pacific, the Near East, and Asia (Malm), *0103*
Music Education Research Council. *Bibliography of Research Studies in Music Education, 1932-48, 0338*
Music Educators National Conference. *Bibliography of Research Studies in Music Education, 1932-48, 0338*
Music Educators National Conference. Bicentennial Commission. "Selective List[s] of American Music....," *0797*
Music for Patriots, Politicians and Presidents; Harmonies and Discords of the First Hundred Years (Lawrence), *0688*
Music from Latin America Available at Indiana University: Scores, Tapes and Records, 0908
Music from the Middle Ages to the Renaissance (Sternfeld), *0511*
Music in a New Found Land (Mellers), *0711*

Music in America (Ritter), *0714*
Music in Art and Society (Lesure), *0126*
Music in Aztec and Inca Territory (Stevenson), *0875*
"Music in Brazil" (de Jong), *0979*
Music in Canada (MacMillan), *0544*
Music in Canada, 1600-1800 (Amtmann), *0555*
"Music in Caracas during the Colonial Period" (Plaza), *1325*
Music in Denver and Colorado (Denver Public Library), *0727a*
Music in Early America: A Bibliography of Music in Evans (Hixon), *0818*
"Music in 'High' Peru" (Stevenson), *0971*
Music in Latin America: a Brief Survey (Pan American Union), *0843*
Music in Mexico; an Historical Survey (Stevenson), *1193*
Music in New Hampshire, 1623-1800 (Pichierri), *0733a*
Music in New Orleans: The Formative Years (Kmen), *0734*
Music in Our Time (Salazar), *0102*
Music in Philadelphia (Gerson), *0739*
Music in Prints (Beck and Roth), *0117*
"Music in Quito, Four Centuries" (Stevenson), *1154*
Music in Texas (Spell), *0745a*
Music in the Americas (List; Orrego-Salas), *0854*
Music in the Baroque Age (Sternfeld), *0511*
Music in the Baroque Era (Bukofzer), *0102*
Music in the Classic Period (Pauly), *0103*
"Music in the Culture of the Jíbaro Indians of the Ecuadorian Montaña" (List), *1150*
Music in the Hirsch Library (British Museum. Department of Printed Books. Hirsch Library), *0378*
Music in the Medieval World (Seay), *0103*
Music in the Middle Ages (Reese), *0102*
Music in the Modern Age (Sternfeld), *0511*
Music in the Renaissance (Reese), *0102*
Music in the Romantic Age (Sternfeld), *0511*
Music in the Romantic Era (Einstein), *0102*
Music in the Southwest, 1825-1950 (Swan), *0724*
Music in the 20th Century (Austin), *0102*
"Music in the United States" (Goldman), *0719*
Music in the United States: An Historical Introduction (Hitchcock), *0103, 0709*
Music in Western Civilization (Lang), *0100*
Music Index, 0289
Music Lexicography (Coover), *0048*
Music Librarianship, A Practical Guide (Bryant), *0363*
Music Libraries, Including a Comprehensive Bibliography of Music Literature and a Select Bibliography of Music Scores Published Since 1957 (Dove), *0366*

Silva Uzcátegui, Rafael Domingo. "Cultura musical," *1310;* "Música y músicos del Estado Lara," *1310*

Simon, Alfred. *Encyclopedia of Theatre Music . . . , 0803; Songs of the American Theater . . . , 0804*

Sing Out, 0615

La siringa [series], *0936, 0940*

"Sistema pentafónico en la música indígena precolonial del Perú" (Castro), *1264*

Škerjanc, Lucijan Marija. *Glasbeni slovarček, 0039*

Śledziński, Stefan. *Mala encyklopedia muzykii, 0034*

Slonimsky, Nicolas. *Biographical Dictionary of Musicians* (Baker), *0175; Music of Latin America, 0840; Music Since 1900, 0112, 0070*

Słowniczek muzyczny (Habela), *0033*

Smith, Julia. *Directory of American Women Composers,* 0789

Smith, W. C. *0248*

Smith, William James. *A Dictionary of Musical Terms in Four Languages,* 0006

Smithsonian Institution. Bureau of American Ethnology. Bulletins. See: Bureau of American Ethnology. Bulletins.

Smits van Waesberghe, Joseph. *Musikerziehung-Lehre und Theorie der Musik im Mittel-alter, 0119; The Theory of Music from the Carolingian Era up to 1400, 0255, 0419*

Smolian, Steven. "Da Capo," *0466; Handbook of Film, Theater and Television Music on Record, 1948-69,* 0503

Snow, Robert J. *Essays in Musicology . . . , 0535*

Social Development of the Traditional Calypso of Trinidad and Tobago . . . (Elder), *1291*

The Social Implications of Early Negro Music in the United States (Katz), *0771*

Social Sciences and Humanities Index, 0300, 0301

Société Française de Musicologie, *0357*

Society for Ethnomusicology. *Directory of Ethnomusicological Sound Recording Collections in the U.S. and Canada,* 0540

Sociología del folklore musical uruguayo (Mendoza de Arce), *1297*

Soeurs de Sainte-Anne. *Dictionnaire biographique des musiciens canadiens, 0576*

Sohlmans musiklexikon . . . 0203*

"Some Drums and Drum Rhythms of Jamaica" (Roberts), *1188*

"Some Portuguese Sources for Early Brazilian Music History" (Stevenson), *1023*

Song Catalogue (British Broadcasting Corporation), *0376*

Song in America, from Early Times to about 1850 (Yerbury), *0766*

Songs of the American Theater . . . (Lewine; Simon), *0804*

Sonneck, Oscar G. T. *A Bibliography of Early Secular American Music (18th Century), 0819; Dramatic Music: Catalogue of Full Scores* (U.S. Library of Congress), *0388; Early Concert Life in America (1731-1880), 0715; Early Opera in America, 0695; Orchestral Music Catalogue: Scores . . .* (U.S. Library of Congress), *0389*

The Sound of the City . . . (Gillett), *0683*

Soundprints; Contemporary Composers (Such), *0577*

Source Readings in Music History from Classical Antiquity through the Romantic Era (Strunk), *0104*

Les sources de la musique canadienne: une bibliographie des bibliographies (Proctor), *0583*

Sources in Canadian Music: a Bibliography of Bibliographies. Les sources de la musique canadienne: une bibliographie des bibliographies (Proctor), *0583*

Sources, Musical (Pre-1450) (Harvard Dictionary), *0002*

Southern, Eileen. "America's Black Composers of Classical Music," *0797; The Black Perspective in Music, 0777a; The Music of Black Americans: A History, 0766; Readings in Black American Music, 0767*

Spaeth, Sigmund. *A History of Popular Music in America, 0659; Music and Dance in New York State, 0738; Music and Dance in Pennsylvania, New Jersey and Delaware, 0728; Music and Dance in the New England States, 0732; Music and Dance in the Southeastern States, 0744*

Speculum, 0330

Speculum: An Index of Musically Related Articles and Book Reviews (Wolff), *0330*

Spell, Lota. *Music in Texas, 0745a*

Spemanns goldenes Buch der Musik (Spemanns), *0204*

Spemanns, Wilhelm. *Spemanns goldenes Buch der Musik,* 0204

Spiess, Lincoln; Stanford Thomas. *An Introduction to Certain Mexican Musical Archives, 1237*

Spoken Word and Miscellaneous Catalogue (Gramophone), *0478*

Sputnik muzikanta (Ostrovskii), *0038*

GUIDE TO USE OF THE SUBJECT INDEX

The filing procedures described for the Author-Title Index are also in effect here. Subdivided headings (MUSIC–PORTUGAL–HISTORY AND CRITICISM) and inverted headings (MUSIC, PORTUGUESE) are interfiled, word by word, without regard for punctuation. Thus MUSIC, AMERICAN precedes MUSIC AND SOCIETY which precedes MUSIC–ARGENTINA. This point is stressed because it varies from Library of Congress practice.

The principles followed in constructing the subject headings were those of the Library of Congress, and most of the headings utilized do appear also in the LC catalogs. Countries and other geographical units are invariably *subdivisions* under musical headings. It is MUSIC–BRAZIL, *not* BRAZIL–MUSIC, which will encompass material on that topic. It will also be MUSICAL INSTRUMENTS, BOLIVIAN; SYMPHONY ORCHESTRAS–MEXICO; MUSICIANS, CANADIAN, etc.

An important distinction is made between headings like MUSIC–BRAZIL and MUSIC, BRAZILIAN. The first encompasses writings about musical activity in Brazil, while the second encompasses actual musical compositions by Brazilians. The latter heading, if subdivided, refers to works *about* Brazilian music: e.g., MUSIC, BRAZILIAN–IMPRINTS (lists of titles of Brazilian compositions, rather than the actual compositions in score).

Ambiguities are avoided through various devices. One is the modifier provided when BIBLIOGRAPHY might be read in two ways. The modifier (further subdivision) COMPOSITIONS or the modifier WRITINGS will be found in such cases. For example: MUSIC, PORTUGUESE–BIBLIOGRAPHY could refer to a list of Portuguese compositions or to a list of books about Portuguese music. In the present index, such an entry is clarified: MUSIC, PORTUGUESE–BIBLIOGRAPHY– COMPOSITIONS, so that it is plainly a list of musical works.

In the same spirit, the somewhat uncertain heading CATALOGS is made specific via four modifiers: LIBRARY CATALOGS, MANUFACTURERS' CATALOGS, PUBLISHERS' CATALOGS, SALES CATALOGS. LIBRARY CATALOGS is used as a main heading (LIBRARY CATALOGS–FRANCE) or as a subheading (MUSIC–LIBRARY CATALOGS–FRANCE).

The terms discography and iconography are here elevated to equal status with bibliography, and all three are used as subdivisions: MUSIC–ITALY– BIBLIOGRAPHY–WRITINGS; MUSIC–ITALY–DISCOGRAPHY; MUSIC–ITALY– ICONOGRAPHY; or JAZZ MUSIC–DISCOGRAPHY, etc.

Details on the use of these and other terms are found in the index itself.

An entry for a person as a subject is made only if there is particularly significant attention to that person in the work cited.

SUBJECT INDEX

AGUINALDO, 1280, 1281
ALMANACS, 0154, 0155. See also:
    MUSIC–ALMANACS, YEARBOOKS,
    ETC.
ALMANACS, CANADIAN, 0558
American Music. See: MUSIC, AMERICAN;
    which covers works of United States
    composers and writings about them. For
    material on musical activity in the
    United States, see: MUSIC–UNITED
    STATES. For music of the American
    continents, see: MUSIC–NORTH
    AMERICA; MUSIC–LATIN
    AMERICA; and see also AMERICAN
    as a subdivision, e.g.: OPERA,
    AMERICAN.
ANDRADE, MARIO DE, 1043
ARCHIVES–MEXICO, 1237
ARGENTINA–IMPRINTS, 0961
ART–THEMES, MOTIVES, 0115
AUSTRALIA–IMPRINTS, 0267
AUTHORS–UNITED STATES–BIOGRAPHY,
    0779
AYESTARÁN, LAURO, 1913-1966, 1305
Aztecs. See: INDIANS OF MEXICO

BALLADS, CANADIAN–HISTORY AND
    CRITICISM, 0550
BALLADS, AMERICAN–HISTORY AND
    CRITICISM, 0636, 0637, 0654
BALLADS, ENGLISH–DISCOGRAPHY, 0918
BALLADS, ENGLISH–HISTORY AND
    CRITICISM, 0550, 0636, 0637
BALLADS, MEXICAN, 1204
BALLADS, MEXICAN–HISTORY AND
    CRITICISM, 1204
BALLADS, SCOTTISH–DISCOGRAPHY,
    0918
BALLADS, SCOTTISH–HISTORY AND
    CRITICISM, 0550, 0636, 0637
BALLADS, SPANISH, 1204
BALLADS, SPANISH–HISTORY AND
    CRITICISM, 1204
BALLET–ARGENTINA–BUENOS
    AIRES, 0943
BALLET–BRAZIL–RIO DE JANEIRO, 1018
BALLET MUSIC–BIBLIOGRAPHY–
    COMPOSITIONS–LIBRARY CATALOGS,
    0388
BAMBUCO (DANCE), 1090, 1097
BAND MUSIC, AMERICAN–BIBLIOG-
    RAPHY–COMPOSITIONS, 0797

BAND MUSIC, CANADIAN–BIBLIOG-
    RAPHY–COMPOSITIONS, 0600, 0602
BARROSO, ARY, 1008
BATUQUE (DANCE), 1001
BAY PSALM BOOK, 0716
BECKWITH, JOHN, 0577
BEECROFT, NORMA, 0577
BEHYMER, LUNDEN, 0724
BEN, JORGE, 1008
BIBLIOGRAPHY. Under this heading are
    writings about bibliography (as an
    activity in itself), or–with subdivisions–
    universal bibliographies and bibliog-
    raphies of bibliographies. Topical bibliog-
    raphies are entered as subdivisions, e.g.,
    CUBA–BIBLIOGRAPHY (for writings
    about Cuba). See also notes under
    IMPRINTS, and MUSIC–BIBLIOGRAPHY.
BIBLIOGRAPHY–BIBLIOGRAPHY, 0168,
    0206, 0207, 0208, 0209, 0210
BIBLIOGRAPHY–UNIVERSAL, 0235,
    0244, 0245
BIOGRAPHY. This is primarily a subdivision,
    e.g., MUSICIANS–BIOGRAPHY. It is also
    a main heading for works about biography
    (as an activity in itself), and with a few
    subdivisions.
BIOGRAPHY–BIBLIOGRAPHY, 0168
BIOGRAPHY–DICTIONARIES, 0185
BIOGRAPHY–DICTIONARIES–INDEXES,
    0516
BIOGRAPHY–INDEXES, 0169, 0170-0173,
    0516
BIOGRAPHY–PERIODICALS, 0184
BIRD MUSIC, 0064, 0068
Birthdays–Musicians. See: MUSICIANS–
    BIRTHDAYS
Black Music. See: NEGRO MUSIC
BLUEGRASS MUSIC–DISCOGRAPHY,
    0645
BLUEGRASS MUSIC–HISTORY AND
    CRITICISM, 0645, 0646
BOLIVIA–IMPRINTS, 0974
BOMBA, 1281
BOOKS–REVIEWS–PERIODICALS–
    INDEXES, 0351, 0352, 0353, 0354,
    0355
BOSSA NOVA (DANCE), 1003, 1007, 1013,
    1014, 1015
BRAZIL–BIBLIOGRAPHY, 0898
BRAZIL–IMPRINTS, 1044, 1045, 1046,
    1047
British Guiana. See: GUYANA, as subdivision
    under specific headings.